Love Needs No Words

Love Needs No Words

What raising my autistic sons has taught me about hope, acceptance and joy

James Hunt

GALLERY BOOKS UK

London · New York · Amsterdam/Antwerp · Sydney/Melbourne · Toronto · New Delhi

First published in Great Britain by Gallery Books,
an imprint of Simon & Schuster UK Ltd, 2026

Copyright © James Hunt, 2026

The right of James Hunt to be identified as the author of this work has been asserted in accordance with the Copyright, Designs and Patents Act, 1988.

1 3 5 7 9 10 8 6 4 2

Simon & Schuster UK Ltd
1st Floor
222 Gray's Inn Road
London WC1X 8HB

For more than 100 years, Simon & Schuster has championed authors and the stories they create. By respecting the copyright of an author's intellectual property, you enable Simon & Schuster and the author to continue publishing exceptional books for years to come. We thank you for supporting the author's copyright by purchasing an authorised edition of this book.

No amount of this book may be reproduced or stored in any format, nor may it be uploaded to any website, database, language-learning model, or other repository, retrieval, or artificial intelligence system without express permission. All rights reserved. Enquiries may be directed to Simon & Schuster, 222 Gray's Inn Road, London WC1X 8HB or RightsMailbox@simonandschuster.co.uk

www.simonandschuster.co.uk
www.simonandschuster.com.au
www.simonandschuster.co.in

Simon & Schuster Australia, Sydney
Simon & Schuster India, New Delhi

The authorised representative in the EEA is Simon & Schuster Netherlands BV, Herculesplein 96, 3584 AA Utrecht, Netherlands. info@simonandschuster.nl

The author and publishers have made all reasonable efforts to contact copyright-holders for permission, and apologise for any omissions or errors in the form of credits given. Corrections may be made to future printings.

Simon & Schuster strongly believes in freedom of expression and stands against censorship in all its forms. For more information, visit BooksBelong.com.

A CIP catalogue record for this book is available from the British Library

Hardback ISBN: 978-1-3985-4858-9
Trade Paperback ISBN: 978-1-3985-4861-9
eBook ISBN: 978-1-3985-4859-6

Typeset in Bembo Std by
Palimpsest Book Production Limited, Falkirk, Stirlingshire

Printed and Bound in the UK using 100% Renewable Electricity
at CPI Group (UK) Ltd

For Tommy and Jude.
You've taught me more than I could ever teach you. This is for you – and for every other family like ours, finding their way.

Contents

	Prologue	ix
1	Jude	1
2	Tommy	15
3	Milestones and Inchstones	27
4	The Unwritten Rules	41
5	The Small Joys	55
6	Love Needs No Words	67
7	A Noisy World	85
8	School, but Different	105
9	The Long Nights	123
10	When Your World Shrinks	137
11	Never Alone	151
12	Co-parenting	169
13	Brothers	185
14	The Most Wonderful Time of the Year	205
15	Finding my Voice	221
16	Carer, Son, Dad	245
17	Becoming an Adult	271

| 18 | What Comes Next | 289 |
| 19 | Choosing Joy | 307 |

| Afterword | 330 |
| Acknowledgements | 334 |

Prologue

It's just gone 8 p.m. and the house is unusually calm.

Charlotte is upstairs trying to get Tommy to go to sleep. I'm downstairs with Jude, who is standing inches away from the TV, his eyes tracking Mickey Mouse across the screen, flapping his fingers in rhythm. One upstairs, one downstairs, the story of our life.

I grab my laptop and sink into the sofa. Tonight's the night. I've been putting this off for too long. If I don't do it now, I never will.

The post is written. I've reread it twenty times. Edited it a dozen. It's honest. Maybe too honest. I hover over the 'publish' button like it might bite me.

I'm not sure what scares me more: that nobody will read it, or that people actually will.

I've written it for friends and family. But other people might read it too.

It all feels so unnatural. Up to now, I've never been one of those people who shares everything online. There's been the odd photo of the boys. Pics from our wedding. The occasional day out. And that's about it. I kept the real stuff private, especially the hard stuff. Which was most of the last three to four years. But recently, something in me has shifted. After years of bottling everything up, of trying to stay strong and figure it all out alone inside my mind, I've felt an urge I can't shake. A need to write. To get it out of my head and onto a page. I can't seem to talk about our lives out loud, I choke up with emotions every time I try, words failing me. So I wondered if, maybe, I could write it down instead.

Not for likes. Not for sympathy. But because I want people to get to know Jude and Tommy. Our life has become more and more isolated of late. People aren't seeing the boys anymore, not really. Perhaps this post, this moment of openness, is one way to change that. But I can't stop the worry spiralling in my head.

Am I oversharing? Will people think I'm attention-seeking? Using my boys for sympathy?

But I also don't know how else to explain what our life is really like.

We've been living in what feels like a different world. A world of diagnoses, therapies, meltdowns, sleepless nights and routines so rigid that turning left at the end of the road instead of right can cause a complete collapse. A world where we're still waiting for first words. For first friends.

But it's a world filled with beauty too. Jude's huge smile whenever he's listening to Ed Sheeran or watching *Mickey Mouse Clubhouse*. Tommy's quiet joy and sense of accomplishment when he completes a puzzle meant for kids twice his age. Moments of pure happiness, buried in the chaos. Moments that feel like they are happening in secret. No one else really sees them. No one else truly sees the boys, not the way we do.

PROLOGUE

And the hard days? The ones where I feel like I'm failing everyone? I'm definitely not talking about those with anyone.

So maybe, if I can't say it all out loud . . . I can write it.

I take a deep breath. Click. The screen refreshes. The post is live.

I shut the laptop and feel like I might be sick. I fight the urge to open it back up and refresh the screen again and again. I manage to hold out for six and a half minutes before checking to see what people think.

There's already ten likes. A name I haven't seen in years. Another one. Then the comments start coming in. They're all positive, encouraging, telling me to keep going. More names. More comments. People I went to school with, old colleagues, friends I haven't spoken to in ages. Most of them had no idea Jude and Tommy were autistic. No idea what our life looks like behind the smiles and carefully selected photos.

And I think that's what gets me most: how little people knew. I've spent so long keeping everything in, trying to protect the boys, protect us and pretend we're coping just fine. Sharing it doesn't fix anything . . . but it makes everything feel a little bit lighter.

And that small shift, that tiny bit of breathing space, is all I need to write something else. Then something else.

A week later I share a post about sleep and how we haven't had a full night in years. Then one about meltdowns. One about Jude's school. I'm not following a plan or trying to build a platform. I'm just telling the truth, one post at a time, in the hope it might help someone else feel a little less alone.

In the weeks that follow, I keep writing.

Not every day but often enough that it becomes something

I look forward to. Something I *need*. A way to process what is happening in our lives. A way to make sense of the chaos, the joy, the grief, the laughter.

At night when I'm up late with Jude, sitting in his bed waiting for him to sleep, I write down my thoughts. On the train home from work, I write some more. Some posts are short, just a few sentences. Others pour out of me like they've been waiting there for years. Some of them I share, some of them I delete.

And every time, without fail, someone messages me with the same words: *'I'm so glad I'm not the only one.'*

That sentence comes up again and again. Different people. Different countries. Same feeling.

It doesn't take long before people start asking questions. I open my inbox to dozens of messages from new followers. Sometimes hundreds. Always on the same themes:

'What were the first signs?' 'When did you know something wasn't right?' 'How did you get the diagnosis?' 'What school does your son go to?' 'How do you deal with meltdowns?' 'How do you cope with the fear?' 'How do you manage to keep going?'

I try to answer as many as I can, writing back in my lunchbreaks at work, on the train or late at night, in bed, one of the boys lying next to me.

I can't keep up with every message, but I understand the need behind each one. Because I've felt it too. That desperation for answers. That longing for connection. That need to hear, *'You're not doing this wrong. You're not alone.'*

That's part of why I wrote this book.

Over the last seventeen years, I've learned more than I ever thought I could.

PROLOGUE

Not just about autism but also about myself. About what really matters when life doesn't go to plan. I've learned that an autism diagnosis can bring with it a lot of fear. And in some ways, that fear is justified. Life can be incredibly stressful and difficult for Jude and Tommy – and for us as their family. There are days where everything feels fragile, where the pressure builds until it breaks.

But I've also learned that this life can be full of love and joy too. Not in the way I expected but sometimes in ways even more meaningful. I've learned that progress looks different here. That milestones don't always arrive on time, or at all, but that doesn't make them any less worth celebrating.

More than anything, I've learned that I'm not failing, even on the days when it feels like I am. And neither are you.

Somewhere along the way, sharing our story stopped being just about helping others understand Jude and Tommy. It became about building something I didn't know I needed: community, connection, a reminder that we're not doing this on our own.

I've lost count of the number of times someone has messaged me and said, *'I found your page at just the right moment. I was lost. And now I feel a bit less alone.'*

I've been that parent too. Lost. Scared. Exhausted. Wondering what the future will look like. Wondering if we're doing enough. Wondering if we'll ever feel OK again.

This book is for you.

It's for the parent lying awake at 3 a.m., Googling traits and therapies and trying to hold it all together. It's for the dad who doesn't know how to talk about what he's feeling but knows something's not right. It's for the families who feel like they've been dropped into a different world without a map.

It's not a guidebook. It's not a list of tips and tricks. It's a story. Our story. And maybe, in some small way, yours too.

I'm not an expert. I'm a dad. I don't have all the answers. But I can tell you what helped us. What we've learned. What we're still learning. I can tell you that it's OK to feel scared. It's OK to feel heartbroken. It's OK to grieve the life you thought you'd have. But I can also tell you there's joy here. Connection, laughter and a love so strong that it breaks you down and builds you back up again.

It's not the life I thought we'd be living. But it's taught me more than I ever expected.

So wherever you are in your own story, at the beginning, deep in the trenches, or somewhere in between, I hope these pages remind you of one thing:

You are not alone.

1
Jude

We'd already missed the turning once. The satnav couldn't find the exact location of the Children's Centre, and the tension in the car was building with every wrong turn. Jude had woken up unhappy, sucking on his dummy and whining in protest. We were already late.

Eventually, I pulled into the Children's Centre, and Charlotte got Jude out of the car. I scooped him up from her. I wanted to do something; I needed to hold him. Jude sucked harder on his dummy, clinging onto his ever-present muslin, rubbing it against the side of his face, probably wondering where we were and why we were taking him into this strange place. On the outside I looked calm and collected, but inside I was falling apart. My chest was tight, my head was spinning, tears felt seconds away.

Somewhere inside this beautiful Victorian building that we'd finally found was a doctor who would tell us what was going on with our little boy. The door buzzed open, and we walked inside, the sound of our feet echoing along the polished wooden floor. A receptionist guided us down a corridor and into a waiting room. Jude wrapped himself around me, scanning the room anxiously. New place. New sounds. New people. All of it too much.

I was slowly getting used to these kinds of rooms. Rooms that contain a small selection of wooden toys and trays filled with books that Jude refused to look at. I loved books as a kid and still do now. Why wasn't he interested in books? Was he supposed to be playing with these kinds of toys by this age? Was it my fault he wasn't interested? Was I not making them fun enough? The thoughts spiralled.

These rooms are always eerily quiet. Nervous parents silently acknowledge each other with a nod or a small smile. Then a child shatters the quiet because they're either overexcited or fed up with being shut in this room and want to leave. Every time there was a sound I looked at Jude anxiously, hoping it wouldn't make him cry. I found myself wondering if there were cameras in the corners. If the people assessing us were already watching. If they were already forming their opinions, not just of Jude, but of us.

The wait didn't last long. A woman appeared and introduced herself as a speech therapist. I forgot her name instantly. Lately, I'd been struggling to retain simple bits of information. Names. Dates. Words. I'd put it down to lack of sleep, but maybe it was stress too.

We followed her up a flight of stairs and into another room, where two more people were introduced to us as a paediatrician and an occupational therapist. I didn't really know what an occupational therapist did, and I was too embarrassed to ask. I just nodded like I understood. I should know this stuff. I knew I'd read about it. Another example of my poor memory. What was going on?

JUDE

I put Jude down and he immediately ran to Charlotte, grabbing at her clothes, desperate to get away from these new faces. The instinct to scoop him up and walk straight back out the door was overwhelming. I didn't want him to go through this. *I* didn't want to go through this. I wanted to take him home and pretend none of it was happening.

But we stayed. We sat on the floor with him for a while, trying to ease him into the space. Eventually, he began to explore the room a little, and we relaxed – or at least tried to.

The paediatrician began asking questions while the speech and occupational therapists attempted to play with Jude. Charlotte answered most of them. She always did in these situations, organised, composed and already several steps ahead in her thinking. She gave them a detailed summary of her concerns: the lack of eye contact, the way he didn't respond to his name, the repetitive play and the lack of interest in social interaction. She'd had these concerns for over a year, she'd listed them off many times before. She was ready for this day.

While she spoke, I watched Jude across the room. He was playing with some toy cutlery, passing it from one side of his body to the other. Each time he paused to hold it up to his eyes, slowly lowering it towards his nose before placing it down beside him. He ignored the cars they pushed his way but popped a few of the bubbles they blew. I eagerly showed them how we'd taught him to clap when he wanted more of something. 'Look!' I said. 'He claps for bubbles!' He did it on cue. I imagined, hoped, that tiny gesture might mean something. That it might prove this was all a misunderstanding. That Jude was clever. That we were wrong to be here. That everything was going to be OK.

We spoke about his restricted diet. About sleep, or the lack of it. With every answer, I could feel more boxes being ticked. It was like they already knew everything about Jude without needing to ask. What he was able or not able to do. What he liked and didn't like.

After a while, they suggested we take a break. A chance for Jude to have a snack and for them to discuss everything they'd observed. A chance to decide our little boy's future. Back in the waiting room I sat Jude on my lap, offering him some crisps, watching him crunch each one slowly, methodically.

Charlotte and I didn't say much. Had it gone well upstairs or not? I had no idea. The silence between us didn't feel tense, just heavy. We were both bracing for what was coming. Both wondering if they were watching us even now, assessing not just Jude but us too. How we parented. How we handled stress. Whether we were somehow to blame.

And maybe we were. Maybe we'd missed something. Waited too long. Not pushed hard enough. Maybe he'd be talking by now or more interested in play if someone else was his dad.

They called us back upstairs far sooner than they had said they would. I remember glancing at the clock. They were supposed to need more time to weigh up what they'd seen. But they were ready so quickly. It felt like a TV drama where the jury are sent out to discuss the verdict, but the decision is so obvious, they don't even need time to deliberate.

We sat back down opposite the paediatrician, the therapists trying once more to engage with Jude so that we could focus on what he was about to tell us. Enough of the small talk and pleasantries, I urged silently, just tell us what we already know and don't want to hear.

JUDE

'So, Mr and Mrs Hunt, we've spoken among ourselves and gone over our findings. Taking everything into account, and even though he is very young, we are sorry to say that we believe Jude has a diagnosis of Autism Spectrum Disorder . . .'

Charlotte and I looked at each other and shared a sad smile. Maybe we held hands, maybe I squeezed her knee. I don't want to over-romanticise the moment, but I think that's what happened. Or perhaps I'm confusing it with images I've seen on TV when families get given news by a doctor. Some parts of that moment are crystal clear. Others are completely lost in the fog. I hope I did. I hope I tried to show her I was there for her.

I remember the uncomfortable silence that followed. One that was probably seconds but felt like hours. How much it said without anyone saying anything. Maybe they were waiting for us to break down in tears. Or to argue with them. But I think that in the short time we'd spent together today, they'd got a feeling that we knew exactly why we were here. The paediatrician shuffled some papers around, waiting for us to respond. But there was nothing for us to say. We were there for answers — weren't they supposed to be giving them to us?

'OK,' I said. 'So now what?'

He started to explain how autism is a spectrum and where they felt Jude sat within it: the severe end. He explained how autism changes as a child develops, how Jude was still very young; in fact, at twenty-two months, he was one of the youngest they'd diagnosed in Essex at that point. Then he mentioned global developmental delay and showed us where Jude was developmentally in various skills compared to what would be expected for his age group, how much younger he was displaying in every test, which stung. He told us about a course we could go on that would give us more information and how various departments would be getting in touch with us. They gave us names and numbers, used acronyms we'd never heard before. I nodded along, pretending to understand, but I wasn't taking any of it in. I couldn't.

Before I knew it, I was carrying Jude back down the stairs, Charlotte beside me, both of us holding a handful of leaflets. That was all we were leaving with. That and a diagnosis: Jude had autism.

We got in the car and just sat there. Jude seemed relieved to be out of the centre, wriggling in his car seat and content with his dummy and muslin, none the wiser. Unaware that everything had changed. Not in him but in how the world might see him. In how I feared the world might treat him. In what our lives might now become.

We had known it was coming, of course. We'd been 99.9 per cent certain that we'd be leaving that room with an autism diagnosis, so it wasn't a shock. But at the same time, we had no idea what it meant for the future. Jude was the same gorgeous little boy he'd been before the assessment but now, officially, he was autistic and also had global developmental delay. Words that, until a few months ago, had meant nothing to us but which now felt like the most important words in the world.

It had been about a year before that appointment that Charlotte had started sensing something wasn't quite right. She'd take Jude to baby groups and watch the other mums chatting while their babies crawled around their feet. Playing, excitedly

pointing at things and babbling their first words. Jude wasn't doing those things. He wasn't engaging like the other kids. He wasn't even interested. He was around nine months old at the time, and Charlotte couldn't shake the feeling that something was different.

I couldn't see it. All I saw was my beautiful, amazing boy. He'd been born seven weeks premature, of course he'd take a little longer to catch up. 'He's fine,' I'd tell her. 'He's just being lazy. He'll get there, you'll see.' I believed it too. Or maybe I just wanted to believe it.

Charlotte, though, wasn't convinced. Jude was often off in his own world, staring out the window at the leaves, rarely responding to his name. At baby groups, he'd avoid the other kids entirely. When friends came over, he wasn't interested in joining in.

She tried to tell me, more than once, but her concerns felt like overreacting to me. It didn't help that on weekends, Jude and I had a great bond. During the week I didn't get to see him much because of work. I was co-owner of a marketing company in London, commuting to and from the office each day, desperate to build a business to provide for our future. But by Saturday morning, we'd be best mates. Our weekends were full of cuddles, smiles and little routines that felt magical. But then, come Monday evening, after I'd been away at work all day, he'd look at me like I was a stranger. I told myself it was his way of punishing me for being away. *Clever little thing*, I thought. I never once considered it might mean something more.

Charlotte eventually took Jude to the GP to share her concerns. He dismissed her pretty quickly. 'He's young. It's nothing to worry about,' he said. Charlotte came home frustrated, whereas I felt reassured. If the doctor wasn't worried, why should we be? But I could see how much it bothered her. She was frustrated with me too, I think, for not seeing what she could. For not being on her side. She tried to let it go, but I knew she couldn't. And deep down, a part of me was worried she might be right.

We agreed to give it a few more months, enjoy his first birthday and see how things progressed. And that's what we did. Jude had started to sleep a little better, the summer was coming and the usual childhood illnesses of winter disappeared. We had an amazing day on his birthday, surrounded by all of the people we loved. In my eyes, life couldn't have been any better.

But Charlotte was still concerned and she wouldn't let it go. She kept pushing for answers, even as our doctor dismissed her concerns again and again. She was certain that Jude was different, but nobody seemed to be listening. Not even me.

That summer, we went to Charlotte's dad's house in Port Grimaud near Saint-Tropez for a couple of weeks. It was a place we loved, calm, beautiful, the kind of setting where life just feels slower. Easier. The canals flowed right up to the back garden, and we'd use her dad's little inflatable motorboat to head to the beach or to pop to the boulangerie for fresh baguettes for breakfast. I could imagine us spending holidays there for years to come, Jude growing up splashing in the water and playing on the beach. Back then, I still believed that's what life had in store for us.

When we arrived, we dropped our bags and opened the

patio doors to let the air drift through the house. We set Jude down in the garden to crawl around, his muslin still clutched in one hand. Next door a German couple were sitting out in their garden with their young daughter, a lively little girl around a year old. She waved at us enthusiastically, smiling at Jude through the slats of the fence. Charlotte and I started making polite small talk with the parents, chatting about where we were all from, the usual back and forth you exchange on holiday with people you'll probably never see again. They were warm and easy to chat to. Their daughter was running around, pointing at things, grinning from ear to ear. But what she was most excited about was Jude. She was fascinated by him.

Jude gave her a quick glance and then went back to what he was doing, rolling a ball across the garden and shuffling after it. She wanted to join him, which we happily agreed to, and her dad lifted her over the low fence that separated our gardens. As she rushed towards Jude, he did his best to get out of her way. She picked up his ball and held it out to him; he took it off her and crawled away as fast as he could. Her parents smiled politely as we told them that Jude was actually older than their little girl, but I could see the flicker of surprise on their faces, although they tried to hide it. Their daughter was interacting, smiling at us, pointing at cars going by and shouting 'Auto!' Jude, meanwhile, was engrossed in rolling his ball, oblivious to the world around him. I laughed it off, making a joke about 'German efficiency' and how they must be much better parents than us. But inside, something was shifting.

The gap between the two children was impossible to ignore.

I couldn't hide behind the excuse of a premature birth anymore. Couldn't dismiss it as Jude being shy or wanting to be alone. Maybe I had been brushing things aside because I didn't want to see them. That day, standing in the garden of this beautiful place, I felt a growing sense of dread. I'd always thought of Port Grimaud as somewhere we could escape the pressures of home, but there was no escaping this.

Later that night, when Jude was asleep, Charlotte and I talked. We didn't dive straight into it, we circled around the subject. We talked about how lovely the neighbours seemed; how clever their little girl was. But we both knew what we were really talking about. I felt awful for not believing Charlotte sooner. I told her I was sorry. That I wished I'd listened sooner. That I could finally see what she'd been seeing all along. I promised her we'd push for answers the moment we got home and that we'd make sure we were taken seriously. But even as I said the words, I felt completely lost. The future I'd imagined for Jude – the school drop-offs, the birthday parties, watching Jude make friends – suddenly felt out of reach. I couldn't see a path forward. All I could feel was fear.

We still had two weeks of our holiday left, and I tried my best to put all of that worry out of my mind and make it feel normal. Looking back at the photos, there are moments that seem perfect, Jude smiling, the three of us laughing together. But I remember what was really happening in my head. How distant I felt. How everything suddenly looked different, because I couldn't stop imagining what we were heading into.

*

JUDE

As soon as we got home from France, Charlotte booked another GP appointment. This time, she didn't go alone, her dad went with her, not just for moral support but because he was friends with the senior doctor at the practice. It was one of those quiet favours that make a world of difference. It shouldn't be like that but in this case, it was. Charlotte had voiced her concerns before and been dismissed. But this time, with her dad sitting beside her, the GP reluctantly agreed to refer Jude to a paediatrician.

Even then, he said it was probably too soon. That children develop at different rates. That boys are slower than girls. That there were many other possible explanations. But at least with Charlotte's dad there, now someone was finally listening.

Looking back, it doesn't sit right with me that this was what it took. That a concerned mother, the person who'd spent nearly every waking moment with her child for over a year, wasn't taken seriously until her father called in a favour. Her instincts weren't enough. Her voice wasn't enough. And she's not alone in that.

In some British counties, assessments won't even be considered until the child is three years old. In others, families can wait two, three, even four years for a diagnosis. Years of fear. Years of self-doubt. Years of being stuck in limbo, trying to hold it all together while feeling like the only person who sees what's really going on. Having to wait, chase, complain and fight to even get your child an appointment.

For us, it took around six months to go from that third GP appointment to our assessment at the Children's Centre. At the time, it felt like forever. Now I know we were incredibly lucky.

In those six months, I did what so many parents do: I turned to Google.

It was 2009. Social media was still in its infancy. Blogging was only just starting to find its way. Most of the information out there was cold and clinical, medical journals, diagnostic criteria, long-form articles filled with jargon I struggled to get my head around.

Autism had been mentioned as a possibility by a family member, and the more I read, the more it felt like Jude ticked a lot of the boxes. But it didn't make sense. Not really. The way it was written about, the type of language that was used, it felt like there had to be some kind of mistake. I couldn't find our family in those descriptions. I couldn't find Jude. And with every article I read, I felt more lost. I'd read and reread the same pieces and retain nothing. It was like my brain refused to let the information in. I'd fall asleep each night with all these swirling thoughts, only to wake up the next morning feeling like I was starting from scratch.

The only cultural reference point I had was *Rain Man*. It was one of those '80s films that was always on TV when I was younger, and I'd seen bits of it over the years, maybe even the whole thing, though never all in one go. I don't remember the word 'autism' being used in the film, but the internet told me that Dustin Hoffman's character was autistic.

And all I could think was . . . that can't be right.

That wasn't Jude. He didn't count cards. He didn't refuse to get on aeroplanes. He was just a little boy. My little boy. I didn't yet understand that autism was a spectrum. That no two 'autistic people' are the same. That it can present in a thousand different ways. That was a lesson I'd learn slowly, over time and through experience, not textbooks.

Now that we had a diagnosis, all I wanted were more answers. I wanted to know what Jude's life would look like. Would he ever speak? Go to a mainstream school? Make friends? Would he be happy? What did autism mean for him?

When they told us Jude was one of the youngest children they'd ever diagnosed in Essex, they said it was a good thing, that early diagnosis meant early support, early intervention, a better chance at helping him progress. But to me, it just made it feel more serious. If early intervention was so key when it came to his development, that made it feel like we were now under enormous pressure. That our lives were now a ticking time bomb, where we had to start making breakthroughs before it was too late.

And I felt ashamed. Ashamed that Charlotte had seen it all so clearly, months before I had. Ashamed that I hadn't backed her up sooner. Ashamed that I might have cost us time that we couldn't get back.

Once we were home and Jude was settled, watching *Mickey Mouse Clubhouse* as always, and Charlotte had taken all the phone calls from people checking on how it went, we finally sat down on the sofa and spoke about it. We admitted we were both scared. Sad. Not surprised exactly, but still shaken. We'd known this moment was coming but that didn't make it any easier now it had arrived.

What struck me most was how little guidance we were actually given. I wanted someone to draw me a map, to tell me what to expect. But of course, that's not how any of this works. What we'd been given instead was a list of difficulties: social communication, social interaction, social imagination. Sensory processing issues. Global developmental delay.

It was a lot. And all we had to try to make sense of it all was a handful of leaflets.

By the time Jude was finally in bed, we were both emotionally drained, too tired to talk anymore about it. But the thoughts wouldn't stop. The questions kept circling, crashing into one another in my head.

How do you raise a child when you don't know what their future looks like? What if the world is cruel to him? How do you parent when every instinct you have feels like it's suddenly up for questioning? What if I'm not a good enough dad for him?

I was trying to hold it together, but I felt completely lost. And yet, somewhere in that mess of emotions, there was also love. Fierce, unshakable love. I didn't know what lay ahead and that terrified me. But I knew we'd do whatever we could. That Jude would get every bit of love and support and understanding we could give him.

That was the starting point for everything.

We had no idea what we were doing, but we had each other. And we had Jude.

But everything we thought we knew about parenting, about the future, was about to be rewritten.

2

Tommy

Three years after Jude's diagnosis, almost to the day, we found ourselves back in that same room, this time with our second son, Tommy. Waiting for an assessment that once again felt like it was going to change everything. I knew we were there to confirm that Tommy was autistic, but a part of me still held onto a glimmer of hope that this time would be different. Tommy was so different to Jude, such a different personality, with such different interests, how could he be autistic too?

Tommy was different to his brother from the second he was born. When Charlotte's waters broke just after midnight, on a summer's evening in June, I quickly called my mum to come round to the house. We needed her to wait with Jude, who still wasn't asleep, so I could take Charlotte to hospital. By this time we had moved to Essex, a forty-five-minute drive away from the hospital, and it was the most nervous drive of my life. Less than an hour after reaching the hospital, Tommy came kicking and screaming into the world. Jude took nearly twenty-four hours to arrive, Tommy was here in two. It seemed he was much more excited to see the world than Jude had been, something that still holds true today.

Like Jude, though, Tommy was born early, six weeks in fact. Which meant he ended up spending five days in hospital before he was allowed home. With the help of my mum and dad I juggled looking after Jude and being at the hospital. After a couple of days, I stayed at the hospital with Tommy while Charlotte went home for a few hours to spend time with Jude. As I sat cuddling Tommy, giving him a bottle, a whole mixture of emotions rushed over me. It had been an eventful six months. In December, Charlotte and I had got married, surrounded by friends and family, in the church of my primary school back in London. We'd had the best day. I can still picture a tiny Jude, with his curly blond hair, wearing a little tuxedo and black Converse. We'd been so worried about how he'd cope that day, with the church, the party and so many people, but he did us proud. Then in April we'd moved house, needing a larger space for our growing family. Now, Tommy was here, and it felt like everything I wanted from life was coming together.

Alongside all of the joy and nerves, I found myself wondering what Jude and Tommy's relationship would be like. I hoped having a sibling close in age would help Jude. That maybe Tommy would be the one to draw him out of his world a little. That Jude might start to feel more comfortable around other kids by learning from and alongside his brother. I knew it wasn't as simple as that, but it gave me hope, the kind you cling to in those early years and the kind I desperately needed.

In part, this desire was tied to my own childhood. I never had siblings close in age; all of mine were from my parents' previous marriages and at least eleven years older. Growing up, it was my cousins who felt like my siblings. I wanted Tommy and Jude to have what I didn't. Someone by their side through everything.

I was so happy and had so much to look forward to, but even then, that day in the hospital, I couldn't help but feel anxious too. Autism still scared me. Some of what we'd been through with Jude over the last few months – the lack of progress with communication and how upset he would get on some days – had my heart in a vice.

I thought back to the day I first held Jude. Here I was three years later, holding Tommy, talking to him, telling him how much I loved him. But I didn't talk about the future with him. I was too scared. Too worried to let myself picture the future in case it didn't come true. Not the big, outlandish dreams, of him scoring the winning goal for England in the World Cup, but the simple stuff. The conversations, the days out, the birthday parties. All the things I'd previously taken for granted. Amid the joy, I was grappling with the fear that, as with Jude, these things might remain dreams for Tommy too. As those thoughts washed over me, guilt did too. Why couldn't I stop thinking about it? Why couldn't I just enjoy the moment and Tommy being here?

Looking back, I was bracing myself for the possibility of what might come. Trying to protect myself from all the emotions I'd been through and was still going through with Jude. But I knew this was beyond my control. When you become a parent, you suddenly become vulnerable, your heart forever walking around outside your body with your child. Here I was about to risk my heart all over again.

*

When you bring your second baby home, it's different. You're more relaxed than the first time. You've done the nappies and the bottles. You know what to expect. That fear of getting everything wrong isn't quite so loud anymore. But what I hadn't expected was just how much harder it would be now that there were two of them.

I'd seen friends struggle when their second baby came along, how the chaos of returning to the newborn stage collided with the demands of a toddler or preschooler. But we weren't just juggling two kids. We were juggling a newborn who relied on us for everything and still trying to learn more about what autism meant for Jude and how best we could support him.

And when it came to sleep, it was like we'd never even left the newborn stage. Jude barely slept as it was and now we couldn't risk Tommy waking him with his cries. Within weeks of Tommy coming home, we'd settled into a routine that felt like survival. Charlotte slept downstairs with Tommy, while Jude slept in our bed with me. Or didn't sleep, more accurately. We were still battling relentless sleep deprivation, just with an added layer now. I look back and honestly don't know how we functioned. We couldn't give each other much of a break as we were both up at different times throughout each night. We were shattered. Living hour to hour. But the adrenaline and excitement of having a new baby, that buzz you get in those early months, is what carried us through.

In the middle of that chaos, Tommy felt like our calm. He fed well. He settled quickly. He wanted to be close to us. There was this warmth in him, this sweetness, that made me think maybe things would be easier this time. But that hope

TOMMY

didn't last forever. Because slowly, quietly, signs began to appear that maybe he was developing differently too.

As much as I tried not to, I couldn't help but keep watching Tommy, analysing every little thing he did, or didn't do. Comparing him to what Jude had been like at that age. Or what friends' children had been like. At first, we told ourselves things were going well. Tommy was more cuddly than Jude had ever been. He wanted to be held. He smiled. He made eye contact. He was curious about the world around him. We couldn't see any of the red flags we now knew so well. Not yet.

I remember clinging to the fact that Tommy would sit beside other babies. That he seemed to take an interest in what they were doing. Surely that meant his social skills were fine? He was curious, observant. He didn't avoid people like Jude did. He wanted to be near us all the time, constantly craving attention and closeness. That had to mean something. That had to mean he was different.

But slowly, I began to notice the cracks in the story I was telling myself.

Tommy might have been sitting *near* other children, but he wasn't really engaging with them. He watched what they were doing but never tried to join in. It was as if they were part of the scenery: interesting but not essential. If they made too much noise or got too close, he'd pull away. Sometimes dramatically. He'd wedge himself behind the sofa, press his body into tight corners, bury himself in cushions. Seeking pressure. Seeking escape.

Then came the head-banging.

It started around his first birthday, and it scared the life out of me. When he got overwhelmed or upset, he'd lie flat on the wooden floor and start hitting the back of his head against it. Hard. The first time it happened, he got upset in the hallway and started doing it out of nowhere. I ran to him, scooped him up, tried to hold him tight and calm him down. But he thrashed wildly, fighting to get free, desperate to return to the floor and continue. I eventually moved him to the sofa, thinking at least the cushions would soften the blows, and sat there with him until the TV distracted him enough to stop. But a few minutes later, he climbed down, walked straight back into the hallway and tried to do it again.

It became a pattern. His way of regulating, of telling us something was wrong. People would say things like, 'He's only doing it for attention' or 'He's not really hurting himself'. But those comments missed the point entirely. I wasn't worried about the attention-seeking. I was worried that my little boy *needed* to hurt himself in order to feel OK again. How could we stop him? What if he damaged his brain?

And still, part of me resisted putting the pieces together. This was just a phase, a frustration at not being able to communicate better. Where Jude had been content to crawl and was not that fussed about standing or walking, Tommy couldn't wait to get up. Starting to crawl wasn't enough for him. He wanted to walk way before he was physically able to. We got him a walker and he'd spend his time racing around the house, crashing from room to room. When we took him out and carried him or put him on the floor, he just wanted to get back in. He was so active, showing a deep desire to be independent. I held onto that: he wanted to take part in the world so much more than Jude had at that age.

TOMMY

But there were other signs. His babbling had stopped around ten months, and his eye contact was inconsistent. That silence crept in again and with it the panic I was trying to keep at bay.

While much more interested in activities than Jude was at that age, if Tommy did something good, like colour in a picture or complete a puzzle, he couldn't handle any type of praise or celebration. If I clapped or cheered him on, Tommy would automatically drop to the floor, lie down and press his body against the surface.

He would only eat in his highchair if he had a book or pencils to colour with and struggled with the textures of wet or soft foods, refusing to touch them. He'd run through a room with his head tilted to the side, scanning every inch of it, making sure things were where they were supposed to be – in his mind at least.

If he was playing and I tried to join in he would let me, but the play had to stick to set patterns. He liked me to build a tower out of his blocks and for him to knock it down, but what he enjoyed most was putting them in and out of their box. Repeating it over and over again. If I added anything to the game, changed it at all, he would simply shut down and go play somewhere else. He loved colouring and could sit for hours at the table, crayons in hand. We were allowed to join in with this; in fact, if I stopped, he'd take my hand and press it back to the page. He didn't talk, but in those moments, he was clearly communicating what he wanted.

That said, there was still little communication between us. No words, no shared moments of 'look at this!' He never used his finger to point at a plane in the sky or a dog on the street, or to show us what it was he wanted. He responded to little of the language that we used, other than 'biscuit', 'drink', 'yes' and 'no'. Just like Jude, he rarely responded to his name, happily continuing with whatever it was he was doing while we called in vain.

When I list these things out it seems so obvious, why was there ever any doubt in my mind that Tommy was autistic? It was all there. I thought Tommy was so different to Jude, and in many ways he was and is, but there were also so many of their traits that were similar.

When the referral came through for Tommy's assessment, it felt like déjà vu. Same building, same waiting room, same anxiety. The only real difference was that this time we knew exactly how the process worked. We understood the language, the looks, the pauses.

If someone had asked me outright, 'Do you think Tommy is autistic?' I would have said yes. Yet there I was, walking into that appointment, with the hope that maybe, just maybe, all the signs were wrong. That Charlotte was wrong, that the health visitor, GP and paediatrician who'd already seen him and referred us on to that stage were wrong. I knew so much more about autism than I did on the day we'd been there with Jude, and yet I couldn't bring myself to fully admit that Tommy was autistic too.

I can't remember Tommy's assessment as vividly as I do Jude's. I know I was there, I've seen my name on the paperwork, proving I was in attendance, but looking back, much of it is a blur. I think that's a reflection of what we were going through during that period. We'd had years of very little sleep because of Jude, and he was starting to experience

TOMMY

huge physical and emotional meltdowns too. Life was intense, every day felt like we were trying or learning something new about Jude, and here we were about to go through it all over again with Tommy.

When we entered the room with Tommy he ran around, scanning the room, taking in everything in this new environment, before squeezing behind the back of the sofa, squashing himself between the sofa, the floor and the wall. We laughed nervously about it, explaining that this was Tommy's way of coping with a new place, his way of showing he needed time to transition and process what was going on. He stayed there for a few minutes while we chatted and then he was back out again and began to play. He sat down and started stacking the toy cups, then moved on to stacking the bricks too. He put them in number order, and again I found myself wanting to comment on how clever he was and how good he was at certain activities. He paid little attention to any of the therapists calling his name. They tried to get him to play with some toy cars, to push them, race them but instead he put them in and out of the box. He climbed on the furniture, getting a good look at the room from every angle. Then he settled with some crayons and paper and scribbled over and over, before he became fascinated with the pen the therapist had and needed that too.

Meanwhile, we went through the same old hoops with the paediatrician, charting the milestones missed, the verbal and social delays. Even at this early stage in our journey, I'd realised how draining it can be talking about all the negatives. How hard it is to keep listing off all the things your child can't do. I'd find myself wanting to highlight what Tommy and Jude *could* do, what they enjoy, what they're good at, even if it didn't fit into a scale of where they 'should' be. However, the truth is that if you want support, if you want public services to help your child, you have to continuously focus on the challenges and the struggles, no matter how emotionally difficult it is for the parent to list them off time and time again.

The assessment was straightforward, almost a given. The longer it went on, the more I watched Tommy in that room, the more any false hope I'd tried to give myself fell away. At each step along the pathway they had listened to us without any pushback. As we already had one autistic child and had been through the process before, it felt like our words carried more weight. In no time at all, we left that room with an autism diagnosis. A plotted development chart just like Jude had, marked off where Tommy sat on this scale. This time there was no need for leaflets, and I barely listened to their assurances of who would be in touch and the support that would follow.

'Tommy has autism.'

Again. And still, it hit me like a punch to the chest.

With Jude, everything had been unknown. The diagnosis gave us a name for what we were seeing and in a strange way, a place to start. But with Tommy, it felt different. I *knew* what autism could mean now, not in theory, not from Google searches or paediatric leaflets, but from the last three years of living it.

I knew what it looked like when your child couldn't speak. I knew the feeling of watching other kids pass yours by socially, emotionally, academically and not being able to do anything about it. I knew how lonely it could feel, even with people around you. How relentless the days could be. How hard the nights were.

And now we were here again. Back at the start, with another chart, another plan, another version of the same uncertain future. I wasn't grieving *Tommy*. I loved him exactly as he was, this quiet, intense, curious little boy with his fists full of crayons and his head pressed into the corners of the sofa. He amazed me each and every day. But I was grieving the life I had thought he might have. I'd been through this process already but that didn't make it any easier. If anything, it made it harder. Because this time, I couldn't pretend I didn't know what was coming.

I remember sitting in the car afterwards, not even starting the engine. Just staring at the dashboard while Charlotte sorted things in the back. Tommy was happy, clutching onto one of his favourite biscuits. Everything was all right in his world. Meanwhile, I was spiralling. Not from shock this time but from *knowing*. Knowing the battles we were going to have to fight. The forms. The funding. The waiting lists. The explaining and justifying and advocating that would now double in size.

I didn't say much that afternoon. I don't think either of us did. We were both already exhausted. We'd barely had time to come up for air with Jude and now everything was about to get harder.

I felt scared for Tommy. Scared for how hard life might be for him, how he'd be treated, what the world might expect of him. Scared he'd grow up misunderstood, just like his brother often was. And alongside the fear, came a creeping sense of helplessness. Worrying about how we were going to cope. How we were going to be enough for not just one boy with additional needs who was already stretching us to our limits but now two.

The thing about a second diagnosis is that it doesn't just echo the first, it multiplies it.

And then the guilt would crash in. For thinking that way. For being scared. For wishing, just for a second, that life could've been easier. For wondering, why Tommy? Why Jude? Why us?

But underneath all of that, I'd look at Tommy and feel this fierce, aching love. Love that made me determined to do anything I could to help him and Jude grow, safe and happy. He was just a little boy, not even two. All he really wanted was to be active, busy, explore, have fun. He just needed me to show up. To keep going. To love him.

And I did. I still do.

It's not that the fear went away. It didn't. It's still there a lot of the time, even now. But I think at that moment I started learning how to hold the fear *and* the love at the same time. To let both be true.

Because the truth is, those early years were hard. And beautiful. And exhausting. And full of moments that broke me and others that stitched me back together.

And this? This was just the beginning.

3

Milestones and Inchstones

Jude was following a different timeline before he even arrived.

I was finishing up at the office one Friday evening, half listening to the others making plans to go for a drink, when Charlotte called me in floods of tears.

She'd been to the toilet. There was blood. A lot of it.

I raced out and jumped into a black cab, calculating the weeks in my head. She was nearly thirty-two weeks pregnant. That meant there were still eight weeks to go. Was that enough? Was the baby developed enough to survive?

The cab crawled across London Bridge. I urged the traffic to move, phoned the maternity unit to let them know we were on our way, then called Charlotte again, just to hear her voice and reassure her that I'd be there soon. I hated that she was alone. Hated the silence that gave my brain too much space to panic.

When I got to the flat, I hugged her tightly, grabbed the hospital bags and we made our way back down to the car. I don't remember much about the drive to St Thomas's, just the pounding in my chest, the sweat on my palms, the hope that maybe, somehow, this would all turn out to be nothing.

But of course, it wasn't nothing. The baby's heartbeat was fine, they said, but Charlotte was admitted on the spot. They were taking no chances. After months of hospital visits and anxiety that the baby might come early, it looked like they'd been right to worry.

For the next week, we lived in a cycle of false starts, to and fro between the labour ward and maternity ward, never quite sure what was going to happen. Charlotte barely slept. I felt helpless, watching her go through so much pain and fear, knowing there was nothing I could do but be there. Keep calm. Stay strong. Stay positive. Pretend I wasn't crumbling too.

A week later, with no signs of the baby coming, she was induced. Labour began. Two failed epidurals, nearly eighteen hours of pain, and just when it looked like we were heading for an emergency caesarean, Jude arrived naturally.

He was blue. Completely blue. I froze. Babies cry when they're born but Jude didn't. He was silent. The seconds stretched like hours. And then, finally, he cried. And we cried too, relief washing over both of us as he was placed on Charlotte's chest for the first time.

It's true what they say, there's no feeling quite like becoming a parent for the first time. It's impossible to explain unless you've lived it. No words that can do justice to the emotions you feel in that moment. You've now got this tiny little human to look after, that you created, who you've brought into this world. It's a feeling of such overwhelming joy, where nothing else in the world matters and it doesn't feel like anything ever will again. Your whole life has just changed. This baby is now everything.

I was twenty-seven when I became a parent, but I think it was only in that moment that I suddenly felt like an adult.

MILESTONES AND INCHSTONES

Jude was small, fragile. Because he'd been born so early, he was quickly moved to the neonatal unit. A nurse, seeing how nervous I was, took pity on me and gave me a crash course in what to do: how to hold him, how to change his nappy, how to feed him. I'll never forget those first moments alone with him. The love. The fear. The quiet realisation that this little boy was completely dependent on us for everything.

Two days later, just when we thought the worst was behind us, they told us he needed to be moved again as he'd developed severe jaundice and his bilirubin levels were dangerously high. He was taken to the Special Care Baby Unit and into the highest-dependency room.

I remember walking in and seeing all the other tiny babies in incubators, many of them no bigger than my hand. There were wires everywhere and the beeping of machines. It was a glimpse into a world I'd never imagined being part of. But now, we were one of those families.

Jude looked so sick. So vulnerable. He had a cannula in his head as they hadn't been able to find a vein in his arm. I kept telling myself it would be OK, kept putting on a brave face for Charlotte. But inside, I was breaking. That night, as I drove away from the hospital, I barely made it 100 yards before I had to pull over, unable to see through the tears.

A few days later, while we were visiting, the alarms went off around one of the other cots. A baby was rushed to surgery. Later, we saw the mother collapse in the hallway. She had lost her baby.

That scream. The utter devastation. I'll never forget it. We were the lucky ones. And I knew it.

Over the next few days, Jude improved. He was moved

from Room 1 to Room 2 and eventually to Room 3. That's when we started talking about taking him home. And it was in those last few days, once he'd stabilised, that I found myself in the relaxation room on the maternity ward. There were a few expectant mothers pacing around, waiting for labour to begin. I was walking Jude in circles, his tiny body tucked into my arms, the sunlight streaming in through floor-to-ceiling windows that overlooked the River Thames, Big Ben and the Houses of Parliament.

It was peaceful. Still. A moment I've never forgotten.

I remember looking out at the incredible view, then down at him and telling him that he could be anything he wanted to be. That I would do everything in my power to help him get there. That the hard part was over and the rest of life was waiting. That I couldn't wait to be his dad, to love him, to raise him and help him have the best life possible. It felt like the start of everything. A quiet promise made to him in the calm after the storm. A moment where I let myself believe that everything would be simple from here.

But of course, life doesn't always go the way we imagine. And sometimes, the hardest parts are still to come.

Back then, I had no idea what lay ahead. Like most first-time parents, I had a picture in my head of what fatherhood would look like. And without even realising it, that picture had been forming for years, shaped by TV, films, books and all of the assumptions I didn't know I'd made.

One of those images came from the film *Jerry Maguire*. There's a scene where Jerry, played by Tom Cruise, is talking to Ray, the little boy in the film, as they're driving along and out of nowhere Ray says, 'Jerry, do you know the human head weighs eight pounds?'

It's funny. It's sweet. It's one of those perfect movie moments. And I realise now, I thought that was what parenting would be like. That's what I wanted it to be like. I thought I'd have kids who were chatty, clever, funny. That we'd have these quirky little conversations in the car and laugh together over things that they'd learned. I couldn't wait to be a dad, to enjoy moments like that. And it sounds ridiculous now, but I remember watching that film with Charlotte and saying something like, 'Our son's going to be like that.' As I held Jude in those early months, visions like that filled my mind. It never occurred to me that life might go another way.

Autism, disability, hadn't touched my life up until this point. It wasn't in the shows I watched, the books I read, the people I knew. It didn't even cross my mind as a possibility.

Of course, I knew life might be different to the rosy images we're bombarded with. But the different I was prepared for was minor: perhaps we wouldn't share the same interests. He might not get as excited as I do about football or sports in general. Maybe he'd have no interest in history or reading books. It never once occurred to me that my son wouldn't be able to talk. That we might never have a conversation like Jerry and Ray in that scene.

When life does end up looking so completely different from what you imagined, it brings a whole mix of emotions that are hard to untangle. Fear. Grief. Guilt. Not because you don't love your child but because you're still holding onto the life you thought you were going to live.

Those expectations run deep. They've been a part of you for longer than you realise, and they will go on to shape the way you interpret everything that happens next. The way you measure progress and define success. The way you feel when your baby doesn't hit the milestones all the other babies seem to be racing through.

When Charlotte first found out she was pregnant, I remember going into Waterstones and buying *The Contented Little Baby Book* by Gina Ford. I wanted to be prepared, get a head start. I wanted to know how to support our baby's development. It all stemmed from wanting to be a good dad, and I thought I was doing the right thing in being prepared. But really, all it did was cement those expectations even further, reinforcing the idea that there was a 'right' way to do things and a 'normal' pace to follow. That if you did everything right, things would just . . . happen.

Then from the moment Jude was born, the questions started. Has he smiled yet? Rolled over? Crawled? Pulled himself up? Started babbling? It's all part of the script. A shared language among parents, grandparents, health visitors, strangers at soft play. All the things a child 'should' be doing. The milestones stack up like checkpoints.

So when Jude started to fall behind those expected milestones, it was hard not to feel it. Every birthday party, every playdate, I was observing, comparing, overanalysing. At one party when Jude was three, I remember following him around the room while the other kids sat watching the entertainer. Jude was circling the edges, pacing, exploring. I kept trying to keep him away from the birthday cake, the only thing he had any interest in, worrying he'd get there before it was the right time. The party games started – pass the parcel, musical chairs – and Jude just didn't get it. I sat with him, tried to help him open his layer of the parcel. He didn't know what to do. All the other kids became more and more excited with every layer that was opened, desperate to see what was inside the present, but Jude couldn't care less. When the other kids were milling around, playing, a few of them came up to him, curious, trying to talk, trying to get him to join in. But Jude didn't respond. He wouldn't even look at them. And then the questions came.

'Why doesn't he speak?'

'Why doesn't he want to play with me?'

'Will he talk when he's older?'

They weren't cruel questions. They were innocent. Honest. The mind of a child trying to figure out why the little boy at the party who was the same size as them wouldn't talk back to them. But every time, it cut through me. Because I didn't have the answers, and I didn't know how to explain. The kids would give up and run back to their own games, and I'd hear them talking among themselves: 'That's Jude, he can't talk.'

Apart from a few sounds early on, for Jude and Tommy the words never followed. Speech was just one of what felt like so many milestones we weren't hitting. Toileting still wasn't mastered by the time they started school. Jude couldn't mark make, let alone start to colour or learn to write. Tommy loved colouring, but he definitely didn't stick to any lines. Cutlery wasn't used at mealtimes, unless it was in mine or Charlotte's hands. With no words and little interest in other kids, there were no early friendships. No bike rides, no games of chase in the park, no waving goodbye at the school gates.

And as each of those milestones passed us by, the worry grew louder in my mind and with it a creeping sense of failure. Like we'd done something wrong. Or not done enough. Like everyone else was racing ahead and we were somehow failing to keep up. It seeped into everything. I started turning every moment into a chance for learning. Every mealtime became a chance to prompt a word. Every playtime an opportunity to practise a skill. Praise became performance, fun became therapy. Even the things the boys did enjoy got turned into tools. Because I was desperate. Desperate to see some kind of progress, any sign that I was doing something right, that things were going to be OK.

But the irony is, in the effort to be the best parent you can be, you can start losing the joy of parenting altogether. It stops feeling like connection and starts feeling like pressure. And the weight of that pressure is exhausting. In trying to chase the milestones, we were in danger of losing the moments that were happening before our eyes. You stop seeing the child in front of you and start seeing the gap. The gap between where they are and where you thought they were 'meant' to be.

It's a painful way to live, always looking for what's missing. And at some point, something in me broke. I couldn't keep parenting like that. I couldn't keep measuring my boys against a version of childhood that wasn't made for them.

At some point I realised the comparisons just felt like grief on a loop. So I stopped looking at the gaps and started trying to see *them*. My boys. Not what they couldn't do but what they *were* doing. The small things. The tiny things. The things most families wouldn't ever think to celebrate.

Jude picking up a spoon and putting it into his yoghurt, even if he still needed help getting it to his mouth. Tommy looking up when I said his name, even if it was only for a second. Jude playing with the beads on his wooden activity cube. Tommy holding my hand when we went for a walk. Jude making a clear choice between two foods. Tommy stacking blocks like a master builder. Jude not getting upset when another child cried. Tiny steps. But to us, they were huge.

I read somewhere of another parent describing them as inchstones, and it just fitted perfectly. So that's what we started calling them. They weren't the milestones the books talked about but they mattered. They gave us hope.

Jude running to us when we got back from a few days away for our honeymoon. A moment that felt like he did actually miss us, that we did matter. Every time Tommy completed a puzzle. Jude rocking side to side to his favourite songs. Tommy bouncing a ball, over and over until he became a natural. Kicking a ball around with Jude in the park for a few minutes. Tommy playing pass the parcel.

Inchstones. No one else would have noticed them. But we did. Each and every time.

Starting to let go of those old expectations didn't just change how I saw the boys, it also changed how I felt as their dad. The pressure started to lift. The constant weight of feeling like I was 'not enough' started to loosen its grip a little. It didn't happen overnight. I still had moments where I found myself slipping into old patterns of comparing, doubting, second-guessing everything. But more and more, over time,

I started to feel it shift. Bit by bit I started to let go of the timeline I was chasing. I let go of the worry about catching up and focused on meeting the boys where they were. And it gave me the space to feel something else instead: joy.

It wasn't the joy you expect to come from the big moments; it wasn't the days out, the holidays, the parties and the achievements. It was the joy you feel from the simple moments. When I'd hear Tommy belly-laughing in the next room, with no idea what he found so funny. When I bounced on the trampoline with Jude, a huge smile on his face. Every time Tommy asked for a piggyback and I'd feel him latch on. Every night as Jude and I lay in bed listening to Ed Sheeran, and he'd rest his foot on my leg. Slowly, I started to see that parenting didn't have to be just about the progress Tommy and Jude were making. Sometimes, it was just about living, about a day that didn't end in tears but instead held small moments of peace or connection that you didn't think you'd get. Those moments were always there and always had been, I'd just been too focused on what was missing to see them.

And as I saw more of them, I softened. I laughed more easily. I played without an agenda. I stopped trying to squeeze meaning out of every moment and just let them be moments. It didn't mean I stopped hoping or that I stopped pushing when it mattered. But I stopped making our entire life about the next milestone. I let go of trying to 'catch up'. Tommy and Jude were already enough. And, slowly, they helped me to see that I was too.

*

MILESTONES AND INCHSTONES

One Sunday morning, Charlotte was catching up on sleep after another rough night and I was downstairs with the boys. Tommy was about one, Jude was four. It was sunny, one of those warm mornings where everything feels a bit lighter, so I took the boys outside. The plan was simple: burn off some energy, try not to wake Charlotte up and survive until lunchtime.

Jude was straight onto the trampoline. Bouncing, pacing, laughing, his version of joy. Trampolining was always an activity that seemed to satisfy his sensory needs, long before I really understood what that meant. But the second I stepped away to check on Tommy, he'd stop. Climb off. Pull me back with his eyes or his hand. He wanted me on there with him. Every second.

But I couldn't just leave Tommy. He was still so little, still wobbly on his feet, fascinated by everything and nothing. So I picked him up and brought him onto the trampoline with us.

It was chaos, straight away. I was trying to bounce hard enough for Jude to feel the rhythm he needed, soft enough so Tommy didn't fall. Trying to keep Tommy from bumping into Jude. Trying to keep Jude in his zone without being overwhelmed by his brother's unpredictability. Luckily, Tommy was already the thrill seeker he still is today and being bounced until he fell over was hilarious to him.

There was no rhythm. No calm. Just bouncing, adjusting, catching, laughing, grabbing, redirecting. Then off the trampoline. Run around the garden. Then back on. Round and round we went.

At one point, all three of us collapsed onto the trampoline

in a heap. I lay down between them, catching my breath. Then I reached out and started tickling them both. They laughed. Really laughed. Jude flapped his arms, kicking the mat with joy. Tommy shrieked with delight, his tiny body wriggling under my hand, and I held my breath hoping the sound wouldn't upset Jude. It didn't.

And I just lay there, looking at them, both of them smiling, both having fun. No goals. No targets. No expectations. Just a dad, and his two boys, figuring it out. For a couple of hours, we made it work. That morning I wasn't thinking about the words that hadn't come. I wasn't worrying about whether Jude understood what I was saying. I wasn't over-analysing, trying to see if there were any signs of progress. We just played.

That Sunday morning wasn't a big breakthrough; it was just a few hours in the garden. A morning with no meltdowns, no disasters and a chance for Charlotte to sleep. Just laughter, bouncing, fun with my boys. But as the weeks and months passed, that day stayed with me. I'd think about it after a tough day or when everything felt overwhelming and scary and let it remind me of how happy Tommy and Jude were in that moment. How happy I was.

This is where the journey really began for me. It was the start of a different kind of fatherhood. One that wasn't built around what I thought I should be doing or what my boys should be achieving. One that stopped measuring everything in milestones and how far behind my boys were and focused on the inchstones instead.

Because this journey didn't really begin with the diagnosis. It didn't begin with the research or the referrals or the leaflets. It began with that slow, uncomfortable, beautiful shift from grief to gratitude, from chasing what was missing to learning to see what was there. From trying to *fix* to focusing on *connection*.

It wasn't just that moment on the trampoline, it wasn't any single moment, but over time I stopped waiting for our life to look like everyone else's and started figuring out what life could look like for *us*.

And those inchstones keep coming. Quiet little reminders that we're growing. That we're learning. That give me strength on the lowest of days. That reassure me we're doing OK.

4

The Unwritten Rules

As I made my way back downstairs from checking on Tommy, I spotted a trail of rice leading from the kitchen to the living room. I followed it and found Jude standing in front of the TV, chewing away, a sprinkle of rice at his feet. Most parents would probably be frustrated finding their six-year-old like this, maybe even a little angry. Instead, I had to contain my excitement, fighting the urge to scoop him up and spin him round. I had to stop myself from making too big a deal of this huge step, overwhelming him and scaring him off from ever doing it again. Jude had just eaten rice!

He paid little attention to me and made his way back to the kitchen. I followed him, all the way to my half-eaten plate of dinner still on the side. He reached for my plate, grabbed another handful of egg fried rice and shovelled it into his mouth. He spun round and headed back to the living room, more rice scattering in his wake.

Up until then, Jude had a very limited diet. There were two dinners that he'd actually eat – a cheese and tomato pizza, and pasta with a Dolmio meatball sauce, and even they were hit and miss. New foods were a no-go, and it had been a stressful topic for the last few years as we battled with improving his daily nutrition. So, trying egg fried rice, unprompted, and going back for more was huge, and I was so proud of him. What mattered wasn't *how* Jude ate, but *that* he ate. That he was trying something new. That he was doing it on his terms.

But for many outsiders, they'd have seen fault. Why was he using his hands? Why wasn't he sitting at the table? Why was he walking around and eating? Why was he taking from someone else's plate? And maybe a few years earlier, that's what I'd have seen too. Until I learned to start picking my battles.

I used to think dinner would be one of those lovely, bonding family moments. You know the kind, everyone sat at the table, eating the same meal, chatting about their day. That's what I saw in films and on adverts. What we got looked nothing like that. Jude would take a few bites, then get up and start pacing, flapping his hands, running from side to side across the room. Tommy would nibble at one piece of food, then flip himself upside down on the sofa, humming happily to himself. Cutlery would be left on the table, quickly swapped out for fingers.

Sometimes dinner was eaten. Sometimes it was pushed away, untouched. Attempts at introducing new foods were ignored. Even favourite safe foods, eaten happily one day, would be snubbed the next. Jude had his pasta and meatballs phase, which I'd have to spoon-feed to him while trying to keep him in his seat, but even then some days he ate only the meatballs, some days only the pasta. Some days, if the stars aligned, both. Some days Tommy would eat just the skin off his sausages, leaving all the meat inside. Other days he'd eat the meat and peel off the skin. Occasionally, he'd eat the whole thing. The same went for chicken nuggets. There was no pattern, no predictability, no logic you could hold onto.

For years, Tommy went through a phase of only eating dinner at my parents' house. There, he'd clear his plate. At home? He'd pick at bits, leave it half-eaten. I tried everything, same meals, same brands, even my mum cooking it at their house and bringing it straight over to ours, just in case she had some magic touch, but it never worked.

The hardest part wasn't even the food. It was the feeling that something was slipping away. Every unfinished meal, every abandoned plate, every battle at the table chipped away at the image I'd carried in my head. And in its place was uncertainty. A life that didn't fit the story I thought we were living. And underneath it all, fear. Fear that they weren't eating enough or that what they were eating wasn't healthy enough. Fear that somehow, all of it was my fault. That if I could just 'parent better', dinners and everything else would magically fall into place.

It took me years to realise that forcing things to look how they were 'supposed' to wasn't helping anyone. Trying to make dinnertime perfect was driving a wedge between us. All it did was make dinner more stressful and make it even less likely that the boys would eat. And at the end of the day, them eating their dinner, however that looked, was what was important. I realised that picking my battles wasn't about letting go of standards, it was about letting go of the wrong ones, the ones that weren't right for our family. It was about doing what my boys needed, not what the world expected.

Because it was, once again, about expectations. It was

about trying to follow a script that wasn't written for our lives. The problem wasn't Jude or Tommy. The problem was the version of 'family life' I was still trying to force us to live up to. And once I started to see it that way, everything shifted. Dinner was just the start. Letting go of the battles that didn't matter gave me more energy to fight the ones that did. It gave me permission to choose joy over judgement. To choose understanding over society's expectations. To choose Tommy and Jude, their needs, their pace, their happiness, again and again. When you're raising autistic children, it's not just dinner that looks different, it can alter everything. And when you stop trying to force your family to live by someone else's rules, that's when you can start trying to build something better.

As with the ingrained milestones, those 'rules' don't just vanish overnight. They cling to you. They're buried deep in the years of life experience you've had and the media you've consumed. They're built into every bit of advice you hear, every sideways glance from strangers, every well-meaning comment from people who don't live your life.

And learning to let go of them, really let go, means first seeing them for what they are.

You don't get handed a rulebook when you become a parent but somehow you still end up carrying one anyway, deep inside. It's stitched into every conversation you overhear. Every article you read. Every throwaway comment from friends, family and strangers in supermarket queues.

Children should sleep in their own beds. Children should eat at the table. Children should say please and thank you.

THE UNWRITTEN RULES

Children should dress appropriately for the weather. Children should sit still and pay attention. Children should behave a certain way in public.

I didn't even realise how many of these rules I was living by until Jude and Tommy started to grow. Until it became clear that our life didn't fit the script. At first, I fought it. I apologised when Jude didn't say hello to someone who greeted him and tried to get him to look up at them or wave. I insisted Tommy wear a coat when he was adamant he wasn't cold. I tried to coax Jude back to the table when he got up mid-meal to stim and run around.

I worried endlessly about how we looked from the outside. What people thought when they saw us. What they thought about my parenting, whether they assumed we were lazy or careless or doing it all wrong.

In the early years I struggled with this a lot, most often in supermarkets. Tommy would run from aisle to aisle and I'd chase after him, narrowly avoiding other shoppers as we zipped past them. More often than not we'd end up with Tommy lying down in the middle of an aisle or buried against one of the product shelves, seeking deep pressure, clearly overwhelmed. And that's when the comments would start. Some were harmless, trying to be funny, some were mean, with no other intention than to let out some of their own frustration and anger into the world. Telling me that they'd never let their kid get away with doing that, that I needed to teach him a lesson. Through gritted teeth I'd focus on Tommy and choose to ignore them rather than tell them what I was really thinking. Choosing Tommy (or Jude) over an argument that would likely distress them even more.

Every time someone stared or gave unsolicited advice, it chipped away at me. Every time I saw a child following all the 'rules' effortlessly, it stirred up doubt. Was I failing my boys? Was I making excuses? If I was more strict, had more boundaries in place, eventually Jude and Tommy would follow the rules too. Wouldn't they?

It took a long time to see the truth clearly. The problem wasn't that Jude and Tommy weren't following the rules. The problem was that the rules weren't made for them. When your child's brain is wired differently, when their sensory needs are different and their ability to communicate is different, it's not just that those rules don't fit, they actually cause harm. They can be damaging, anxiety inducing and meltdown triggering.

Trying to make them sit still when their bodies needed to move wasn't 'teaching discipline', it was ignoring their needs. Forcing eye contact wasn't 'building social skills', it was demanding something of them that felt invasive and uncomfortable. Pushing them to behave a certain way in public, just to make a random person in the supermarket more comfortable, wasn't preparing them for the world, it was asking them to be someone they're not.

Eventually, I had to confront my way of thinking and how I was parenting. Whose comfort was I protecting when I forced these rules upon them? Theirs? Or mine?

It's not easy, unlearning the narrative you've been told all your life about what a 'good parent' looks like. It's not easy feeling judged or misunderstood, knowing people think you're 'letting them get away with it' when you're actually fighting for their dignity. But little by little, the discomfort started to fade and was replaced by something stronger: a deeper understanding of my children than I knew was possible and a pride in who they are.

Because once you stop trying to force your child to meet the world's expectations and start meeting them where they are, everything changes. You stop worrying so much about what other people think and you start focusing on what really matters most: your child.

Letting go didn't happen all at once. It happened in a hundred tiny moments. Moments where I had to stop and ask myself, what actually matters here? What am I trying to achieve? Who am I trying to prove myself to?

Does it matter that when we drive to the shop each night Tommy is barefoot and will only wear a T-shirt, no matter if it's July or January? Or is it more important that he feels comfortable enough to go out and face the world that day?

Does it matter if Jude eats with his hands and will only use cutlery for one or two mouthfuls at most? Or does it matter that he's eating, nourishing his body and staying regulated enough to get through the day?

Does it matter if either of them stim in public, flapping their hands, bouncing, hopping, vocalising, even if it causes people to stare? Or is it more important that they have ways to cope with a world that often feels overwhelming?

The more I thought about it, the more I realised it wasn't just about a few things here and there. It was about pretty much everything. And I could either choose to make changes to my own mindset, focusing on the battles and challenges that were truly important and needed changing, or I could let others determine how we live our lives and make my boys a lot less happy because of it.

I didn't realise how tightly I was trying to follow these invisible rules until I started to let go of them. And when I did let go, little by little, I felt it in my own body too. I breathed easier. My shoulders dropped. My mind stopped racing. I was no longer spending every day trying to control the uncontrollable. I was finally living alongside my kids, not against the reality of who they were.

So I made different choices . . .

- Letting them pace around the living room while they ate dinner if they needed to, because sitting still feels like confinement to them. Letting Tommy eat his dinner sitting on the sofa, in his bedroom or at the table when he chooses to. There's a reason why he's making those choices each day; he might not be able to explain it to me, but I can believe it's important to him.

- Letting Tommy keep his jumper or coat on, even if I think it's too warm, because he's making a choice based on his sensory needs. Trusting that he knows what he needs in that moment.

- Letting Jude have unlimited screen time each day. Realising that it is a safety net for him that he needs to help him regulate and cope with the world. And understanding that while there's not much Jude is able to control himself, not much that he truly enjoys, the iPad fulfils both of those criteria. In a world where so many choices are made for him, it is something he can work independently, and he can choose what he wants to watch or listen to. Would I love him to spend less time on screens? Sure. But in a world where he has so little control and that can be so overwhelming, I can see how important that time is for him.

- Saying yes to hour-long showers, or multiple baths and showers a day, because the feel of water helps regulate their nervous systems better than anything else could. Water is important to both Tommy and Jude, and if they're seeking that activity on any given day, there's a reason behind that. Do I wish Tommy wouldn't splash so much water out of the shower every night, and that I wouldn't have to mop up after him? Of course. Am I more focused on making sure he lets me wash his hair and clean his teeth every night? Definitely.

- Choosing happy, familiar foods instead of forcing variety and tears at the table. Choosing sustenance over ideal nutrition when the latter means foods that they are just unable to eat.

- Letting them be barefoot indoors and outdoors, whether that's in the house, in the car or in the park. Every time we sit on a bench by the river, watching the world go by, Jude wants his shoes and socks off, and that's fine.

- Letting Jude be topless at home. As soon as he was physically able to take his own T-shirt off, he did. The second he gets home from school or wherever we've been, it comes off, every single time. For him to do it that regularly is a sign of a clear sensory need. So I stopped trying to put his shirt back on.

- Responding to communication however it comes – gestures, noises, glances – and not forcing words.

- Accepting stimming is not a problem to fix but a part of who they are. Stimming is shorthand for 'self-stimulating behaviour' and usually involves repetitive movements, sounds or actions. Autistic people might stim to gain sensory input, to reduce stress and anxiety or simply for enjoyment. For Tommy and Jude that might involve hand flapping, bouncing, jumping or rocking back and forth. Humming, or replaying certain parts of their favourite cartoons or songs, over and over and over again. Recently Tommy has started licking his lips a lot, which seems partly a sensory need and partly a sign he's feeling anxious. Most of us stim without even realising. Maybe you shake your leg while sitting, bite your nails or twirl your hair. For autistic people it's often more intense or more frequent, but as long as it's not causing distress or discomfort, to them or to others, there's no need for it to be stopped. So when Tommy is sitting in among the stones, the bark and woodchips, and the sandpit, seeking the feeling of them between his fingers and flicking them, I am OK with that. Do I wish we got fewer weird looks in public? Definitely. Do I care more about my boys feeling safe, happy and free to be themselves? Always. So I make sure he's not bothering anyone else, not flicking sand over anyone and ignore the stares.

- Letting Jude have his dummy until he was seven years old as it was a huge sensory comfort for him. He sought it out whenever he was upset, it helped him self-regulate and get to sleep. He gave it up when he was ready to move on.

- Focusing on toileting when it was right for Tommy and not when he 'should' be nappy-free. We tried at various stages, realised he wasn't ready and waited until he showed more signs of progression, choosing to have that battle when it was the right time to do so.

Every time I made one of those choices, something changed. They relaxed. I relaxed. We found more joy, more connection; less anxiety and more peace. I never lowered my expectations, just re-evaluated them around what my boys needed. And that isn't giving up, it's picking the battles that actually matter.

Some things are non-negotiable, not because they match someone else's idea of 'good parenting' but because they matter to the boys' lives. Safety is one of them. I'll never stop fighting for my boys to be safe at home, at school, out in the world. That means teaching them, in their own way, about dangers they might not naturally pick up on. Road safety has always been a challenge. Whenever we're walking near traffic, I'm on edge, keeping myself between them and the danger, ready in case they bolt. In many ways it's become easier as they've got older and grown in their understanding and experience, but I know that in a moment of anxiety or meltdown, both Tommy and Jude are still likely to move unpredictably, without thought of safety or control. And with them both being much bigger and stronger these days, it can be a challenge to keep them safe. Or it can be as simple as something catching their eye. Tommy had one near miss where I had to drag him out of the path of traffic, because he had spotted a cat on the other side of the road. Usually, he runs the other way if a cat comes anywhere near him, but for some reason, this particular cat he just had to go and see close up! So it means holding boundaries when it comes to roads, water, strangers, even if it means trying to carry Jude across a car park while he's kicking and screaming because he doesn't understand why we have to move quickly.

Communication is another. I never try to force speech, but I'm always supporting the way Tommy and Jude communicate. That means honouring every gesture, every sound, every glance that tells me something about what they need, being patient, enthusiastic and encouraging them to communicate more. It has also meant fighting for Augmentative and Alternative Communication (AAC) when it's needed and trying to make others respect non-speaking communication just as much as spoken words. Because everyone deserves to have a voice, in whatever form works for them.

Their dignity is non-negotiable too. I'll always stand between them and anyone who treats them like they're less. Whether that's a teacher who underestimates them, a stranger who stares too long or a system that tries to shut them out. I'll advocate. I'll push back. I'll speak up when needed and I won't back down.

Sometimes, the battles worth fighting aren't the big obvious ones. Sometimes they're quiet, daily acts of belief. The world sees bravery in the big battles, the tribunals, the protests, the meetings where we advocate until our voices shake. But there's a quieter bravery too. The kind that happens at home, every time we choose trust over control. Every time we let our children show us who they are, not who the world expects them to be.

Choosing to believe Tommy when he says he's not cold and refuses to wear more clothes, even when it's freezing outside. Choosing to respect Jude's autonomy when he refuses to walk into a room, even when it looks fine to me. Choosing to respect their sensory needs, even when the world tells me to 'toughen them up'. Choosing to trust that my boys know their bodies and their needs better than anyone else.

For me, that's what 'picking battles' actually looks like. It's asking different questions. Not 'How do I make them fit in?' But 'How do I make sure they're respected, supported and safe?' Not 'How do I get them to do what everyone else is doing?' But 'How do I help them thrive on their own terms?'

I once thought that being a good parent was about helping shape my boys to fit the world. Now I know it's about creating a life that fits them and that works for our family. It's not about sitting quietly at the dinner table, getting dressed quickly in the morning or saying the right thing at the right time. It's about feeling safe, feeling understood, knowing they don't have to be someone they're not just to be loved.

It means questioning those invisible rules, asking, is this about growth or is it about appearances? Am I teaching them something important or am I teaching them to hide who they are? Am I parenting for them or parenting for the people watching?

LOVE NEEDS NO WORDS

And once you start living by *those* questions, something beautiful happens. You start seeing your child for who they are, their needs, their strengths, their struggles and everything that makes them *them*. And you realise that even if the life you're building looks nothing like you once imagined, it's still good. It's still yours. And it's exactly the life your child needed all along.

5

The Small Joys

There's a moment I always come back to. Jude was two. We were on a day out at Tropical Wings, a little zoo and garden park, with birds and butterflies, rabbits in pens, even meerkats. We'd gone with a group of families Charlotte had met through baby groups, so our kids were all born within a few months of each other and the parents were new friends in our new hometown. That first year, Charlotte and the other mums had spent a lot of time together, and I'd met some of them at the odd weekend meet-up, but this was the first time we'd all got together as a group.

I was a little nervous, hoping Jude would have a good time and enjoy it – and that Charlotte and I would be able to relax and have fun too. But that day the differences between our children cut right through me.

Their kids were running around, calling out to each other and their parents, chatting away, asking questions, pointing at animals. They were curious, noisy, social, everything you expect of toddlers at that age. Jude was quiet. Floating on the outside of it all. He wasn't interested in the animals, didn't want to hold my hand or join in. He didn't really interact with the other children either, most of the time looking confused if they came up to him or simply choosing to walk away from them. He spent much of the time either being carried or wandering on his own path. Already I could see we were having to work hard to keep the experience enjoyable for him, where it just seemed so easy for everybody else. Their kids just seemed to turn up and automatically start having fun. I watched the other parents laughing, chatting, snapping photos of their kids. So at ease. All I could think was: we're not really a part of this anymore.

It was one of those days where the grief crept up on me. The kind where you smile and nod and make polite conversation, trying to get to know the other parents better, trying to get to know the dads. All the while trying not to stare at what the other kids are doing. Hoping my face wasn't showing the torrent of emotions that were rushing around inside. Spending time with so many other kids of Jude's age just emphasised to me how different Jude was to them. How different our paths were becoming.

And then, we found the water tray.

Simple plastic containers, filled with a few inches of water. Nothing fancy. No instructions to follow, no complicated games. Just water. But to Jude, they were magical.

His face lit up. He darted over, hands in straight away, splashing and feeling and watching the water trickle between his fingers. He was laughing, really laughing, in a way I hadn't seen all day. Just like the other kids had been laughing throughout the day. His arms went in deeper and deeper; his sleeves were soon soaking wet no matter how much I rolled them up. I had to stop him from climbing in fully a number of times. But it didn't matter. I knelt beside him and played too. Watching the way his face lit up, I felt that ache in my chest loosen just a little.

Something about water has always drawn Jude in. Wherever there was water, a river, a fountain, even a garden feature, I'd have to stop him climbing in. Where the rest of the day had felt confusing and overwhelming, this made sense to him. It grounded him. It wasn't what I'd imagined days out would look like, but in that particular moment, Jude was happy. And for the first time that day, so was I.

We left the zoo still feeling the sting of comparison, still noticing the gap between our world and theirs. But I also carried something else with me: the sound of Jude's laugh at the water tray. The light in his eyes. That moment of joy, it stayed with me.

I didn't know it then but it was the start of something new. The start of learning to see happiness differently.

Water has always brought out something special in both of the boys. Not swimming, that's still a skill we're yet to master, just moving, splashing, feeling. There's something about the sensation of water on their skin, the way it moves and flows, the sound it makes and the patterns it creates, that lights them up like nothing else.

We've had moments in swimming pools where nothing else in the world matters. Jude circling around the shallow end, flicking water up into the air. Watching me splash. Letting me lift him up and crash him down into the water. Not under, never under, that's too much for him but the splash and the waves it creates, that's what he loves. Tommy's the braver one.

Inching down towards the deep end, going as far as his tiptoes will allow. Jumping in the pool over and over again. But mainly, splashing and flapping. That's what both of them love, and they can do it for hours.

Paddling pools are another favourite. Tommy spends pretty much his whole summer in one even now, and it's only in recent years that Jude's enthusiasm for them has lessened. But Tommy loves nothing more than to slide around on his knees in there, splashing water over the top. It never gets old for him.

It's the same with the bath or shower. Jude will be in and out of there multiple times a day. Which on occasion has been frustrating, having to dry him and help him get dressed over and over again. But whenever I've felt like that I've just had to remind myself how important it is to him, how much it helps him calm his nervous system. Sometimes it helps to just stand outside and listen to all the happy vocal stims coming from inside the bathroom. Tommy has a slightly different approach: less often, longer duration. He goes from the bath to the shower, time after time. It's like his own mini-spa in there. It soaks the bathroom floor every time and makes the paint peel off the walls but again, the joy he gets from it, the relaxed state he's in when he leaves the bathroom, it's always worth it.

Tommy also finds puddles impossible to resist. He can't walk past one without stopping to explore it. Not just stomping, although that happens plenty, but crouching right down to play with his fingers, feeling the ripples, watching the reflections and the light dance across the surface.

There's something about water that feels freeing for both

of them, as though their bodies can let go and their minds can rest. And some of our best interactions have come in those moments. Playful, close, unforced. Just connection. Joy.

And water wasn't the only place I began to notice it. For Tommy, there are also puzzles. He has loved them since he was just a year old. While the rest of the world can seem difficult for Tommy to navigate, puzzles provide no such issue. He was soon completing puzzles meant for much older children. He'll mix multiple puzzles together and make all of them simultaneously. He'll make puzzles image side down, not using the picture on the box as a guide but going just by the shapes of the pieces. Boxes get thrown to the side, the image he's trying to create already committed to memory. Occasionally, he'll get bored with them and not touch them for months at a time. Then, just when I think he's done with them, he'll start making them again.

While he does love completing puzzles, he also loves scattering the pieces around the room. Flicking them, dropping them, causing a huge amount of mess with multiple puzzles and hundreds of pieces. I could see it made him happy, but in the early days it would stress me out. I'd worry that pieces would get lost, which would then annoy him when he came to make them again. And the mess annoyed me. I was much happier watching him make them, which to me signalled how clever he was. I loved nothing more than when he'd complete one, turn around to me and wait for me to clap and cheer. But, I had to admit, he really loved stimming with them too. Maybe even more so. And so, I stepped back, got out of my own head and chose to try to see the joy through his eyes.

LOVE NEEDS NO WORDS

Now, every night, Tommy gets out a 1,000-piece puzzle and empties it onto the rug. He gets down onto the floor and starts to pick the pieces up, flicking them across the room, stacking them up into mini-towers and letting them fall like raindrops through his fingers. Sometimes he'll lie face down on the floor, head tilted, watching how they move as he scatters them. There's a rhythm to it, a kind of dance, and even though the pieces end up everywhere, it brings him peace. And these days, as I watch through the glass doors into the annexe, I don't care whether he finishes the puzzle or not. I care that he's happy. That he's calm. That he's found something that helps him wind down from the world.

Because this moment on the floor with scattered puzzle pieces and a quiet smile is the beautiful moment. One I might have missed, if I hadn't learned to look a little differently.

It took time for me to make that change. In the early years, I sometimes felt embarrassed when people saw Jude or Tommy play in ways that looked 'different'. If Tommy flicked sand or Jude ignored attempts to interact from the other children and just ran backwards and forwards across the grass. When Tommy would lie down at the very top of the slide or Jude would be more interested in the wrapping paper than the presents. Back then I thought it was my job to teach Jude and Tommy how to play. To show them the 'right' way. To help them move on from the repetitive things they were doing and guide them towards something more purposeful. More typical.

If Jude was pacing the room or flapping at the radiator, I'd try to tempt him over with a toy. If Tommy was stacking puzzle pieces into little towers, I'd encourage him to finish the puzzle instead. I'd suggest we make the blocks into a shape, instead of a straight line or swap the bottle Jude was tapping for a ball we could throw back and forth.

I never did it to be unkind. It all came from love and from a belief that I was helping. That if I could just get them to engage with the world the way other children did, it would make their lives easier in the long run. I thought I was showing them something better. I was scared they'd be seen as 'different'; I wanted them to be more like everyone else.

Around that time we were really struggling: big meltdowns every day and with little connection. Something had to change. I didn't realise for a while that what needed to change was me. Then we did a course called the Son-Rise Programme, a type of therapy we'd discovered after many late night Google searches in the desperate hope of finding something that would improve Jude and Tommy's lives. In simple terms, it's a parent-led, relationship-first approach: you join your child in what they love, keep things calm and low-demand, celebrate any attempt to connect and build from there. We didn't stick to it religiously and not all of it was right for us (a little too 'American' in style for a more laid-back Brit), nor did I agree with all that the programme taught. But one simple idea from it shifted everything for me.

What if, instead of trying to change Tommy's and Jude's behaviour, I joined them in what they were doing and what they enjoyed? Here I was trying to force Tommy and Jude to do things that I wanted them to do or that I thought kids their age 'should' be doing but that they clearly had little interest in. That simple question 'what if I joined them instead?' flipped a switch for me. So I gave it a go. If Jude was running side to side across the room, I ran too. If he was tapping the radiator, I'd sit at the one next to him and tap too. No pressure. No demands. Just being with him. When he grabbed a bottle and wandered around tapping it, so did I. I lay on my back humming when he did, I threw blocks with him, flapped my hands when he did and rocked back and forth in sync, dancing together. And sometimes, I'd see it, the glance, the flicker of recognition. Even a smile. The smallest sign that we were connecting.

When Tommy was stacking his puzzle pieces into towers or letting them fall like rain, I started doing the same beside him. If he was making a puzzle I'd grab another one and lie down near him to make it. At first, he looked confused or would take the puzzle off me, in which case I'd move onto something else. But over the weeks I persisted and eventually, he smiled. Soon he was taking my pieces and joining in, making it for me. Taking control but letting me be a part of it with him. I was allowed to join in.

One of the things that has always amazed me about Tommy and Jude is how much joy the simple things in life bring them – water, puzzles, music, the same YouTube video on repeat. For my boys, that's because of the way their brain is wired, part of them being autistic.

The same brain that struggles to filter out background noise or sudden changes also seems to experience joy more vividly, more fully, when something feels good. It's as if they don't just like something, they *feel* it, in their whole body. The right music. A splash of water. A favourite video. It lights them up from the inside out.

They don't care if it's the 'right' thing to enjoy. They don't worry about what other people might think. It doesn't matter if they've done it or seen it a thousand times before (in fact, that often seems to make it even more fun). They're not trying to fit in. They're just being themselves in a way few of us ever experience. And I think that's one of the unexpected gifts of autism. A kind of emotional honesty. When Jude is happy, you *know*. When Tommy is excited, it's contagious. There's no filter. No holding back. Just pure, unfiltered joy.

When you become a parent you assume you will have to teach your kids how to be in the world. But the truth is, Tommy and Jude have taught me just as much about this, if not more. They've taught me that joy doesn't have to be complicated. That it's OK to love the same thing again and again. Repetition can be comforting. Happiness can come from a puddle, a YouTube clip, a stretchy string. And maybe the world isn't made better by fitting in but by embracing what makes you different.

The more I joined Tommy and Jude in their world and the more they saw me enjoying what they enjoyed, the deeper our bond became. We weren't just co-existing anymore, they actively wanted to be around me and let me in. They trusted me and felt more relaxed, now that I wasn't trying to stop their fun or make them do something else instead. And the funny thing was, the more they trusted me and the more relaxed they were, the more open they were to trying something different too. Like playing with a ball, trying a flash card game or looking at a book.

That course and the many, many moments that followed, taught me that connection doesn't come from pulling your child into your world. It comes from stepping into theirs.

Tapping the radiator. Stacking the puzzle pieces. Rocking back and forth. Not because you're trying to make it stop but because you want them to know: I see you, I'm with you and I love doing this too.

That change of mindset, from redirecting to joining in, didn't just help the boys, it changed me too. It helped me to see the joy in moments I used to overlook. Whenever I'm with Jude and he's dancing, rocking back and forth, I'll jump up and do the same. There have been hundreds of moments now, beautiful, special moments that fill my heart with joy, that are just me and him rocking around the room. Me spinning him around in circles like we're on *Strictly Come Dancing* (I used to pick him up and spin him but with a seventeen-year-old as tall as me, those days are long gone). Jude's face is full of joy in those moments, his eyes open wide, looking deep into mine, his face beaming. Moments like that wouldn't have happened if I'd stayed in my old mindset. If I hadn't spent months tapping radiators and flapping hands beside him. That's where the trust came from. That's where the connection began. Those moments were the heart of our life together.

Once I opened my eyes, I started to see the beauty in moments everywhere I looked, every day. Every time Jude and Tommy flap their hands with excitement. When Jude taps my nose and stares into my eyes, his face full of joy. When Tommy bounces his ball down the ramps at the skate park, chasing it with delight. When I hear Jude humming in the shower. The way Tommy lights up whenever he opens a present, not just one meant for him but for anyone. Watching both boys bounce on a trampoline, their whole bodies feeling each jump like it's the best sensation in the world. Every time I've pushed them on a swing and seen their faces tilt to the sky, smiling.

The photos we get sent home from school, Tommy grinning mid-activity, Jude relaxed in sensory play. The McDonald's trips where chicken nuggets are devoured with the kind of joy most people reserve for a gourmet meal. The river walks that once felt impossible and are now familiar and calm. The moments spent kicking a ball with Jude in the park or watching Tommy flick stones into the air or letting sand fall through his hands like it's magic.

The rhythmic, happy pacing. The gentle foot resting on my leg as they drift off to sleep. Every time Tommy uses his AAC device to ask for something and smiles when I understand. Every time Jude climbs into my lap, his way of asking for 'Row Row Row Your Boat'. The moments of quiet closeness that once felt so far away.

The list could go on forever.

Because in among the anxiety, the meltdowns, the sleepless nights and the constant worrying, there has always been joy. Pure, unapologetic, childlike joy. The kind of joy that grabs your heart and reminds you what matters. And even now, at fourteen and seventeen, it hasn't faded.

When I watch my boys in those moments, lost in water play, watching their favourite clips, singing along to songs they love, I honestly envy them. I wish I could enjoy anything the way they do, *as often* as they do. That moment when Arsenal score a last-minute winner? That surge of joy that takes over my body? They get that feeling five hundred times a day. And these days, I see it. And, maybe not as deeply as them, but I feel it too.

Right now, as I write this, I can see Tommy in the garden. He's hopping on one leg, flapping a stretchy string in his hand as he goes. He stops at the table, flips the page of his Smyths Toys catalogue (his current favourite), then hops off again, completely in his element. It might not make sense to anybody else, but to him, it's pure joy. And that's the thing I've come to understand most of all: if it makes you happy, it doesn't have to make sense to anybody else.

Joy lives in the quiet moments. The messy ones. The ones no one else would even notice. These are the moments I used to overlook, too focused on what was missing to notice what was right in front of me. But when I stopped chasing someone else's version of happiness, I started seeing ours. It's not picture-perfect. It's not always easy. But it's very real.

And now, when I think about the kind of parent I want to be, the kind of life I want for my boys, I don't picture milestones, I picture moments. The kind of moments I'll remember forever. The kind that don't need words. The kind that get you through the harder days. The moments that matter the most.

Like that day at Tropical Wings. What began as a punch of grief and sting of comparison ended with Jude at the water tray, sleeves dripping wet, laughter spilling out of him.

6

Love Needs No Words

One Saturday afternoon we were in my parents' garden, making the most of the warm weather with the paddling pool. The second my dad got the pool out, Jude was standing right next to him, desperate to get in. There's no explaining to him that it needs time to fill up, he doesn't have the patience for that. Before the hose had made even a puddle's worth of water, he was starting to undress.

Of course, this meant the water was freezing cold. Jude didn't seem to mind, happily sliding and splashing around, but my dad and I decided to warm it up for him. To and fro we went, carrying buckets of warm water from the kitchen to the garden, filling the pool bit by bit as Jude played. Seeing how happy he was, I stopped, grabbed my phone and started recording. It hadn't been the best of weeks, so seeing him relaxed and having fun was a relief.

My dad came back with another bucket and poured it in. Jude stopped splashing and looked up at him. He pulled himself up onto his knees and kissed my dad on the cheek. It was completely spontaneous, Jude's way of saying 'thank you'. Unable to say the words out loud, he wanted his grandad to know how grateful he was for warming up the water, for making the pool even better for him.

Tears filled my eyes. We were all a little shocked. Spontaneous moments of communication like that were very rare with Jude. For more than seven years I'd been waiting to hear his first words. I was desperate to hear his voice and would have given anything to know what he was thinking. To have a conversation with him. The silence of those years had been heavy. Our house was full of love, laughter, noise from toys and TV but still, there was that absence. That gap where words were supposed to be. And here he was, showing us exactly what he felt in a way that needed no words at all. That kiss spoke louder than any sentence ever could.

It was also a turning point for me, one of the first times I remember truly believing that communication is so much more than just speech. This was proof that it's about connection and listening, really listening to what our kids are trying to say without words. Jude kissing my dad like that showed us that love needs no words.

A few years later, I shared the video of that moment on my Stories About Autism page and it went viral. The video had millions of views, was shared by celebrities and people from all over the world commented on how beautiful it was. To many of those viewers it was a glimpse into the world of a non-speaking child. For others it was a reflection of their own lives. I reshare it once or twice a year, and every time it goes viral again, viewed by millions. Confirmation of just how special a moment it was.

Moments like that taught me to rethink everything I thought I knew about communication. Like most parents,

I'd started out with a very fixed idea of what communication looked like: it was spoken words, plain and simple. I expected Jude and Tommy to start babbling when they were babies, that their first words would be 'Mum' and 'Dad' and more words would follow. In no time we'd be having full conversations about what they want to do today, what they like and dislike and how their day went. We would be explaining the world to them and listening to what they've got to say about it.

So when Jude wasn't saying his first words or reaching those early speech milestones, naturally I worried. While we were exploring his autism diagnosis I held onto the idea that he was just a late developer and that the words would come in time. But as time went on and Jude grew older, I started to see there was a chance he may never speak.

In the early days, I tried to stay hopeful. He used to love watching this DVD, a kind of picture flashcard show, where they'd slowly say words alongside images on the screen. 'Apple.' 'Ball.' 'Dog.' I remember how he would watch it, completely absorbed, over and over again. At the time, I was convinced he was taking it all in, that the words were quietly building inside him, just waiting for the right moment to come out. That one day, they'd all tumble out at once.

Looking back, I think he just found it soothing. The rhythm of the voice. The predictable pace. The calm visuals. The repetition and knowing what to expect. It probably helped him regulate more than it was ever going to help him speak. But I clung to it at the time because, like most parents, back then I believed that speech was the goal and that spoken words were the key to unlocking everything else.

I'll be honest, realising that Jude, and later on Tommy, might never speak was one of the hardest things to accept. When the paediatrician who diagnosed Jude told us that, I was shocked. I couldn't imagine a world where my son wouldn't be able to speak.

How would he tell us what he needed? How would I know what he liked or didn't like? What made him happy or sad? How would we connect if he couldn't talk to me? How would he make friends? Would he get bullied and teased at school?

At the time, I thought words were the only way to have those connections. It was what the world had taught me up to that point. Which meant for many years I carried a heavy sense of guilt with me, wondering whether Jude's and Tommy's lack of progress in developing speech was my fault, because I wasn't doing enough or wasn't doing it 'right'. The countless speech therapy sessions, the research, the attempts to mouth simple words with them, none of it seemed to 'work'. Other families made progress, other kids suddenly began to speak, so the problem must be me, right?

It's taken time, but ten years later, I've let go of much of that guilt. It still creeps in now and again, on the harder days, especially when I've not been able to understand Jude or Tommy or figure out what's wrong. Maybe there will always be days like that, but the vast majority of the time, I focus on all the ways we *are* able to communicate. Because communication isn't about meeting other people's expectations, it's not about hitting milestones or fitting in. It's about finding ways to understand each other, even if that doesn't involve spoken words.

Jude's kiss that day in the paddling pool showed me something I couldn't fully grasp at the time: that my boys didn't need to speak to connect with me. They were already telling me so much, I just needed to learn how to listen. Unfortunately, the rest of the world doesn't always see it that way. Spoken language is often tied to intelligence and worth. Over the years I've seen that time and again in the way people treat or judge my boys, and it can be hard to take.

But over time, I began to notice all the ways Jude and Tommy were communicating with me, even without words. The way Jude takes my hand to guide me. The way Tommy gives me a thumbs up or thumbs down for yes and no. When speech doesn't come naturally, we need to look at alternative methods. Jude and Tommy have shown me that communication can take countless forms. For Jude, it might mean handing me his drink bottle when he's thirsty or tapping the pocket where I keep my car key when he wants to go for a drive. For Tommy, it's often about using his AAC device to request something specific or saying the first syllable of a word out loud. These moments are every bit as meaningful as words could ever be, because that's how my boys connect with me and the world around them. Every gesture, sound or action holds meaning, and it's down to us to figure out what that is.

Finding the right tools or communication method can be life-changing. For some kids, it's sign language, the Makaton sign and symbol system or gestures. For others, it's visuals like PECS (Picture Exchange Communication System), AAC devices or even simple routines and symbols. The options can feel overwhelming. How are you supposed to know which one to use? What if you choose the wrong one? If my boys weren't going to be able to speak, I desperately wanted someone to tell me what alternative they should use, with some kind of guarantee that it would work for them.

For Jude, our journey began with PECS. I remember sitting at the table with laminated pictures of his favourite snacks, bananas, crisps, biscuits, hoping this system would give him a way to tell us what he wanted. Progress was slow. At first, he wasn't interested in the pictures; he just wanted the food. I'd gently guide his hand to the card, say the word and show him how to exchange it for the snack. Some days it felt like we were getting somewhere and then the next day, it would feel as if we were starting all over again. We worked hard on it at home and school worked on it with him every day, but over time, it became clear that PECS wasn't a natural fit for Jude. His understanding of the pictures didn't quite click and was inconsistent, and the physical actions required to exchange them didn't come easily. Instead, we began focusing on gestures, body language and other ways Jude naturally tried to communicate with us. School began to use objects of reference with him and that seemed to make more sense to him. Locations and activities had different objects assigned to them. It helped him understand where he was going next and enabled him to make simple choices. Every time we were going for a drive I'd show him the car key. He'd hand me his shoes if he wanted to go out. We had a different object for my house, my parents' house, swimming, trampolining. It made communication between us a little easier. A little clearer.

And sometimes, out of nowhere, a moment would stop me in my tracks. I remember clearly when Jude was about two and we were in the kitchen. He walked over to me, took my hand and led me across the room. At first, I didn't know what he wanted but then he stopped in front of the cupboard, threw my hand towards it and looked up at me. The biscuit cupboard. He didn't say anything. He didn't point. But it was the clearest request he'd ever made. He remembered where the biscuits were. He knew what he wanted. And he found a way to ask. A Jammie Dodger was now his.

It probably wouldn't have meant much to most parents but to me, it was huge. It felt like a breakthrough. Like connection. Like progress. We celebrated like he'd just said 'Mum' for the first time. Because in a way, he had. It may not have been spoken words but he was communicating. And it meant the world.

For Tommy, it was a completely different story. When it was time to introduce him to PECS, he quickly picked up on the connection between the pictures and the objects they represented. Within weeks, he was selecting the correct cards and, eventually, constructing short sentences. Watching him make progress gave me hope.

There was one day at school where the cake symbol had gone missing from Tommy's PECS folder. Most kids might have just given up or got frustrated but not Tommy. He ran over to another boy's PECS folder and took his cake symbol instead, then brought it straight to the teacher to ask for cake. It still makes me smile – because it showed not only how much he understood the system but how determined he was to get his point across. Cake has always been a key motivator in our home!

Then one day I came across a video of a child using an

AAC device, and I immediately knew it was something we needed to explore. Knowing how comfortable Tommy was navigating an iPad, I felt optimistic that this could be the right tool for him. I arranged a meeting with school and asked if they could start working on it with him. Within a few weeks of introducing the Proloquo2Go app, Tommy was using it to request his favourite foods and make choices. Soon he was constructing simple sentences.

I'll never forget the first time he used it to ask for something at my parents' house. He tapped out, 'Dad, I would like cake' and when I handed him a cherry Bakewell, his whole face lit up. My parents' faces did too. They'd never seen him use it before and were shocked at what he was now able to do. I'm not sure who was prouder, me, them or Tommy!

Looking back now, I think that moment planted the seed of something I've come to believe deeply. If someone needs help walking, we give them a walking stick, a frame or a wheelchair. If someone needs help seeing, we give them glasses. So if someone needs help communicating, why wouldn't we offer them different tools to support that too?

I'll admit, when PECS was first suggested for Jude, I was hesitant. Part of me worried that if we focused too much on pictures or symbols, it might discourage him from developing speech. Like we'd be sending a message that we didn't believe he'd ever talk. That by giving him another option, he'd stop trying to use words altogether.

But I've come to learn that this fear, while understandable, is one of the biggest misconceptions about AAC and other communication supports. These tools don't replace speech, they support it. Often, they're a bridge to progress, not a barrier. They open the door to language, to connection, to confidence. They give our kids a voice when speech alone isn't enough.

AAC, PECS, gestures, signs, objects, none of it is a 'lesser' form of communication. It's just a different path to the same goal: being able to understand each other. But the journey has been far from straightforward, as sometimes even with the best tools in place our kids can't tell us what's wrong. That's when you have to become a detective. There have been plenty of moments when Tommy and Jude have become frustrated at not being able to communicate what they want the world to know. There have been hundreds of meltdowns over the years, which I know wouldn't have happened if they'd just been able to express themselves clearly.

Even now, as good as Tommy is at using his AAC device, sometimes it's as if he just cannot get the words out. Like he knows what he wants to say but is unable to find the right icon or phrase.

One Sunday a couple of years ago Tommy and I were at our local park, going through all our usual games and routines. Tommy was on top of the climbing frame, looked down at me and said, 'Cuh'. Usually this means he's trying to say a word and wants me to repeat it back to him. Less than a minute before that I'd told him to 'be careful' as he was climbing up, so I opened with 'careful'. I was met with a firm thrust of his arm downwards, a resounding 'no'.

I worked through at least ten other 'c' words that made sense but all of them were a no, with Tommy getting more stressed every time I got it wrong. I reached into his bag, offered him his AAC device and he started to type. Whatever word he was looking for, he couldn't find it and was unable to spell it. He gave the AAC back to me even more frustrated.

I tried more words, but I couldn't get it right. By this time he was crying, kicking the climbing frame over and over, getting more and more upset. Over the next fifteen minutes I tried every 'c' word I could think of, before managing to convince him to leave and head back to the car. After we drove around for a while he snapped out of it.

I still think about that moment. I'll never know what the word was or why it was so important. What I *can* imagine, though, is how frustrating it must be having all of these things you want to say, all these words spinning around in your head and not being able to say them out loud and be understood. How challenging that must be each and every day.

I've often wondered what's really going on inside Tommy's and Jude's minds in moments like that. Does Jude have all these words in his head, talking to himself in a way I can't hear? Or is he just 100 per cent in the moment, completely absorbed in what's right in front of him? Do they see past memories and future dreams, or is their world all about the here and now? The truth is, I don't know, and I probably never will. What I have learned, though, is that less than 50 per cent of the population as a whole – neurotypical or otherwise – have an internal monologue. Many people think in pictures, emotions or sensations rather than words. Maybe it's the same for Jude and Tommy, maybe it's a mix of both. What I wouldn't give to spend a minute, an hour, a day inside their heads getting to understand better how they see the world and what they think.

There have been times when, like the boys, I've felt frustration too, wondering if we were using the best tools or if we could be doing more. Frustrated that I'm not able to understand my sons, especially in those difficult moments that escalate into a meltdown. In the hardest moments, when Tommy or Jude are upset or angry and I don't understand what they want, I try to remember I'm doing the best I can. I'm not always going to get it right or know all of the answers, but I can keep trying, keep listening and showing them I want to help. I want to understand.

One of the hardest things about raising a child who is non-speaking or has limited communication is the guessing game that comes with it. When Jude or Tommy are upset and can't tell me why, it can be heartbreaking.

Is it pain? Are they tired? Did something happen yesterday that they're still thinking about? Or is it something else completely?

Every cry, every scream, every moment of distress leaves me desperately searching for answers. We have to be detectives so often throughout the day, deciphering every little action and never knowing for sure what was wrong.

I remember a particularly tough week when Jude was six, filled with lots of huge emotional meltdowns. One minute he'd be happy, the next the tears would be flooding down his face. He'd be screaming, throwing himself around the room, slapping his knees. We gave him Calpol to ease the pain we imagined he must be feeling. It worked, and he was happy again. Only we still had no idea what the source of the pain was. This went on for two to three days, sudden spikes in emotion, eased by the medicine, before we managed to find out he had a tooth infection. He had been unable to direct us to the source of his pain.

Moments like that are distressingly hard. As a parent, you'd give anything to know what's wrong or how you can help. Not being able to figure that out can make you feel so guilty.

For both boys, supporting their understanding of communication has been just as important as helping them express themselves. For Jude it has been about keeping communication and instructions as simple as possible. I don't say, 'OK, Jude, let's get your bag, the bus is here, it's time for school.' Instead, I'll show him his school bag and say, 'Jude, time for the bus.' I pair words with objects that relate to an activity. I keep things in the same place so it's easy for him to access and use, such as making sure his drink bottle is always at hand for him to request a drink. It's about keeping my instructions clear and giving him time to process what I'm saying. I've had to slow down, simplify my language and focus on gestures to help him feel secure and understood.

Visual schedules have been a game-changer for Tommy. As a boy who thrives on routine, they give him a sense of predictability, help him process what's happening and prepare for what's coming next. The first thing he does when he arrives at school is check his schedule so he can prepare himself for what his school day looks like. He marks off what day it is, selects what the weather is like outside, then as he completes each activity throughout the day he takes the relevant picture off his schedule and puts it into the 'done' folder. These simple images help reduce his anxiety and give him a sense of control.

LOVE NEEDS NO WORDS

Over recent years Tommy's comprehension of language has really improved, far beyond the level of his expressive language. Time spent with his AAC device, playing around with words, has really helped. I feel like he understands everything that I say to him now, and I can use much longer sentences and more complex words. Whether or not he wants to listen to his dad or do what I've asked him, well, that's another story!

But his expressive language is progressing and changing too. Over recent years, he's said some of the most beautiful things, both through his AAC device and using his voice. 'Happy Birthday.' 'Merry Christmas.' 'I love you.' Vocally, it's just shortened sounds from each word, 'Ha . . . Buh . . . Da', and I'll say it back to him, watching his face light up at being understood. Other times, he taps it out on his device, crystal clear. It still takes my breath away, every time.

Every night, for the last five years, we've driven to the shop together. It started during the Covid-19 pandemic lockdown, something small to break up the long days where all of his regular routines had been stripped away and it stuck. A trip out, just the two of us, forty-five minutes in the car to a petrol station, when the world was so quiet. And it's become one of the best ways we've practised communication.

Tommy uses his device to ask for what he wants: 'Dad, I would like white milkshake' or 'green sweets' or 'gold cake'. Then I go into the shop and try to find it. When I get back into the car, he'll say the first syllable of each word, and I'll repeat it out loud with a smile: 'Da, I, Wou, Luh, Whuh, Muh' with a 'Puh' for 'please' thrown in at the end. We do it every night. Come rain or shine. Christmas Day, New Year's Day, it doesn't matter. And I've filmed hundreds of those little exchanges, sharing them to our page.

This repetition has become more than just a routine for Tommy, it's helped build the rapport between us. The predictability of those interactions means the demands on him are low, which raises the chance of connection between us. It's one of the most engaged moments we share each day. In these exchanges he's not just asking for a treat but connecting, expressing himself, enjoying our back-and-forth rhythm in a way that only we understand.

There are also times when I've found completely unexpected ways in. Jude doesn't enjoy spoken language; too much talk can confuse and overwhelm him quickly. But if I sing? Especially a theme tune from one of his favourite shows, *Special Agent Oso* or *Mickey Mouse Clubhouse,* he lights up. Singing doesn't carry the same pressure as talking. There's rhythm, repetition, predictability and no demand. Sometimes I'll sing to him when he's getting agitated or when I need to help him transition to something new. And more often than not, it works. His head turns. He smiles. We connect.

What I've come to realise is that communication is never static. What works today might not work tomorrow, and every new stage brings new challenges and opportunities. Jude doesn't use PECS anymore; instead we rely largely on him physically guiding me and my interpretations of his gestures and sounds. Tommy's AAC device on the other hand has become an essential part of who he is. It helps him tell people what he wants, how he's feeling and even show his cheeky sense of humour. The tools for both boys are different, but the goal always remains the same: to help them feel heard and understood.

A huge part of that is almost acting as their interpreter when they need it and helping others to understand their different ways of communicating. It might be explaining to someone in a shop what Tommy's AAC device is and asking them to be patient while he takes the time to find the words he wants to say. Or explaining to a friend how Jude wants to tap people on the nose as his way of connecting or how a certain sound and gesture means he wants you to leave the room as he needs some space.

Public interactions can be challenging. When you step outside of your safe little bubble at home, you realise how little the world knows about non-speaking people. There have been so many times when someone has said something to Jude or Tommy, at the park, in a shop, at a family gathering, and waited for a response that never came. I can see the confusion in their eyes, wondering if they're being ignored, before an awkward pause as they look to me for an explanation.

'He's autistic and non-speaking,' I'll say, trying to keep it casual, never quite knowing what will happen next.

Some people are kind and understanding, taking the time to try to engage with Jude or Tommy in ways that work for them. Others are dismissive, awkward or even rude:

'There wasn't all this autism in my day . . .'

Sometimes even the innocent questions hit hard.

'Oh, will they ever speak?'

I don't know.

'My aunt's neighbour's son has autism and he started speaking at six, so maybe your son will too.'

Yeah. Maybe.

'You need to make sure you talk to them more.'

In my experience, most of the time these questions and opinions come from a good place. But when you've heard them hundreds of times before it can be pretty tiring. Some days you just don't want to talk about it. But it's also one of the most important things I can do. Because every time I explain, it helps make the world a little more understanding of what our lives are like.

There are the moments when I've doubted whether I've explained enough or prepared people enough or if I've done the right thing in that interaction. Could I have handled it better? Should I have said more? It's easy to feel like you need to have all the answers, especially when there's so much advice and so many opinions about what you 'should' be doing. All I ever wanted was a definite 'follow this therapy and in two years your son will start speaking'. But that doesn't exist. What you can do, though, is keep showing up. Keep experimenting. See what feels right for your child, for your family.

Sometimes, especially in those early years, I used to dream of them talking. I'd be deep in sleep and there they were, Jude or Tommy, chatting away. Telling me how their day was. Asking questions. Laughing at something I said. It felt so natural, so easy. And then I'd wake up.

There was always a moment of hope, just for a second, before the truth caught up with me. That it was just a dream. That those conversations hadn't happened. And for a while, those mornings really hurt. I don't have those dreams as often anymore. Maybe it's because I've found more peace in where we are. Maybe I've stopped hoping for words so much and started celebrating all the other ways we connect. But those dreams, as painful as they sometimes were, came from the same place as everything else in this chapter: a longing to understand and be understood.

And that's something we've built, slowly, steadily, over time.

When I think about the future for Jude and Tommy, I'm no longer clinging to the desperate hope that they will talk one day (although any progress in spoken language would be a huge bonus). What I hope for now is that they'll continue making progress in their own ways, in how much they're able to communicate and how much others are able to interact with and understand them.

For Tommy, I hope his communication becomes more spontaneous. That he continues to grow and feel more confident using his AAC device in more situations. Not just at school when doing his work, not just at the shop when choosing a treat but in more places and with more people. I still believe more words will come one day. I can see how he experiments in the mirror and how he repeats certain sounds over and over. I know there are so many words on the tip of his tongue, so I hope one day more of them will flow for him. Above all of that, I just want him to feel understood. Tommy can be quite complex and become frustrated easily, and I know a lot of that is down to the communication barrier. If we can help ease that, life will be a lot happier for him.

For Jude, I hope we find more ways to help him express what he's thinking and feeling, what he wants, what is making him upset or where something hurts. I want to revisit using an AAC device with him again. He's so capable of navigating and using an iPad, yet for some reason we're yet to have much success with it for communication. I hope that he feels confident enough to communicate more with others around him. To engage more and be himself, rather than sit back and watch. I just hope he feels understood.

If there's one thing I hope this chapter has shown you, it's that communication isn't just about spoken words. It's about connection.

No matter where your child is right now, there will be progress. There are so many children and adults out there, non-speaking or with limited speech, living full, meaningful lives. Communicating in their own way. Surrounded by people who understand and love them just as they are. Jude and Tommy are two of them.

7
A Noisy World

When Jude was three, we went to a birthday party for one of the children from his baby group. I remember watching the other kids, excited from the second they walked in. They understood it was time for fun: the entertainer, the music, the food, the games, they just got it.

Jude didn't. He wandered the room, unsure of what was happening. Galloping from side to side. Tapping a paper plate against his hand. Circling the food table, picking up and putting down different items. He was completely uninterested in the entertainer, who had every other child captivated, and he avoided every attempt the other kids made to interact with him.

Within fifteen minutes, he was in meltdown. Not a little cry that might settle with a cuddle but the full, body-shaking, inconsolable crying that I already knew by heart. The type of cry where everyone starts looking at you, confused as to why your child isn't calming down. I tried everything. His dummy. His muslin. Some of his favourite snacks. I took him into another room, hoping the quiet might help. But nothing worked. I remember the heat rising in my face, knowing everyone could still hear him and were wondering what was wrong. Knowing they didn't understand.

Eventually, I put him in his buggy and left to walk him along the river. Charlotte stayed behind, trying to lose herself in conversations and fake smiles that must have taken everything she had to muster. I hated leaving her there. Hated feeling like we were falling apart when everyone else was so at ease.

We just wanted Jude to have fun. We wanted to spend time with the other families, watch our kids play together and eat too much cake, before heading home with an overexcited child. I'll admit, in that moment, I just wanted Jude to be a little bit more like everyone else.

I had assumed our life would be filled with birthday parties. It would start with friends and family and the parents from baby groups and then move on to nursery friends and eventually school friends. There would be soft play and balloons, little paper plates with cake crumbs and half-eaten sandwiches. I pictured Jude chasing his friends around the garden, squealing with excitement. I thought we'd be booking entertainers, making party bags, figuring out who to invite, not wanting to leave anyone out.

I'd lived it growing up (although a lot more simply than the birthday parties you see today. Party at Wimpy, anyone?). And before Jude was born, when I worked as a tennis coach, I ran kids' birthday parties and watched first hand how excited the children would get. That's what I thought parenting would look like.

I remember walking along that river, knowing if I picked up the pace, Jude might eventually regulate himself. And after half an hour of walking back and forth, he fell asleep, exhausted. Not just from the crying but from the overwhelm of it all. When I returned, Charlotte was waiting outside. We made our polite excuses and went home.

It felt like a disaster. But it was also a turning point. We didn't know at the time but that party would end up being the last we ever took Jude to. Because as we slowly started to understand more about autism, more about sensory processing and anxiety, we realised something important: for Jude, they weren't fun. They were overwhelming.

It wasn't just parties, either, it was the same at playgrounds, soft plays or family gatherings. The things you're told are supposed to be the fun parts of childhood. The moments you're supposed to look back on and have happy memories of. And so, we kept trying. Sometimes we made it through and got home in one piece without any upset. Sometimes we didn't even make it inside. Sometimes the hardest part was getting ready at home, willing myself to try, even though deep down I was pretty sure it wasn't going to work.

Over time it began to feel cruel, dragging Jude into situations he couldn't cope with. But there was always that voice in my head, echoing the well-meaning comments of friends, family, even strangers, telling us: *'He just needs to get used to it.'* *'You need to keep putting him in those environments.'* *'He'll never cope if you don't push him.'* Because when enough people say these things, you start to believe it and start to doubt your instincts. And so I thought that if we kept turning up to these events, little by little things would get easier, until one day he'd be fine around the other kids. In fact, he'd learn to love it.

But no matter how much I wanted that for Jude, the evidence was right in front of me: Jude wasn't refusing to cope. He *couldn't* cope. Exposing him to all these different experiences wasn't a solution; all it was doing was exposing him to more fear and more upset, making him increasingly anxious.

I wanted nothing more than to protect him. But I desperately wanted him to experience the world too. More than that, I felt that he *had* to, that it was a crucial part of how kids learned and how he would develop. And figuring out how to balance these two apparently conflicting desires has been one of the hardest and most important parts of our journey with autism.

It hadn't sunk in back then, but Jude was battling something invisible. The noise. The unpredictability. The unfamiliar food. The children running and shouting. The bright lights. The smells. The pressure to socialise. The sensory overload.

For a long time, I didn't fully understand what sensory processing differences meant. I thought sensory issues just meant not liking loud noises or perhaps being picky about food. I didn't realise how deep it went or how much it coloured every part of Jude's experience of the world.

The birthday parties, the playgrounds, the trips we thought would be fun, it wasn't that he didn't want to enjoy them. It was that his body and brain were working overtime just trying to survive them. With sensory differences the world can feel overwhelming. Unsafe.

A balloon popping can feel like a shockwave that rattles through your whole body. A crowded room can be unbearable, every sound hitting you all at once with no way to filter it. Being touched unexpectedly can feel painful, violating, like your whole system is under attack. And that's before you even get to the bright lights, the strong smells, the unfamiliar textures or all the social expectations layered on top.

Sensory differences aren't just about feeling things a little more or a little less, although that is a part of it. Some autistic people are *hypersensitive*, meaning their senses are turned up so loud that everyday things can feel overwhelming or even painful. Others are *hyposensitive*, meaning their senses are dialled down, and they seek out more input just to feel grounded. And sometimes, the same person can swing between both, craving noise and movement one minute, shutting down from it the next. It's not predictable. It's not deliberate. It's just how their nervous system processes the world.

Once I began to understand this better, it changed how I saw my boys' behaviours and how I responded to them. For Jude, sensory overload could look like crying, bolting, covering his ears, and as time went on, it would lead to aggression and self-injurious behaviours. This often looked like 'bad behaviour' to the outside world, who just saw a naughty kid, a spoiled kid, a bad parent. It might be a child refusing to join in or having a meltdown in the supermarket. Or clinging to the doorframe rather than going inside somewhere new.

There were many times when even I misunderstood what was happening, when I thought he was being stubborn or that he just didn't like the activity we'd chosen. Sometimes I thought, *If I just encourage him enough, maybe he'll enjoy it. If we can just get him there and show him it's fun, maybe he'll realise that he likes it.*

But he wasn't being difficult or naughty. He was completely overwhelmed, trying to survive in a world that wasn't built for him. And the heartbreaking part? He couldn't even tell me that was what was happening. There was no way for Jude to say, 'Dad, it's too loud.' Or 'I don't feel safe.' Or 'My body can't handle this right now.' So instead, he showed me the only way he could, through his behaviour: through the crying, the lashing out at himself, the meltdowns that left him exhausted and left me feeling like I was failing him.

Sensory processing had been mentioned in the parenting autism course we had attended after Jude's diagnosis, along with a hundred other things we were supposed to learn, understand and act on straight away. But back then, it had all blurred together. In order to understand it, it wasn't another item on a checklist I needed. It was experience.

It was watching how Jude reacted in different places. It was seeing how Tommy sought out movement and pressure to cope with the world around him. It was reading accounts from autistic adults explaining what certain things felt like to them and why it made them feel anxious. It was hearing other parents' stories online and thinking, *That's us too.*

Slowly, through daily life with my boys, the pieces started to click into place. First with Jude, then, as Tommy grew older, his sensory needs started to show themselves too but in a completely different way. Where Jude would retreat or melt down when overwhelmed, Tommy sought more. He craved movement. He needed to bounce, to spin, to jump. His sensory seeking was constant and intense.

We'd be out for a walk and he'd be darting from side to side, climbing anything he could, jumping off every step he saw. Always hopping, stomping, landing with as much force as possible. At home, he'd bounce on the beds, flip cushions, climb onto the kitchen counter or the sink. He'd donkey-kick backwards against walls, radiators, furniture, anything that gave him that feedback through his feet and legs. If he didn't get enough movement and deep pressure, everything became harder: concentrating, coping, even sleeping. And then, when it had all become too much, when he'd had too much sensory input or the anxiety of transitions built up, he switched to the opposite. Burying himself into corners of the room, in the gap behind the sofa, in between the sofa cushions, pulling a blanket over his head.

It wasn't 'bad behaviour', even though I know it looked like it; it was his way of regulating. His way of calming the storm going on inside his body.

And once again, the answer wasn't trying to stop it. It was going with it and adapting, finding ways to meet that need safely. Trampolines. Soft play. Big squeezes. Walks where climbing wasn't just allowed, it was encouraged. It was realising that the goal wasn't to force Jude or Tommy to 'cope' with the world, it was to help the world make space for them. Because, underneath it all, it was the same story: two little boys trying to make sense of a world that didn't always feel right to them.

We needed to adapt the environment to Jude and Tommy, rather than trying to force them to adapt to the environment. Those changes started showing up in the smallest of ways. Like still doing things for them that they could probably do themselves. Putting Jude's shoes on and taking them off when he comes in from school each day. Helping Tommy get dressed. Opening packets or zipping up a coat. Not because they aren't capable but because I know how much those tasks take out of them. If me doing it for them helps them save that energy for something that actually matters, for joy, for play, for peace and also reduces their anxiety levels, then I'll keep doing it.

Even once we started making changes to support Jude's and Tommy's sensory needs, there were still days that caught us off guard. Days when everything seemed fine one minute and the next, they were in complete distress. There was no obvious sensory trigger, no loud noises or bright lights, just sudden panic and subsequent meltdown.

At first, it made no sense to me. I thought if we avoided the things we knew were overwhelming, the noisy places, the crowds, the smells, then everything should get easier. But it wasn't that simple. Because sensory overload was just one part of the problem. It was anxiety that was the real challenge. I didn't realise how much fear Jude was carrying every day. How anxiety, invisible as it is, was driving so much of what we were seeing. It's only now, looking back, that I can see how it was at the root of so many of the challenges. And the more I learned, the more I realised that anxiety is behind so many autistic behaviours that people misunderstand.

Rigid routines? They're not about being controlling. They're about feeling safe.

Repetitive play? It's not about being stuck. It's about finding comfort in predictability.

Meltdowns over seemingly 'small' things? They're not about being difficult. They're about the world suddenly feeling too unpredictable to handle. Or a culmination of things that have

A NOISY WORLD

built up and built up across the day and then lead to a meltdown. Anxiety can build quietly underneath the surface, and then one tiny thing – a missed turn on a car journey, roadworks, the iPad running out of charge, the wifi not working – can tip it over the edge. It's easy to see the last 'small' thing that happened as the trigger, when really it's been a combination of multiple factors.

For Jude, it was largely social anxiety that was the problem: being around other children and not knowing what they would do next, whether they'd get too close or make too much noise. Other children crying, screaming, shouting or even just having fun, could all set him off. He couldn't cope with the unpredictability. Dogs are another one. If a dog came too close at the park, a happy day out could turn in an instant. And I get it. In Jude's eyes this animal comes bounding towards him, and he doesn't know that it's going to turn away at the last second and go back to its owner when called. Or even worse, the dog might come right up, walk around him, sniff him or even jump up. I'd always make sure to put myself between him and any dogs or even change direction and walk off if we saw one in the distance. But as much as I tried, it was impossible to protect him from everything. I remember taking Jude on a tour of a mainstream school, when we were still trying to figure out what would be best for him. We were wheeling him around the grounds in his buggy when the bell for breaktime went off. It upset him so much we had to leave. And the time we went to the park and hadn't even been out of the car for thirty seconds before we had to head back. A crying toddler had come past in their pram, and it had sent Jude into a meltdown.

As Tommy got older, his anxiety started to show itself too, albeit in different ways. Sometimes it was loud and immediate, a refusal to get out of the car, a full-body protest if a plan changed without warning. Other times it was quieter but just as intense, clinging to routines, needing everything to happen in a certain order, melting down if something small didn't quite go as expected.

In the early years a lot of it didn't make any sense to me. With Tommy unable to tell us what was going on, we were left guessing most of the time. We'd only figure it out after the third or fourth time it happened. The problem was, anxiety wasn't always easy to spot from the outside. It didn't always look like panic or fear. Sometimes it looked like stubbornness. Sometimes it looked like avoidance. Sometimes it looked like a sadness they couldn't explain. Which often meant that by the time we realised what the problem was, it was too late to prevent the meltdown that inevitably followed.

But slowly we were learning that the common cause behind all of these behaviours was anxiety. It showed up everywhere. It shaped everything. In truth, it was probably the biggest challenge of all.

For Tommy and Jude, anxiety made the world feel unsafe in ways they couldn't communicate. It explained why Tommy needed such strict routines, why he panicked if we had to take a different route to the shop because of roadworks and why he needed countdowns for everything, from finishing a meal to transitioning to bedtime. He needed a sense of control over what was going to happen.

And for Jude, it explained why even the 'fun' days – swimming, trampolining, the park – could spiral so quickly without warning. When you live with that level of uncertainty inside your body, anything unfamiliar, unexpected or new isn't exciting. It can feel terrifying. And no amount of reassuring him, *'It'll be fine,'* could make it better. Anxiety isn't rational. It's not a thought, it's a survival response.

That is why so much of our life is controlled by things that most people never think twice about. Whether the iPad is charged. Whether there's going to be a crying child in the park or a dog off-lead. The beep of a reversing car. These things might seem small but for us, they can determine whether the next few hours go smoothly or spiral. That's what anxiety does, it makes the world feel like a minefield, where even the tiniest sound or change can set everything off.

Recognising this, life became a process of trying to prevent that anxiety from building too high. Because when the sensory overload, communication struggles and unexpected changes combined, that's when the meltdowns happened.

To a lot of the world, when a child is having a meltdown, the first thing they see is behavioural problems: a child throwing a tantrum and a parent unable to keep control.

But Tommy, Jude and the many families I've met along the way, have shown me that couldn't be further from the truth. Meltdowns aren't a sign of a child being naughty or of throwing a tantrum when they don't get their own way. They're what happens when there are no other options left, when the brain says: *'I can't take anymore.'* A floodgate bursting open, no longer able to withstand the pressure. A full-body signal that says something isn't right. It's communication, just not in the way the world is used to seeing.

For Jude, this has often meant explosive, angry outbursts, full of tears and self-injury. For Tommy, it could be intense, impulsive behaviour, lashing out, running, jumping, screaming, throwing things, doing anything to try to regulate a body that felt completely out of control. And then, when it was over, he'd come crashing down, bury himself away and cry.

Seeing your child go through those moments is scary. Sometimes they can seem so out of control that you wonder if they'll ever come to an end. You'll do anything to stop them happening again. And so, we tried everything we could: sensory diets, occupational therapy, changing the food we ate, reducing demands, ear defenders, audio therapy, play therapy, visual schedules, countdown timers, first-then boards. All attempts to prepare them for every transition, even the tiniest ones, to try to build predictability into every part of their day.

Some of it helped. Some of it didn't. Ear defenders, for example, have helped both boys so much over the years. One of the most visible signs of overload has always been how often Tommy and Jude cover their ears. It's not just about noise, it's anticipation. They press their fingers in tight before the noise even happens. Tommy does it when he knows something's coming: a surprise, a song, even when we're handing him a food he's asked for. The ear defenders reduce that overwhelming noise, but also free up their hands. Tommy wears his most of the day at school. Jude stopped wearing his around age ten after loving them for years. Which has been a shame, as he definitely would benefit from them, but more recently, he's started using noise-cancelling headphones with music when we're out, and already they've made such a difference.

Visual schedules, too, have been a great help for Tommy. They give him more stability and help him to understand what is going on in his world. He craves routine, and creating and following these schedules helps make his days feel so much more predictable and, as a result, happier. But there's another side to that, too, when the routine becomes so rigid that the smallest disruption causes huge distress. When something doesn't go to plan, he can't move past it, as he can't process why the routine has gone wrong.

For Jude, these schedules made little difference. He struggled to understand the visual supports and showed no real signs that they were making his days easier. So instead we have had to reduce the demands we make of him, trying to make his environment as calm and quiet as possible. Because no matter how much love we showed him, no matter how much we adapted and tried to keep him safe, there were still times when the anxiety became too much. This could lead to days, weeks, even months of meltdown after meltdown. And that's when the really hard conversations began. The ones we didn't want to have. The ones that brought up all kinds of guilt, fear and grief. That's when we started to wonder: if love, patience, support and every strategy we could find still weren't enough, should we consider the thing I was most afraid of – medication?

The first time someone suggested medication for Jude, I shut down. It was during a meeting at school, the kind where there were more professionals than I could keep track of. It was impossible to remember what role each different person actually had and why they were there. Ten people, maybe more, were all sitting around a table, discussing what to do about my six-year-old son, and I felt completely lost.

One of them gently asked, 'Have you ever considered medication?' Inside my head, the answer was loud and instant: *No. No way. There's no f*cking way I'm turning my little boy into a drugged-up zombie.* I had a scene from *One Flew Over the Cuckoo's Nest* playing out in my mind and that was what I associated medication with. Of course, I didn't say that out loud, I just mumbled something about it not being the route we wanted to take. Because back then, medication felt like giving up. It felt like admitting that we weren't good enough, that our love wasn't enough. And I wasn't ready for that path. Not for my little boy. He was only six years old, how could we have reached that point?

But the reality we were living was impossible to ignore. Jude was having multiple meltdowns a day, big, aggressive ones where he would hurt himself, slapping his arms, hitting walls, punching his own face until the skin was red and swollen. There were nights he would wake up screaming, lashing out before he was even fully conscious. We would go for long drives at all hours of the night, trying to help him snap out of it. Then there were mornings where we'd sit together on the sofa, him crying and rocking, me holding onto him and just wishing I could take all the pain away.

And it wasn't just Jude who was left bruised. Some days I would turn up to work with cuts or purple marks on my face and arms, the aftershock of trying to protect him during a meltdown. Sometimes I looked like I'd been attacked by a cat that we didn't have, so deep were the scratches. I'd find myself adjusting my sleeves, brushing off questions, avoiding the truth. Not because I was ashamed of Jude but because I didn't know how to explain. How do you tell someone your six-year-old son hit you in a moment of complete distress? That it wasn't about naughty behaviour but his pain and you were the safest person he had to let it out on? It's something no one prepares you for and is a conversation the rest of the world isn't ready to have.

Unless you've been through it, I really don't think anyone can understand how heartbreaking it is to watch your child do that to themselves over and over, day after day. How helpless you feel when nothing you do can console them, and their first instinct when upset is to try to hurt themselves. Especially when they're unable to tell you why or what's wrong. I couldn't wrap my head around why he'd hurt himself like this. I mean, he was only six, why did he think of doing that?

That's when the idea of medication stopped being a hypothetical and became a question we couldn't ignore anymore. It wasn't an easy decision or a quick one. It's a big decision and not one that should be taken lightly. It was months, years, really, of slow, painful conversations. Meetings with doctors. Research late into the night. Talking to other parents. Hearing the stories of what had helped and what hadn't. Reading about possible side effects and contrasting them to the quality of life Jude currently had.

There was so much guilt tangled up in it. If we tried medication, were we betraying him? If we didn't try it, were we failing him? I was afraid he'd become drowsy, more subdued, not be himself, but was I being selfish in clinging to my fears while he suffered? If Jude had a physical illness,

I wouldn't hesitate to give him the medicine he needed. Why was this any different?

We didn't want to change who Jude was or alter his personality in any way. We just wanted to ease some of the weight he seemed to carry. We wanted to give him a chance to be happier and to live a life with less fear, less pain. All you want to do as a parent is find a solution. You want your child to be happy. You want your child never to feel the need to hit themselves ever again. You want to stop living in fear of your child breaking a bone from slamming his hands against a radiator in anger. I fully accepted that autism is a part of who Jude is and the medication was in no way trying to 'cure' or change that. I also knew that his life could be so much better than it was right then. Watching him hurt himself every day, looking so lost, angry and out of control, surely he deserved more than that?

And so we kept talking about it. With each other. With school. With professionals. His school was incredible, open, honest, compassionate. They shared stories of other pupils who'd benefited, but they also told us about the ones it hadn't helped. They were honest and that really mattered.

Eventually, after almost two years of wrestling with it, we made the decision to give medication a try. When risperidone was first suggested it terrified me. It's an antipsychotic medication and that word alone conjured up all kinds of images. But the more it was explained to us, the more we came round to giving it a go. Medications like risperidone aren't treating autism itself; they act more as though turning down the dial on the really dangerous stuff that comes with the overwhelm Jude feels every day: the explosive aggression, the self-injurious behaviours and the full-body meltdowns. With the hope that this was the impact risperidone could have, we were willing to give it a go.

We started with the lowest dose possible, monitoring everything, worrying about everything. And as we watched, gradually, something shifted. The meltdowns came less often. The bruises started to heal. There were longer stretches of calm. Smiles that lasted more than a few seconds. Walks by the river that didn't end in tears. It wasn't a miracle cure. It didn't erase his challenges. But it gave Jude, and us, room to breathe.

It took the edge off just enough for all the other things we were doing, the sensory supports, the routines, the adjustments, to have a chance to work. And over time they began to. Soon Jude was completely unrecognisable from the boy he was before; he was sleeping better, enjoying and coping better in school and having much happier days. Life became much lighter – for Jude, for Charlotte and for me too.

It wasn't until a couple of years later that I realised how rarely people actually talk about this. Both the theory of why medication might be an option and the emotional part too. The fear. The judgement. The silence in parenting circles. People are scared to talk about it; sometimes I guess I still am too. So many people have a negative view about medication, the same kind of opinion I had before we started down this path. And when you're trying to find out more information, when you're brave enough to ask in a Facebook group or another forum, there are people all too ready to shoot you down. It's hard to admit you're considering something that so many still see as a last resort. But it was only through sharing our story online and talking with so many other families, that I realised how commonplace it is. I wish I'd known how many parents have faced that same huge decision and how medication had helped so many. It might have made things a bit less scary and would have helped me feel less guilt as a parent too.

A few years later, as was so often the case, we found ourselves having the same conversations about Tommy. Different struggles, different challenges but possibly the same outcome.

Tommy's meltdowns were loud, impulsive, destructive. He was like a whirlwind, and there were days when keeping him, and everyone around him, safe felt like an impossible task. Again, we tried every other solution first. And again, it wasn't enough.

When we went to the paediatrician appointment to discuss medication, Tommy didn't stay still for a single moment. As she asked us questions and Charlotte tried to answer, Tommy gave her a very clear example of what was going on for us. For the whole of the appointment he fixated on me: hitting me, spitting at me, kicking me. He'd clearly decided I was to blame for forcing him to spend time in that room, and he wanted me to know it. Watching him that day, relentless and overwhelmed, made it clear that this wasn't something he would just grow out of or that more patience could fix. It was bigger than that. And he needed help.

This time, the decision came quicker. Not because it was any easier but because we had already lived through the fear and seen the positive impact medication had made in Jude's life. We knew what it meant to be at breaking point. And we knew that sometimes, the bravest thing you can do for your child is to admit that you need help.

Tommy began a course of risperidone, just like Jude. It took some heat out of the days, the pent-up aggression eased and those explosive moments reduced pretty quickly. But the restlessness didn't budge. By then Tommy's ADHD traits were front and centre: never still, impulsive, always chasing more sensory input. Risperidone wasn't touching that. With Tommy in a steadier place, and with our paediatrician's support, we slowly transitioned off risperidone and onto clonidine. The aim wasn't to change who he is, just to lower the volume on the impulsivity to make it easier for him to sit still, to focus, learn and be less impulsive. Within a few weeks we started to see some changes: he could sit long enough to finish short tasks, was less likely to run off or lash out when his frustration spiked. Even car journeys felt calmer. We kept the doses small, reviewed regularly and kept a close eye on the usual things: appetite, weight, blood pressure and any drowsiness. It's not been a magic switch but alongside structure and sensory input, it has given Tommy a bit more control over his day.

Medication hasn't been a 'cure' for either Tommy or Jude. It hasn't made everything easy. But it's now part of our toolkit that helps make life a little more manageable, a little more joyful and gives our family a better shot at happiness. It's lowered their anxiety enough to make the hard days less hard and opened up the world a little more for them to enjoy. It's helped us hold onto the boys they've always been, the boys underneath the struggle. And for that, I'll always be grateful.

There are still plenty of social occasions we don't attend

and some 'fun' things we skip because they'd be too overwhelming or anxiety inducing. We still lean on ear defenders and wireless headphones to take the edge off the world. But over time we've found what works for Tommy, for Jude and for us as a family: walks, drives, park trips, supermarket runs, McDonald's takeaways and, when the stars align and the adaptations are right, even the odd family get-together. We work hard on reducing anxiety every day, figuring out what helps Tommy and Jude feel more regulated. It doesn't always work out, but we're much better at understanding and predicting what will.

8

School, but Different

When I imagined becoming a parent, school was part of the dream. The first day at the school gates. The little uniform, slightly too big, sleeves needing to be rolled up. The photo on the doorstep, backpack slung over one shoulder, a slightly nervous but excited smile. The chats on the way home about who they played with, what they learned. The school plays. The certificates for effort and kindness. The birthday party invites filling up the fridge door.

I wondered what Jude would enjoy most about school. Would he like history, like I did, would he be creative and like writing and drawing or would he be more logical and enjoy maths and science? Would he be sporty? Would he make lots of friends? I didn't dream of grand achievements, I just hoped he'd enjoy going. That he'd find something he was good at. That he'd belong.

It never crossed my mind that school might not be like that for us. School was one of those things that just . . . happened. You look at the schools in your local area, read the reports about them, listen to what others have to say about them and make a choice. You pick a school, you buy the uniform, you send them off and the rest just falls into place. Or at least, that's what I thought.

But when your child's development looks different, school stops being so straightforward. Instead, it becomes something to worry about, a decision so big it feels impossible to get right. You're not just wondering what bag to buy or what their favourite subject will be. You're wondering if anyone will understand them, whether they'll receive the support they need and how the other kids will react around them. You're wondering whether your child will even understand why they've been left there each day. You're wondering if you're setting them up to thrive or setting them up to fail.

School becomes a minefield of decisions. Mainstream or Special Educational Needs (SEN)? Push for inclusion or prioritise support? Try to help them fit in or find a place that fits around them? I thought someone would help guide us through it all. But there was no one. It was up to us to figure it out. With nothing but instinct, a pile of reports and a growing fear that, whatever we chose, it might not be enough.

When the time came to start looking at schools, we decided to visit all the different options available to us, both mainstream and SEN. I still held onto a small hope that a mainstream school would be possible for Jude. A part of me wanted him to have the kind of school experience I had growing up. I thought maybe, with the right support in place, he could find a way to fit in and that being around all the other children who were talking, writing, reading, learning at a 'typical' rate, would help him to do the same. I knew it wouldn't be easy, but I hoped it might be possible. Looking back, I feel embarrassed that I

SCHOOL, BUT DIFFERENT

thought that way. But I've also seen many other parents hold onto those hopes too.

That hope disappeared almost instantly during our first visit. Within minutes of stepping inside a mainstream school, I knew it wasn't going to be right for Jude. We walked into bright, busy classrooms packed with thirty children. Noise was bouncing off the walls and there were visuals and displays everywhere. I felt like *I* was struggling with how overwhelming it was, never mind how Jude would feel. If this was what a 'normal' school day looked like, how could Jude survive it, let alone enjoy it?

When we walked into the Reception class and the teacher got the children to stop and say hello to us and the headteacher, it struck me how everyone was sitting calmly, listening, following instructions. Memories flashed back of my own school days, doing exactly the same. Then I thought about Jude. He couldn't sit still for more than thirty seconds without constant support. Even at nursery, a far more free and flexible setting, he needed the space to move, to explore, to regulate himself. There, he was allowed to move in and out of the garden, wander around, run up and down. How was he ever going to cope with this?

The more mainstream schools we visited, the clearer it became: Jude wasn't going to survive in an environment that expected him to 'keep up' quietly in the background while the teacher managed twenty-nine other children. He needed more. He needed space, understanding, flexibility. He needed people who could really see him. As we discussed his needs and the fact we had a statement (as it was called back then before EHCPs – an Education, Health and Care Plan), we were met with mixed levels of enthusiasm. We discussed his entitlement to one-to-one support, and what that would look like. But instead of reassurance, we got uncomfortable glances and comments like, 'We had an autistic child a few years ago . . .' as if that was enough experience. No one left us feeling confident that Jude would fit in, that they'd be able to support him or that they had much knowledge or experience when it came to autism at all. One particular visit stays with me, where we saw the one autistic child in the class sitting at the back with his one-to-one, working facing the wall. The teacher casually told us that this boy spent very little time in the classroom. Which left us feeling disappointed. Was this what happened? Was this what inclusion looks like?

From there we moved on to looking at special needs schools, carrying with us a combination of hope and fear. At the first SEN school we visited, the buildings had been upgraded a few years before. The rooms and corridors were wide and spacious, built for purpose. But the feeling I got walking around was a little too sterile. The feeling we got from the staff was similar too. The SEN classrooms were so different to the mainstream ones, much smaller and quieter, with only eight kids in each class and four to five teachers and support staff. The rooms were less colourful, less stimulating. Clearly this was on purpose, to help make the environment more suitable but still, it was a stark contrast to what we'd seen the week before and to the picture I'd carried in my head for so long. It all felt a bit heavy, as though the fun of school was being sucked out of the room.

I'll be honest, that first visit to a SEN school felt scary, like we were stepping into the unknown. After three and a half

SCHOOL, BUT DIFFERENT

years of knowing Jude and hearing a few stories from other parents we'd met along the way, suddenly I was looking at a whole school full of kids similar to him. From kids just a few months older than him, to teenagers, to young adults. It suddenly felt so real, seeing all these different, beautiful kids, and the realisation hits you that there are so many of us out there. So many families living similar lives. So many kids similar to Jude. And, at the time, it was overwhelming.

I found my eyes scanning each classroom, looking for any kids who seemed similar to Jude. Who flapped like he did, moved like he did, vocalised like he did. I was trying to catch a glimpse into the future and find some reassurance that if he came to this school everything would be OK. I saw kids who made me smile, which brought tears to my eyes. I saw kids who were putting together their first words, which made me hopeful. I could feel the tension in the air in one class, where the teacher signalled to us not to come inside and heard a meltdown in another class nearby that brought a lump to my throat. I knew how hard those moments were for Jude and wondered how many kids had meltdowns in school each day.

Maybe it was a reflection of where I was at the time, but I walked away from that visit feeling disappointed, and I know Charlotte felt the same. Was this what going to a SEN school would be like? Was this the only option we had for Jude?

I've spoken to many parents since who have confronted similar emotions after visiting a SEN school for the first time. Emotions I felt ashamed of at the time but also emotions that were real. And that day I was also confronted with the fact that, although that particular school wasn't the right one for

Jude, it emphasised how much mainstream wasn't either. At this school I had seen 150 kids all with similar lives to Jude; some talking, some not, some who had learned to read and write and some who hadn't. This would be Jude's journey. I don't know how to explain it other than to say I smiled a lot, but I wanted to cry a lot too.

I wasn't expecting it to be so hard. It felt like such a permanent, irreversible decision, as though we were carving out a path we'd never be able to step back from. We wanted to make the right choice for Jude, but we just didn't know yet that sometimes there isn't a perfect choice. There's just the best choice you can make, with what you know and who your child is, right now.

So we kept visiting schools and tried to keep open minds. And then, one day, we walked into a school that felt different. It wasn't shiny or new. The building was old and a bit worn in places. It felt more like the type of school we'd both been used to, growing up in London. The classrooms were small and a little chaotic. But the moment we stepped through the door, the feeling in the air was lighter and the energy completely different, warmer, more positive.

The staff were friendly, putting us at ease straight away. They wanted to know more about our family. They asked questions about Jude, real questions that made sense. What did he like doing, what did he struggle with? What were our worries and concerns about him starting school? How had he been getting on at nursery?

And the more we shared, the more we could feel how real that interest was. They smiled when we talked about what made him happy. They gave a knowing nod when we

SCHOOL, BUT DIFFERENT

mentioned his struggles, not surprised, not fazed, just understanding. It wasn't anything they hadn't seen before. That alone was a huge comfort.

The deputy head took us on a tour of the school, stopping to talk with any pupils or staff we passed. With some of the kids it was a simple hello, a smile and a high five. With others there was a lot more interaction and laughter. She seemed to know what each child needed and how much to engage with them. She knew all of their names and encouraged those who were comfortable enough to say hello to us too. I can't put into words how at ease that made me feel. Here were teachers who clearly loved what they do but also knew how different each child was and adapted to their needs.

We toured a few classrooms, before reaching the Year 1 class, the one that Jude would join the following year if he went there. The class teacher couldn't have been more welcoming. Covered in paint, with a huge grin spread across her face, she showed us what the class were working on as the kids buzzed around the classroom. The teaching assistants were spread out across the room, all working with different kids in different ways. It was busy, yes, noisy even, but it felt like organised chaos. Every child was taking part in their own way; some were more able than others, some more relaxed than others, but they were all happy. Within minutes we just knew that everyone working in that classroom adored the kids who were there. Those kids were loved and cared for, no matter how much support they needed every day.

As we made our way back to reception and spoke about the next steps, the deputy head said to us, 'Jude sounds like a wonderful little boy, I'm sure we could meet his needs here, we'd love to have him join us.' I nearly burst into tears and said yes on the spot, desperately trying to keep my cool on the way back to the car. They wanted him there. They weren't scared of everything that he couldn't do or everything that he struggled with. They knew all of that and wanted him anyway. After so many months of fear that no one would be able to see beyond his diagnosis, beyond his needs, the relief was overwhelming.

We arranged a second visit, this time bringing Jude with us. As much as we loved the school, there was still some fear remaining. We'd still be sending our non-speaking little boy out to school each day, and he would be unable to tell us if he liked it or if he was struggling. And that's a barrier that's petrifying for any parent with kids like ours, who is relying on others to look after them. But it was as if the school staff knew how we must be feeling. From the reception staff, to the teachers we passed in the corridor, they couldn't have made Jude feel more welcome. They *awwwed* at his curly blond hair and made sure not to overwhelm him. Nikki, the Year 1 teacher, couldn't wait to take him in, and before we knew it we were being ushered out of the classroom while Jude was left behind to explore. He wandered, tapped windows and plastic bottles. The teachers engaged with him where they could but let him lead the way and relax into his surroundings. Meanwhile, we spoke with the deputy head and asked all the questions we could think of, ending with, 'What do we need to do for Jude to come here?' Our minds had already been more or less made up, and the way they treated him just confirmed it. This would be the school for him.

This school was a place that would help him learn, to progress

SCHOOL, BUT DIFFERENT

as much as he could but would do so by helping create a safe, fun environment, one he'd want to go to each day. It was a place where he could belong and be accepted for who he is. And that, more than anything, was what we were looking for.

By the time it came to thinking about schools for Tommy, you'd think we would've been ready. We weren't new to this world anymore. We knew how the system worked and all the questions to ask. We knew what a good fit felt like and what it didn't. But that didn't make it easy.

Because Tommy wasn't Jude.

His needs were different. His strengths were different. And deep down, a small part of me wondered if his path should be different too.

We deferred his school start by a year to give ourselves, and Tommy, more time. He was always so engaged in learning. He loved to look at books, build and complete puzzles. He was curious and focused. And I kept thinking that maybe, just maybe, he'd start talking soon. It always felt as though his words were right there, waiting. And maybe if that happened, a mainstream setting could work for him.

But as that deferral year passed, the words didn't come and the clarity didn't either. We still didn't know what was best. And so, once again, we began visiting schools. This time we cast the net wider, looking at mainstream but also Moderate Learning Difficulties (MLD) schools, for children with moderate learning disabilities. Places that, in theory, might meet Tommy where he was. Somewhere that might be better for his academic potential.

We visited an MLD school that we were recommended

and couldn't wait to see it. We'd heard good reports about it from other parents, and hoped this might be the middle ground between mainstream and Jude's school that would work for Tommy. Yet it was obvious from the moment we arrived that they didn't want Tommy there. They hadn't met him yet, they hadn't seen him but as soon as I mentioned he was non-verbal, you could see the lights go out. The challenge was one they didn't want to take on. Which I'd have expected to some extent if it had been a mainstream school but it wasn't. This was a SEN school. It didn't make sense to me how a mainstream primary was more optimistic about how Tommy could develop there than a school designed to work with kids with additional needs. They seemed to write Tommy off within seconds of meeting us, as if the fact he wasn't talking by four years old meant he'd never talk and therefore couldn't be taught in their classroom. The teacher made it very clear she thought he wouldn't cope in her class and wouldn't be able to keep up.

We left that day angry, frustrated and hurt. Because Tommy – bright, inquisitive, full of potential – deserved so much more. We could have complained, we could have pushed back, but deep down, I knew there was no point battling it. There was no way I was handing my son over to a school that didn't want him to be there.

I felt like we were back at square one. Like we'd wasted months searching for something that didn't exist. And all the while, the answer had been staring us in the face.

We arranged a visit back to Jude's school. A place we knew so well. A place that for the last three years had cared for Jude with patience and love, had given him room to grow and

SCHOOL, BUT DIFFERENT

supported him through the ups and downs. But still, I had doubts. I'd always seen that school through the lens of Jude's life, and while it worked for him, the two boys were so different, I couldn't get my head around it being the right place for both of them.

The school invited Tommy to spend an hour in the classroom, to let him explore and see how he coped. And what happened that day still brings a lump to my throat. The staff welcomed him like he already belonged. There was no awkwardness, no rushing past, no judgement. He bounced his way down the corridor, excited and free. They didn't try to stop him. They joined him. When he pulled on a teacher's hand to go outside, she ran with him, up and down the playground, lap after lap. Not dragging him back but meeting him where he was, knowing this would help build a bond between them.

Back inside the classroom, he explored happily. He sat for snacktime with a little encouragement. He joined in with the activities in his own way. One of the little girls in the class took him under her wing, held onto his hand and walked around the playground with him, smiling.

It was everything we could have hoped for. That hour was more than enough to rid me of any doubts. Tommy showed how much he loved the structure and being set tasks to do. The teachers saw him as he was, not a checklist of what he couldn't do. The label of being non-verbal wasn't scary to them, nor the diagnosis. They saw Tommy: a bright, energetic, curious little boy who just needed people willing to meet him halfway.

When we walked back through the school to leave, members

of staff came out to say hello, wanting to catch a glimpse of Jude's little brother. They knew he was coming in and wanted to see him. It gave us a real sense of the school being an extension of the family. By the time we left the decision was an obvious one. This would become home for Tommy too.

Both boys have been at the school for several years now. Like so many parents, on the first day of term, we try to capture that back-to-school moment in a photograph. It's not usually on the doorstep, though, more often it's on the way to the bus or in the kitchen as they grab breakfast to go. Jude will have a furrowed look on his face, shocked at having to get up so early after a lazy summer, still processing that he's actually going back to school. Tommy is usually a whirl of energy, excited to get out to the bus. A few years back I asked Tommy to stand by the door for a photo, just as we were about to leave. And he did. Only he stood facing the door, with his back to me. Like most things in life, he'd taken it literally, done exactly as I asked. I got my photo, and for me it stands out more than any other back-to-school picture. A perfect reminder of our lives: different, not less.

For Jude and Tommy, starting school felt like passing a finish line at the time. Like we'd made it through the hard part, the decisions, the paperwork, the visits, the endless uncertainty. But really, it was only the beginning.

Because school isn't just about getting a place. It's about handing your child over every day, sometimes with confidence, sometimes with a knot in your stomach, trusting that the people on the other side of the gates will understand them, care for them and meet their needs. That's a huge ask for any

SCHOOL, BUT DIFFERENT

parent. But when your child is non-speaking, it's something else entirely.

We can't prepare them for school and what's to come. We don't get to hear about their day on the walk home. We can't ask if they had fun or what they did in class. We don't know if they made a new friend or felt left out, if someone upset them, if they were hungry or overwhelmed or had a brilliant moment of connection. We don't know if they like their teachers or how they're being treated.

There's a silence at the end of the day that never quite gets filled and that silence demands trust. Trust in the teachers, the teaching assistants, the lunchtime staff, the transport team who take them to and from school. A whole group of people who become part of your child's world in ways you'll never fully see. And for us, that trust has been earned, growing over time. I no longer spend my days worrying, checking my phone constantly, waiting for a call. I can put them on the school bus in the morning, and I can breathe. I can work. I can juggle all the other demands life throws at us, knowing they're somewhere they belong.

Jude and Tommy's school has been a constant in a life that can feel anything but. We have worked steadily with a team of people there who don't just see the boys' diagnoses, they see *them*: their quirks, their joys, their patterns, their potential. It hasn't always been perfect, and some years have felt easier than others. Some teachers have clicked with the boys straight away, while others have taken a little more time. There have been moments where the class mix hasn't quite worked, where something has unsettled them or there's a kid they're really struggling to be around. Whenever we've seen a spike in unsettled behaviours at home, our first port of call is always school to see if they're noticing similar signs or have any idea why that might be. Then, between us, we've tried to figure it out, whether that means a change in the structure of their school day, an increase or decrease in certain activities or even changing class to find a better fit.

From the very beginning, the lines of communication have been open. With Tommy and Jude going to and from school via transport, it's meant we're not at the school gates every day, so we've had to make sure that we can still have that contact by phone or email. We've had quick check-ins, honest conversations and longer, deeper meetings. We've shared what's working at home, and they've done the same from school. They've helped us with transitions, sensory strategies, even building visuals to help prepare Jude and Tommy for holidays. When we've taken the boys on days out, they've created social stories to help them understand what's going to happen. Social stories can be invaluable for some autistic kids, adults too. They're short stories that create clear and simple explanations of an event or routine, helping them understand and know what to expect. When Jude struggled with personal care, they supported him with showers and brushing his teeth. In recent years they've played a huge part in helping to build the bond between the boys, planning activities they can enjoy together during school time.

There was one year where things got so hard with Jude, we nearly pulled him out altogether. He was so unsettled, having constant meltdowns at school and at home. Nothing seemed to be working. We wondered whether he was in the wrong setting, whether we were asking too much of him even to go to school. We had emergency meeting after emergency meeting.

But we stuck with it. We worked with the school, adjusted routines, trialled new strategies and, slowly, things started to shift. A few years later, he wasn't just coping, he was thriving. In 2022, the school nominated Jude for a Mencap Award at an event organised by the Southend branch of Mencap, to celebrate the achievements of people with a learning disability. Nominations come from teachers and professionals, and Jude's teacher had nominated him for all the progress he'd made that year. Charlotte and his teacher took him to the ceremony, and Jude stood proudly on stage while his teacher shared the story of everything he'd overcome. I wasn't able to be there, which stung a little. I had to be at home with Tommy, as changing his fixed schedule, even for something as special as his brother receiving an award, just wasn't possible. But I got to see the videos and heard the stories. And I still get teary thinking about it now.

That moment, of being seen and celebrated, of Jude standing on stage (and not getting upset), meant more than any certificate I'd ever imagined pinning to the fridge.

We've been very fortunate with the school Jude and Tommy go to, I know that. I'm reminded of it every time I speak to another parent who's still fighting just to get their child seen, supported or even placed. But that's the thing. It shouldn't come down to luck. And recently I've been trying hard to stop using that word. I often catch myself saying it whenever I describe our school journey, especially when talking to another parent who's struggling in that area.

Because really, we shouldn't feel *grateful* just for finding a school that welcomes our children. For getting a place in an environment where they can be happy, where they can thrive. That should be the *baseline*, not the exception.

Do parents of neurotypical kids feel lucky just because their local mainstream school meets their child's needs? Or do they just expect it? Expect it to be accessible. Expect it to be safe. Expect it to work. Because that's what education is supposed to do. That's what all of our children, every single one, should be entitled to.

And yet, for so many families like ours, that's not the reality. Even the basics, like the distance travelled, become complicated. Most of the children where I live walk to school or are a five-minute drive away. For Jude and Tommy, their school is forty-five minutes away in the car. And we're lucky that it's only that far. I know families who travel over an hour each way, every single day. Because that's the *closest* place that can meet their child's needs.

Again, something that should be expected, something that should be *local*, becomes something you feel you have to be grateful for. And that's the problem. The more we're forced to accept scraps, the more we see so many other families having to fight for the basics, the more we're made to feel lucky for things that should be standard.

I hear from parents every single week, in my inbox, at events, through the SAA Clothing community, who are living a very different story. Families pushed to breaking point trying to navigate the system. Children left out of school for months, sometimes years, or forced to home school. Children who are in the wrong setting, stuck because there's no other space available and seeing their mental health suffering every day because of it. Tribunals that drain every ounce of energy and every penny of savings. Parents who are told that their child is too complex, too challenging, too expensive.

And all the while, their bright, beautiful children are being failed. Not because they can't learn but because the system won't make space for them.

I saw this up close in 2023 when I joined the SEND Reform protests and again in 2025 with the Fight for Ordinary SEND Rally. Parents standing shoulder to shoulder, demanding better. Holding placards not because they had time to spare but because they had no choice. All of them tired and fed up because their kids were being let down. The stories I heard from the other parents will stay with me. Parents having to quit their jobs. Kids out of school for over a year. Families drained emotionally, financially, completely on their own. All just trying to get the *bare minimum*. And nobody seemed to care.

Jude and Tommy were both given places in the school they needed straight away. There were no battles, no appeals, no legal fees. I had no idea these were even issues that people faced. I was blissfully ignorant: I expected to get a place, we applied and we did. That's increasingly rare now. And that is wrong.

It's not OK that getting the right support has become a postcode lottery. Or a legal battle. Or something only the loudest or most privileged get access to.

Just because the system worked for us doesn't mean I get to sit back now. I *can't* sit back. Because I know how different our lives would be if Jude and Tommy had ended up in the wrong school or if we'd been forced to home school.

So I'll keep showing up, I'll keep speaking up, trying to use my platform to amplify what's happening to other families. Because every single child deserves what my boys have had, a school that gets them, sees them, believes in them. A team that knows how to support them. A place where they can feel safe and be themselves.

Without realising it, we were lucky. But luck shouldn't be part of the equation when it comes to education. And until it isn't, until *every* family can access what their child needs without a fight, the work isn't done.

9

The Long Nights

I was woken by a slap to the face and my hair being yanked. In that foggy moment between sleep and consciousness, I had to fight every instinct in my body urging me to react. But even in sleep, I never fully switched off. Somewhere in the back of my mind, I already knew. This wasn't a nightmare or an intruder. It was my five-year-old son. My world. My Jude.

It wasn't the first time he'd woken me like this. For months, I'd been sleeping with one eye open, always half-alert. And as rough as it was to be pulled awake in this manner, it was still better than the alternative, hearing Jude slap himself across the face or pound his thighs as hard as he could, over and over again.

I sat up, rubbing my cheek, blinking through the dim glow of the nightlight. Jude was already upright, his eyes wild with distress, his face twisted in confusion and anger. He looked at me for a second, before turning his frustration inwards, slapping his legs and wailing. I grabbed his iPad, searching for the right episode of *Mickey Mouse Clubhouse*, not just any one, the one that would work in this particular instance. But I was aware that what had calmed him yesterday might be the very thing that sent him further into meltdown today. And it was 3 a.m. My brain wasn't exactly firing on all cylinders.

'It's OK, darling . . . it's OK,' I whispered, even though I didn't know if it really was.

I handed him his dummy, which he snatched from my hand and shoved into his mouth and found his muslin cloth, soft, worn, familiar. These two items had soothed Jude since he was a baby and were his essential tools for regulating. For me, they were a source of anxiety. I was constantly searching for them, terrified of the fallout if one ever went missing. He'd hurl his dummy across the room when he was done with it, never worried that he might need it again.

Despite my efforts, the tears kept coming. His cries grew louder. It was decision time. Stick to the sleep advice: stay in the room, teach him that waking up doesn't mean getting up. Or take him downstairs, break the pattern, try something else and pray we didn't wake up the rest of the house.

I scooped him up, grabbed the iPad and carried him down the stairs, whispering to keep him calm, hoping Charlotte and Tommy would stay asleep.

We tried the sofa. Warm milk. Soft music. Nothing worked. Jude kept crying, flapping, hitting himself, slamming the radiator, throwing himself onto his knees. Watching him hurt himself like that . . . I can't explain the pain of it. It's a kind of heartbreak you never get used to. In these moments I tried to stay calm and follow what the professionals said, but all I wanted to do was wrap him in my arms and make it stop. I'd tried everything: holding him close, putting myself between him and his fists, letting him hit me instead. Anything, to stop him hurting himself.

Eventually, I gave in to the only thing left that sometimes worked. I grabbed the car keys, threw on my coat and bundled Jude up in a blanket. As we passed the glowing Christmas tree in the hallway, it struck me once again: this wasn't how the holidays were supposed to feel.

Outside, the cold bit at my face, but the fresh air seemed to jolt Jude out of his spiral, just enough for me to get him in the car. As always, the combination of music and motion worked its magic. Jude swayed along to Ed Sheeran in his car seat in the back, his tear-streaked face softening into a smile. The contrast was almost unbearable.

We drove through the empty roads, the only people awake in a sleeping world. After a while I pulled over, stepped outside and sat on the bonnet, head in my hands. Then I screamed. And cried. And cried. And cried.

For years, sleep ruled our lives. Or more accurately, the lack of it.

Even when Jude did sleep, I rarely did. I was always on edge, waiting. Listening out for the smallest shift in his breathing, the shuffle of covers, the whimper before the storm. And when he wasn't with me, when Charlotte was the one lying next to him, trying to calm him, I'd lie in the room next door fighting the urge to rush in. We'd swap sometimes, not because the other one needed a break but because we couldn't bear not being the one trying to help. Even when we were exhausted, there was this desperate instinct to protect, not just Jude but each other too.

There's a different kind of tiredness that comes with this life. Not just the physical tiredness, although that's brutal but the mental exhaustion of constantly being on alert. The emotional weight of seeing your child suffer and not knowing how to stop it. The fog that settles over your days, the way it seeps into your work, your relationships, your ability to even hold a conversation. You go from surviving on broken sleep to surviving on autopilot.

There's a reason sleep deprivation is used as a form of torture. When you're that exhausted from a lack of sleep, it's not just your eyes that feel heavy, it's your whole life. It turns you into someone you don't recognise. I'd feel it in my bones, the mornings where just getting out of bed felt like an impossible task. I'd turn up to work after three or four hours of disturbed sleep and try to act normal. To lead meetings. To run a business. I'd sit on the train in a daze, nodding off against the window, waking up with a jolt and a damp patch of drool on my shirt. Some mornings, I'd drive Jude to school and have no memory of the journey when I arrived. I've found myself standing in the kitchen, wondering why I went in there or putting the boys' iPads onto charge, then spending ten minutes wandering around the house looking for them. I'm not a coffee drinker, but I've come to understand why so many parents are. For me, it's energy drinks that get me through the day.

I've spoken to so many parents who've said the same thing: they don't recognise themselves anymore. They've forgotten what it feels like to wake up rested. They live in a permanent state of survival, constantly pushing through, feeling like they're failing even when they're doing everything they possibly can.

Sleep deprivation doesn't just affect how we feel, it changes how we connect – with our children, our partners, ourselves. When you're exhausted, your patience wears thin and the

THE LONG NIGHTS

tiniest things become triggers. Conversations become shorter, snappier. You're quicker to argue, slower to forgive. Charlotte and I were sleeping in separate beds for years, not because we wanted to but because it was the only way to get through the night: Jude needed someone with him at night; Tommy needed someone who could be alert early in the morning. So we split the shifts. We did what we could to survive but it took its toll.

Friendships suffered too. I cancelled plans more times than I can count: too tired, too overwhelmed, too empty. Texts went unanswered. Phone calls were left to ring out. I wanted connection, but I didn't have the energy for it.

And then there's the ripple effect of sleeplessness on other children in the family. It can mean siblings experience broken sleep too, woken up by their brother crying or their sister using the bed like a trampoline at 3 a.m. Tommy didn't just lose sleep when Jude was unsettled, he also had to watch it unfold. The slapping, the screaming, the crashes in the middle of the night. He couldn't understand why his big brother was in distress. And he couldn't understand why I had to leave his room to go to Jude. Sometimes it scared him. Sometimes it made him anxious. Sometimes it just made him feel less important.

I know from the other families I speak to that this is one of the hardest parts: trying to meet the needs of the other children, while also being up throughout the night with their autistic sibling.

I spent years blaming myself for the boys' sleep struggles. Was it something I'd done wrong? Had I missed something? Not been strict enough with routines? Given them too much screen time? Or not enough exercise?

It wasn't until I started learning more about autism, not just from professionals but from other parents, autistic adults and my own boys, that I began to realise how complex the relationship between autism and sleep really is.

Take melatonin, for example. I didn't even know what this was until a paediatrician explained it to us. It's the hormone that helps regulate the body's sleep-wake cycle, and for many autistic people their melatonin production is either delayed or disrupted, which means they're wide awake when the rest of the world is winding down. That explains why Jude could be bouncing off the walls at midnight like it was midday. And why Tommy, even when he's clearly exhausted, still fights sleep like it's the enemy.

Melatonin can be given as a medication and is often suggested for autistic children or adults who struggle with sleep. After various consultations with professionals, we decided to give melatonin a try with Jude when he was about five. I needed a lot of persuading and did a huge amount of research, but knowing that it's a natural hormone and that the body processes and eliminates it within twenty-four hours, we felt more comfortable giving it a try than we did with some other medications.

We had mixed success. Firstly, melatonin comes as tablets. Jude has never swallowed a tablet in his life, so we had to resort to crushing them, meaning he wasn't taking it in the ideal form. It is possible to get melatonin in liquid form, particularly in the US but where we live it just doesn't seem to be a prescribed option. At first we put the crushed tablets in Jude's night-time bottle of milk (which he held onto a lot longer than most kids). Within half an hour he was asleep. It had worked! We felt like all our prayers had been answered.

THE LONG NIGHTS

Only for him to wake up again four hours later. Melatonin is really about helping someone fall asleep, not necessarily staying that way!

Over the years we've come on and off melatonin. Currently, we're on it again, and he has the tablets crushed up and mixed in with a yoghurt. At times it seems to do the trick; he will be asleep within thirty minutes and get a decent amount of rest. Other times, not so much. Last Saturday I gave him his melatonin at 11 p.m. and he fell asleep at 3.15 a.m. It did nothing that night.

As for Tommy, he refuses to take any form of tablets. If a crushed tablet is mixed in with a drink or food, he's too aware of the change in taste or texture and will refuse to take it. So we haven't got very far with melatonin for him, and after the mixed results it's had for Jude, it's a battle I choose not to pick with Tommy.

The fact that their bodies are producing less natural melatonin or producing it differently, means that for Tommy and Jude their energy levels don't naturally drop throughout the evening as they do for most of us. Even now, at fourteen, Tommy's energy at bedtime is off the scale. He'll be laughing and leaping across the room – until suddenly he stops. There's no winding down period, he doesn't gradually get sleepy like I do; he's either going full pelt or out like a light.

And then there's what I've come to call 'the switch'. Or rather, the absence of one. So many autistic children struggle to switch off mentally. Even when they're physically exhausted, their minds are still buzzing. Whether it's excitement over a favourite TV programme or sensory input from the day that hasn't been processed yet, it keeps them in this heightened state, overstimulated, overtired, unable to find that quiet place inside themselves where sleep lives.

I see it in Jude when he's flapping or humming or rocking just before bed. That's not him being disruptive, it's him trying to self-regulate and find calm in the chaos of his own body. And as a parent, watching that, knowing he's trying so hard just to settle, it breaks your heart. Because you realise this isn't something he can just grow out of. It's something we have to learn to live with and support him through.

We've tried more sleep strategies than I can remember. Some came from professionals, others from desperate Google searches at 2 a.m., and plenty from fellow autism parents swapping survival tactics as if they were ancient family secrets. Most were tried with hope, some with scepticism and all of them because we were exhausted. I gave up much hope of help from local services when we finally got an appointment for Jude when he was seven. After many months of waiting, the sleep specialist came to the house to observe Jude and ask more questions. I had high expectations, hopes that things were about to change and we'd finally start to get some sleep. Instead, after we'd gone through all the history, all the explanations and spent half an hour observing him, her brightest solution was to tell me to leave Jude with the TV remote at night and let him watch telly, so I could get some sleep. It took every ounce of my self-control not to kick her out of our house.

We kept trying everything. We bought blackout blinds. We stuck to the same bedtime routine every night: warm bath, calming stories, soothing music, dim lights. We followed the textbooks, until the textbooks stopped working. We tried lavender sprays and magnesium creams. Weighted blankets.

THE LONG NIGHTS

Visual schedules. Calming apps. Compression sheets that hugged their bodies just enough to feel more grounded. I'd sit on the floor next to their bed, lie down beside them, wait in the hallway. Some nights I'd have to message Charlotte to come and take my place in the bed so I could use the toilet, knowing that if a sleeping Jude felt my absence he'd wake up and we'd have to start the process all over again. Nothing was off the table if there was even a slim chance it might help.

And slowly, we found things that did work. Jude needs his music. Always. At one point, he would only fall asleep with Ed Sheeran playing; I must have listened to his first album a thousand times. Or it's nursery rhymes on loop, playing softly from the Alexa by his bed, helping him regulate. He'll have multiple devices, one in his hand, the others laid next to him, creating a clash of sounds but sounds that he is in control of. Experts would argue that's the worst possible thing he could do before bed and for most people, maybe it is. But for us, it's the only thing that helps him feel relaxed enough even to try to get to sleep.

For Tommy, bedtime is a process of managing anxiety about tomorrow. Every night, he gets me to list his routine for the next day: 'Breakfast, bus, school, bus, Daddy's house, dinner, shop, shower, bed.' Some days I only have to say it once. Other days, ten times. It's how he calms the uncertainty. Until he hears those words, in that order, the idea of sleep is out of the question.

Tommy used to be a better sleeper than Jude, until he suddenly wasn't. On Christmas Day, when he was seven, out of nowhere, he refused to go into his bedroom. There was no warning, no explanation. He just stood in the hallway, thumb down, shaking his head and saying 'no' over and over again. I tried coaxing him. Begging. Bargaining. But he was adamant. So I gave in. I carried him into my bed that night, assuming it was a one-off. It wasn't.

For three months, I co-slept with him in his room every night. He'd only fall asleep if I was lying next to him, and he'd cry if I even tried to leave the room. Eventually, I moved into his room and gave him mine. It was such a simple switch and suddenly, things improved. The routine fell back into place and he started sleeping on his own again. I still don't know what changed or why. But sometimes, that's just how it is.

None of the tactics we've ever tried has been a silver bullet. Some have worked for a while, some not at all and some even made things worse. And what worked for one boy never seemed to work for the other. That's the thing no one tells you: even within the same family, sleep can look completely different.

There's nothing quite like the guilt that hits you at 3 a.m., when your child is still awake and nothing you've tried has worked. When you've Googled every possible solution, read every forum thread, followed every expert's advice and you're still here, bleary-eyed and defeated, wondering what you're doing wrong. But over time, I've come to realise for us it's not been about finding a magic solution, a lavender spray or a weighted blanket, it's been about flexibility. It's giving up the idea that there's one right way to do this and instead focusing on what works tonight, for Tommy or for Jude, in this moment. And accepting that tomorrow, it might be different again. I also realised that Jude and Tommy weren't just struggling with sleep, they were showing me what they

THE LONG NIGHTS

needed. Teaching me, in their own way, what regulation looks like for them. That rest doesn't always mean stillness. Their way of decompressing from the day might involve hopping, dancing, jumping off furniture and craving sensory input. That's what helped them wind down. They've taught me to pay attention. To adapt.

So we adapted. We had to. We let go of a lot of expectations during those years. The house was rarely tidy. Screen time crept up. Plans got cancelled. But survival mattered more than routines. Trying to get what sleep we could when we could. Getting Jude to school each day, going to work. And learning to let go of that guilt, even just a little, made a big difference.

Because I've learned, through trial, error and years of exhaustion, that sleep isn't a puzzle with a perfect solution. Not for us. Maybe not for you either. Sleep isn't a challenge because Charlotte or I didn't try hard enough. It's difficult because for many autistic children, the way their brains and bodies process the world is different. The signals that tell most of us it's time to rest just don't arrive in the same way. Understanding this hasn't fixed everything but it's lifted a weight. It's helped me to stop blaming myself. It's helped me to stop blaming them. And most of all, it's helped me to let go of what sleep is *supposed* to look like and start to figure out what's best for them.

These days, sleep isn't quite the all-consuming battle it once was but it's still fragile. Jude can go through good spells. So can Tommy. And then, just like that, a small change, an illness, a routine disrupted, a bad day at school and we're back to nights of pacing the floor, trying to hold everyone together.

There aren't many nights where I'm asleep before 1 a.m.

Sometimes I co-sleep with Tommy. Sometimes Jude stays up humming to his iPad and I gently coax him to lie down in bed fifty times before he finally gives in and passes out. I still lie there waiting to hear if he'll stay asleep or get up, needing me again. I wake up most mornings to the sounds of his door opening and open my eyes to him looming over me. During school holidays it's always worse. The routine of school, the stimulation they both get each day, helps with the bedtime routine. By the time we're a few weeks into the summer holidays there are nights where Jude doesn't fall asleep until 5 a.m., breaking me or Charlotte for the day that follows.

Sleep is still unpredictable, but it has changed over the years for the better. The 3 a.m. drives are a thing of the past, as is the co-sleeping with Jude. I used to worry endlessly about how we'd break that particular habit, until one night, without warning, he simply pushed me away. I went to lie down beside him and he physically pushed me out of his bed. It felt brutal at the time, but I followed his lead. That night, he slept alone for the first time in years. And over the next few weeks, it became our new normal. If he wakes in the night, the first thing he'll do is get out of bed and come search for me, and he still needs me to guide him back to bed and tuck him in. But that's my job done. He wants his own space, and I can return to mine. Something I spent years agonising over, he figured out for himself.

Tommy needs me beside him for bedtime, as we go through the many tiny steps of his complicated routine. But once he's settled, I can close the door and walk away. Sometimes it takes five minutes, sometimes half an hour. He still wakes early, but

THE LONG NIGHTS

now he knows the routine – breakfast, bus, school – and that gives him comfort.

And me? I still live in that strange in-between place, ready to jump up the moment I'm needed but learning to rest when I can. And my standards are much lower; for the last three years I've been sleeping on a sofa bed, which we'll come to shortly, and these days I just long for my own bedroom again. For the last few months, once Jude and Tommy have got home from school and we're in that post-shower, pre-dinner period, where they're chilling with their iPads and watching TV, I'll crash out on the sofa for twenty minutes. When they were younger, that was impossible to do, the risk of what they might get up to was too great. Now, with full-blown teenagers, I can afford to close my eyes for twenty minutes at the right time. If they need me, they'll soon wake me up anyway.

I always used to think a good sleep routine meant eight hours of uninterrupted sleep and that anything less was falling short. Social media is constantly reminding us how important sleep is for our bodies. But I've learned to measure success differently. I no longer chase perfection. I don't expect a full night. If I get six hours, I'm grateful. If everyone's calm, I'm relieved. If I wake up and no one's upset, I call that a win.

Being sleep deprived and overtired can make you start to question everything. But it doesn't mean you're not doing enough. It means you're doing more than most people can imagine, day after day, night after night. You're allowed to be tired. You're allowed to struggle. You're allowed to ask for help. And you're allowed to forgive yourself when things fall apart.

No one prepares you for this part of parenting. But if this chapter has shown you anything, I hope it's this: you're not alone. Not in the guilt. Not in the exhaustion. And not in the love that keeps you going, even on the hardest nights.

Over the years, I've heard from hundreds of parents about their own battles with sleep. Different families, different routines but the same exhausted bodies and minds, the same midnight pacing, the same desperate Google searches, the same guilt when nothing works. Messages from mums trying to hold it together after three hours of sleep, from dads napping in the car outside work because it's the only quiet place they'll get all day, from parents taking shifts, passing each other like ships in the night, both worn down but still going.

They'll read something I share about sleep and feel like I'm describing their household. They'll read the hundreds of comments and realise it's not just their child who doesn't sleep. And it helps, it really does, just knowing you're not the only one, that somewhere out there, another parent is lying awake at 2 a.m., humming the same lullaby for the hundredth time, just hoping that tonight might be different. There's comfort in that kind of connection, even if it's quiet and invisible. Even if it only comes in the form of a message, a like, a comment that says 'Us too.'

So if you're reading this chapter in the middle of the night, your phone in your hand, your child curled up next to you, too scared to move in case you wake them: I see you. I've been there too. We might not sleep like other families, but we love just the same, and we find the energy to keep going each night no matter what. And some nights, that's enough. It has to be.

10

When Your World Shrinks

One morning, not long after Jude had started school, I was sitting in a café near our house. I'd dropped Jude off, late as always and left him walking down the corridor with his teaching assistant, before heading back to work from home, with a quick stop at the café to grab some breakfast. A table nearby was filled with other parents, chatting easily, laughing as they sipped their coffees. I couldn't help but overhear.

They were swapping stories about World Book Day costumes and school discos. Red Nose Day, swimming lessons, football matches. Complaining about how exhausting it was keeping up with all the different social events. The after-school clubs, the party on Saturday that clashed with football training, and how they were looking forward to having a break from it all in the Easter holidays. All the normal stuff that parents talk to each other about.

Listening to them, I wasn't ready for how much it would sting. I felt angry that life sounded so easy for them, so straightforward; angry at how insignificant their 'problems' sounded. Jude was at school but still not speaking. He couldn't tell me anything about his day, what he liked or why he was sad. And here they were, complaining about school admin and having too many birthday parties to go to. It all felt so unfair.

These particular parents were strangers, but I knew my own friends were probably having similar conversations elsewhere, talking about similar 'problems and worries', discussing difficult weekend decisions like whether to go to a birthday party or football training. That was the life they were living, and it hit me how different our lives really were. These were conversations I'd never have.

No one really prepares you for this part. That while you're just trying to keep your head above water, trying to make sense of everything, trying to help your child in the best way you can . . . your phone goes quiet. The group chats slow down. Invitations stop coming. Sometimes it's because people assume you'll say no. Sometimes they don't know what to say. Some friendships fade gently. Others go quiet after a single awkward comment or judgement that you can't ignore. But either way, it's hard not to take it personally. Because in the middle of all the grief and exhaustion and change, you start to wonder . . .

Where did everybody go?

And the truth is, it wasn't always about other people pulling away; sometimes *I* was the one drifting. It's not that I didn't care, I just didn't have the energy to keep explaining everything, trying to help people understand, trying to voice what we needed – it was exhausting. So I stopped trying. I didn't chase. I didn't always reply. And after a while, it felt as though too much time had passed to pick things up again.

For Charlotte, it was more obvious and more immediate.

In the early years, most of her friendships were with other mums she'd met at baby groups or been introduced to locally. These were people she spoke to most days, shared coffees with and swapped stories about sleep routines and weaning. They had babies the same age. Toddler tantrums at the same time. They were all figuring it out together. But when autism entered the picture, things started to change.

The conversations started to feel harder. More distant. When people talked about challenges, theirs seemed to have solutions – he'll grow out of it, try this routine, stick with it. Ours didn't. And when Charlotte tried to explain what was going on with Jude or Tommy, she was often met with silence. Or unhelpful advice. *'How's he going to get used to noise and being around lots of people if you don't try?' 'All the kids love it there, I'm sure he'll be fine.'* It became easier to say less, to pull back. And as she did, so did they. There was no big fall-out, no harsh words. Just fewer replies, fewer invites, people she spoke to every day slowly drifting away, until one day they didn't speak at all.

For me, it was a bit different. In those early parenting years, most of the social occasions were built around and by the mums. The dads were there too, of course but more in the background. The WhatsApp chats weren't ours. The playdates weren't usually organised by us. So when Charlotte's social circle shrank, it rippled into mine. Even more so after we separated.

My closest mates were and are the ones I grew up with, the ones I've gone through each stage of life with. They have always been solid, but we only ever really met up in the pub, at football or at parties. And when parenting happened, that naturally shifted. It wasn't that those friendships ended, it's just that the rhythm changed. The chances to see each other got fewer and further between and the meet-ups became family-oriented. But those spaces where you'd usually bring your kids and hang out – soft plays, garden parties, family barbecues – didn't really work for us anymore.

At first we were just trying to come to terms with the fact that our future lives were going to look very different to the ones we had thought we'd be living. We were putting aside our own expectations and trying to figure out how to be the best parents to Jude – and later on Tommy. This meant we were becoming more and more restricted in where we could go, who we could see, what we could say yes to. It all started to shrink. We didn't want to hide away, it just made Jude's life easier. Calmer. Safer. We started living in a world that looked so different to the one our friends were in, it was hard to know how to bridge the gap.

Saying yes took more planning than most people would ever see. Making sure we had the right snacks, the ear defenders, the bag full of essentials. Figuring out whether to arrive early, before everyone got there so it was quiet or come later so that everyone was already there and settled, with no surprises. We would do everything we could to make the day as calm and stress-free in the run-up, and a morning meltdown could have us questioning whether it was even worth giving it a go. By the time we'd even arrive at any sort of social gathering, it had already taken up so much energy. And then we would remain on high alert throughout, so busy trying to avoid triggers and trying to help Jude or Tommy navigate the social interactions, that we didn't get a chance to talk to anyone anyway. We wanted to be there, and we wanted all of us, the whole family, to have a good time but that simply isn't always possible.

The more we tried to explain, the more misunderstood we felt. So eventually, we stopped going. We stayed home more. I wanted us to be out in the world, but home was where the boys were happiest. Home was predictable. Calm. It worked. And that's the part people don't always understand: that the isolation isn't always forced. Sometimes it's chosen. Because your child's peace becomes more important than your own fear of missing out. Their regulation starts to shape your routine. Their boundaries become your boundaries. Their limitations soon become your limitations too.

These days, on the rare occasions when I go to those meet-ups, I'm always on my own. I look around and see the kids all chatting, playing, forming their own friendships. And I think about Jude and Tommy. I used to think they were missing out on this part of life, and I'll be honest, it would really upset me. Now, it's not so much that I think they're missing out – they're happy with their life how it is, they have no desire to be there. But I long for them to be there with me. My family. I want them in the group photos. I want to show them off, talk about how well they're doing at school, the football match they played in the week before. I want to see them making friends, having fun. I want them to be part of it all. And that's never been our reality. I don't dwell on it too much. But every now and then, I feel it, the space where something could have been.

I thought me and my friends would be raising our kids alongside each other. I thought they'd all grow up together, the way that we had. That we'd be hanging out in each other's gardens, kids running around, piling into the paddling pool, stealing crisps off the buffet table. That I'd get to know their kids, and they'd get to know mine. And that is what happened, just not with us. And that's the bit that hurts. I see the photos on Facebook or in the WhatsApp groups, and it stings. A reminder that life isn't quite what I thought it would be.

Me and my mates still catch up when we can. Generally once a year, maybe more if things align. It's always great when it happens; there's no awkwardness, no need to catch up on everything. That's another reason why the social isolation felt different for me to how it did for Charlotte. Me and my mates, we talk about football, work, golf, TV. We take the mick out of each other. And yeah, we'll ask how the kids are, but that part's usually done and dusted in about thirty seconds. There's a Micky Flanagan sketch where he talks about how when he comes home from the pub, his wife asks how his friend's partner is, and he realises he didn't even ask. He doesn't know how his mate is, let alone his mate's wife. That's pretty much how it was with us. We just didn't really ever go there. We'd hang out and have a good time. That was enough. Or it always used to be.

So when things got hard at home, when the sleep deprivation kicked in, when life became full of assessments and therapies and worries, I didn't really bring that to them. It's not that I thought they wouldn't care but because we never spoke like that. We didn't do long phone conversations, and I wasn't going to talk about these problems on a night out and bring down the mood. I didn't have the language for *'I'm not coping'*. Or feel brave enough to say it out loud. Even if I did, I wouldn't have known where to put it between talk of football and work. That's not how men like us spoke back then. Certainly not the men I knew anyway. We'd rather make a joke than admit we were drowning. I didn't know how to open up, and it never felt like the right moment. I never thought about how they might be able to help, never realised how much talking about things can make a difference. So I kept it in. I got on with it. I've got no blame for the people around me, I never really gave them the chance to help or listen. But looking back, I wish I'd opened up more.

Charlotte's experience was very different. Like so many mums I've spoken to over the years, friendships meant something else to her. Her friends were her outlet, her connection and support system. The conversations went deeper and the expectations were higher. So when friends drifted, it wasn't just time spent together that was lost, it was that whole network of support. For me, it's not that the support wasn't there. I just never expected it to be or knew how to ask for it in the first place.

In those early months and years, I assumed my family would be the safe space we needed. They'd known us forever. They loved us. They loved the boys. So surely, they'd get it, even if they didn't understand everything; they'd be the ones who stood by us. And they were. Especially my mum and dad. From the very beginning, they were there for us and for Jude and Tommy in every way that mattered. They never hesitated to help. They showed up, again and again, with love and patience and support.

But even with all that, there were still moments where things didn't quite go how we needed them to. Sometimes it was the optimism, the hopeful comments: 'He doesn't do that at our house.' 'He seemed fine earlier.' 'Did you hear that? He definitely said "Dad" just now.' They weren't trying to dismiss or minimise what we were going through. In fact, they were trying to do the opposite. Trying to offer comfort or hope that things weren't as bad as we feared and protect us from the full weight of what they could see we were starting to carry.

And I get that. It always came from a place of love. From wanting things to feel normal. They knew even less about autism than we did, and it took time for them to even begin to understand it. But in those early days, it sometimes felt like they didn't believe us and perhaps thought we were being overly cautious or reading too much into things. And when you're still trying to come to terms with what's happening, when you're still doubting yourself at every turn, even a well-meant comment can feel painful. The 'He doesn't do that at our house' or even telling us all the 'good' things Tommy or Jude did with them, sometimes left me feeling like I was failing, even more than I already felt. If Jude and Tommy were doing so well at their house, not having meltdowns, close to saying words, surely that meant the problem was our house. That the problem was us. The problem was me as a dad.

I didn't fully appreciate it back then but my parents needed time to learn and to adjust too, just as we had. If I'd had thirty years of expecting life to be a certain way, well, they'd had more than double that. Over time, though, those conversations shifted. As the differences became more visible, more undeniable, the optimism softened into understanding. There was no need for explanations anymore, we were all on the same page. I've always been and always will be so grateful for how my parents were there for us. For the way they talked to the boys, loved them, cared for them, without ever expecting them to be anyone other than who they are. Their levels of patience were never-ending. Their home became an extension of our home. A safe space where the boys could stim, bounce, hop, flap to their hearts' content. A place they could have multiple showers and splash the water everywhere. A place that had a swing in the garden, then a trampoline and a paddling pool. A place that forgave the mess, the beheaded flowers, the scattered puzzle pieces and the torn books. A house that was full of their favourite foods and where they could have the same dinner each night without hesitation. A place where they were loved deeply and unconditionally, exactly as they are. A place where, until the physical side of caring for Tommy and Jude became too much for them, the boys could be without me or Charlotte, to give us a few hours' break.

And I know from hearing so many stories over the years, through our online community, through DMs and quiet conversations in our shop, that this isn't always the norm. So many families talk to me about relatives who've pulled away. Who've made rude or ignorant comments. Who've refused to learn, refused to accept. Who show up with judgement instead of support. That's never been our experience. It might not always have been perfect (which families ever are?) but it's always been rooted in love.

I've come to learn that often those closest to us don't know what to say and inadvertently say the wrong thing. And in those early days, I think that's what we were all trying to figure out. How to talk about it. How to sit in the uncertainty. How to be there for each other, without pretending things were easier than they were. Because as parents we're not always looking for solutions from our friends and family, we just need them to be there with us. To say, *'I hear you. That must be hard.'* To acknowledge what is happening, even if they don't have the answers either. I'd much rather that than *'I don't know how you do it.'* Or, *'I really don't think I could cope with all that you do.'*

I know those sentences are meant kindly. People don't know what else to say. But when you're barely holding it together, they don't feel encouraging. They feel like your life is being seen by others as something extreme or unimaginable. A life they wouldn't want to live. When really, it's just your life. Your family. Your child. You do it because you love them. You do it because what other choice do we have. But those phrases remind you that your life looks so different to theirs, they can't even picture being in it. And that can hurt.

There's been a shift in the conversations as the people we know try to accommodate this. When my friends talked about football matches or school awards or their kids getting into a certain school, I never felt jealous exactly. I was happy for them. But an awkwardness would creep in, on both sides. I could feel them hesitate sometimes, almost apologising for their good news. Trying not to sound like they were bragging when they shared the very thing I was still aching for. And in turn, I'd overcompensate, laugh it off or be extra enthusiastic. If they wanted to moan about the lack of sleep or something their kids were struggling with, I could sense how uncomfortable they'd become, as if they shouldn't be complaining around me. That they'd suddenly remembered how we were only ever getting three or four hours of sleep a night. I never wanted them to feel bad or as if they had to filter what they said, just because I was there. But it was still sometimes hard to navigate.

The isolation can spread beyond friends and family, into public spaces too. I used to take Tommy to the park every Saturday morning, early, before it got too busy. Partly to avoid the noise and the crowds but also to avoid the stares and the confusion. A spotlight we never asked for. If we went later, the place would be full of other families, kids his age running around in little groups. Parents sitting on benches, chatting, relaxed.

For Tommy, waiting his turn on the swing didn't make sense. Sharing the slide, letting go of the roundabout, those things weren't easy. Some days they're still not. He'd want to flap at the top of the slide or flick sand across the whole sandpit or sit underneath the swing and play with the woodchips for twenty minutes straight. And while *I* understood that, the world didn't always. He wasn't misbehaving; he was regulating. Finding calm in the chaos of the world around him, the best way he knew how. I'd find myself desperately trying to explain to him that he needed to come down the slide. Debating whether I'd need to climb up there myself and try to carry him, while also knowing that would probably make things worse. When that didn't work I'd be trying to explain to a group of confused six-year-olds that Tommy would get down soon and that getting up there with him wouldn't be a good idea.

So going early took the pressure off a little; it meant he

could be himself and I didn't have to spend the whole time getting between him and other kids, apologising and explaining. It gave us a better chance of a meltdown-free morning. But it also meant losing another of those moments of being social or even making new connections. Sometimes, if we were there for a while, other families would start to arrive. Their kids would all start playing together, the parents would be chatting on benches. It all seemed so easy. For us, it felt more like a mission: get in, avoid any upset and meltdown, then get out while he's still happy.

It was the same with Jude. If we were out walking by the river and bumped into someone I knew, I'd smile, nod and keep moving. If I stopped for a proper conversation, Jude wouldn't understand why I was talking to someone else. He'd get overwhelmed, confused and anxious. I think he found the unpredictability of those moments too much, unsure if the person would try to talk to him, unsure of what was expected. There was too much language for him to cope with in the back and forth of a conversation. So we avoided people.

When Jude was ten there was a playground we used to go to that overlooked some tennis courts. There was rarely anyone else there, and it had a roundabout and large nest swing that he liked. One Saturday, we'd been having a tough day, and after a long drive that had seemed to cheer him up, I took a chance and stopped off at the park. As we pulled into the car park I was relieved to see that the playground was empty.

Jude ran around for a bit, from one side of the playground to the other, before awkwardly clambering onto the swing and waiting for me to push him. I rocked him back and forth, and he broke into a huge smile, swinging higher and higher.

WHEN YOUR WORLD SHRINKS

A huge wave of relief swept over me. The kind that parents whose kids often struggle in public but are having a good time today, will know all too well.

As I pushed him again and again, my focus was drawn to the tennis courts behind him, to a group of kids having a tennis lesson. I recognised some of them and some of the parents sitting chatting and watching. The contrast hit me. Our day had been so tricky, so finely balanced and had involved a lot of tears. Other than Jude, I hadn't spoken to a soul that day. We hadn't spent any time with anybody else. And there right in front of us were kids Jude's age and their parents, living the kind of life I'd once expected us to have. I tried to concentrate on Jude's smiles, on how happy he was in that moment, but it was a battle to separate all the other emotions that were surfacing. The comparisons and the feelings of isolation. Of loneliness.

Eventually, we stopped going to parks with Jude. It wasn't that he didn't enjoy them, some of our happiest moments have been out in parks, they simply became too overwhelming and unpredictable.

It felt like we were trying to squeeze into places that were never built with our family in mind, surrounded by people who didn't really understand. So we withdrew. Bit by bit. Not out of choice but out of necessity.

Our world got smaller, quieter, more scheduled, more structured. There were no impromptu park meet-ups. No last-minute barbecues. No lingering on the pavement catching up with someone we'd bumped into. Those things slowly disappeared. And in their place came more of a pattern: days that looked the same, routines that worked. A life that wasn't exciting but was steady, predictable and safe. One that has felt lonely at times and has taken some getting used to, but in time, it has come to feel like enough.

It's rarely one big moment that changes everything. More often, it's the slow, quiet fade. The gradual realisation that the life you imagined is no longer yours, and you don't quite know where you fit anymore. The ache of feeling left behind. But that's not where the story has to end. Because somewhere in that quiet, new beginnings start to grow too. A message from someone who gets it. A smile from another parent at the playground who says, 'My daughter's autistic too.' The first time you realise you're not the only one standing on the outside. There are plenty of others out there, living versions of the same story, and as you find them, little by little, the silence lifts. The world doesn't suddenly get bigger again, but it starts to feel less empty. And in its place, something else takes shape, new connections, better understanding and the start of finding your people.

11

Never Alone

We were meeting her for a coffee.

Charlotte was excited – nervous but hopeful. She'd been given Sophie's number by a mutual friend. Sophie had an autistic son, a couple of years older than Jude, who was two at the time and had only recently been diagnosed. Sophie was someone who'd been through the diagnosis, who might understand, who was just a little further down the road we suddenly found ourselves on.

I wasn't quite sure what to expect. I didn't really see the point, if I'm honest. Meeting someone new, talking about everything we were going through – I just didn't have the energy. Not back then. I was running on four hours' sleep a night, barely holding it together most days. The idea of small talk, or worse, big talk, with a stranger wasn't high on my list of priorities. I had too much work to catch up on.

But I went. Because it mattered to Charlotte. And because a small part of me was curious too.

We met Sophie at a café halfway between our two homes. The conversation started slowly, like they always do when you're both trying to work out how much of your story is safe to share. But within a few minutes, something shifted. Sophie just . . . got it. All of it. The stress. The confusion. The grief you don't talk about. The love that doesn't look how people expect it to.

Charlotte looked like she could finally breathe. Like someone had lifted some of the weight she'd been carrying for months. She could ask questions without needing to explain every single detail. She could talk about the things that felt too raw or too complicated to say out loud to anyone else. And Sophie understood.

She spoke about Oliver, her son and the journey they'd been on. How he'd only recently started to speak aged four. How she'd had to fight for support but had found people who listened. She wasn't sugar-coating anything, but there was something in the way she spoke that made it all feel a little more possible. And as I sat there, drinking my juice, watching the two of them talk as though they'd known each other for years, I felt something I hadn't felt in a long time. Less scared. More confident that we could do this. Not alone.

Not long after that café meet-up, Sophie invited us to her house for Sunday lunch. It should have felt daunting – a new house, new people, unpredictable kids, the worry about how Jude would cope in a new environment and whether it was even worth going. Normally, I'd have spent the whole time on edge, counting down the minutes until we could leave. But this felt immediately different. There was just an ease to it.

We went out into the garden and Jude wandered round, before a bucket full of clothes pegs caught his eye. He sat down next to it and emptied them out. Picking up each peg one by one, running them down his nose, eyes transfixed on them, before passing them from one side of his body to the other. Over and over and over again. And that was fine. There was no pressure to play with something else or to play how he 'should' be playing. There were no sideways looks when Jude avoided the other kids, no expectation for him to join in or behave a certain way. No awkward silences when we had to cut a conversation short to stop a meltdown. The boys didn't play together and Jude mostly kept to himself but that didn't matter. We just let the kids be who they were. That was eye opening for me.

Sophie and her husband Alex had been where we were. They understood the noises, the stimming and were aware how unpredictable our day might be. Their home felt calm. Jude was relaxed and so were we.

And I couldn't help but watch Oliver, searching for clues of what Jude's future might be like. Watching him smile, watching Sophie and Alex love him so fiercely, so proudly. Hearing all about how the words had started to come in the last few months after they'd spent so long thinking he'd never speak, gave me something I hadn't had in a long time: hope. It planted a thought in my mind that maybe one day this would happen for Jude too.

The conversations flowed as the day wore on. They didn't have all the answers. They weren't some perfect family who'd figured everything out. But they were real, honest and willing to share what they'd learned. We talked about the hard bits, the process of finding a school, sleepless nights, meltdowns, the overwhelm of it all but also about the wins. The joyful moments. The ways they'd adapted their lives and still found happiness in it. It felt doable. And for the first time since we started this journey, I didn't feel so alone.

I didn't realise how much tension I'd been holding in, how guarded I'd become, until I was in a space where I didn't need to be. We didn't have to apologise when Jude didn't want to sit at the table. Or explain why we couldn't stay long. Or overcompensate to make everyone else feel comfortable. There were no polite smiles masking confusion. No questions that felt more like judgement than curiosity. There was just another family, making it through in their own way, who saw us and accepted us for who we were.

I let Charlotte do most of the talking, as I still felt unable to find the words to describe Jude, and I listened intently whenever Sophie and Alex had something to share. I smiled at stories shared and chimed in here and there. But even without saying much, it just felt easier. There was no need to explain, no need to pretend. And that, in itself, was a kind of support.

Looking back, I think Charlotte knew how much she needed that kind of friendship. She'd been aching for it. But I hadn't realised how much I needed it too. I didn't open up to Alex straight away; that's never really been me. Instead, we bonded over football and stories about living in London. But it was reassuring to be around another dad who had been where I was. Another man who knew what it felt like to carry all this worry, all this uncertainty and just keep going.

Before meeting Sophie and Alex, I didn't know any other parents who had a child like Jude. I hadn't grown up around disability. Autism was something I'd barely heard of, let alone understood. None of my friends had kids with additional needs, and it felt like no one in our lives could truly relate to what we were going through. They cared, they really did, but they couldn't possibly know. How could they? And I didn't yet have the words to explain it.

When Jude was diagnosed, it felt like we'd been dropped into a parallel universe. One that ran alongside everyone else's, close enough to see but never quite touching. The conversations at family gatherings didn't land in the same way anymore. The friendships we'd built on shared experiences suddenly felt out of sync. I remember desperately wanting someone to say, 'Yeah, that happened to us too.' Just one person who could take away the fear that what we were going through was completely unheard of.

Meeting Sophie and Alex made a huge difference, but I still struggled to talk about things, even with people who were in the same boat. At around the same time, we'd been offered a place on a course called Good Beginnings, an introduction to autism for parents run by the local authority. Each week focused on a different topic: sleep, communication, sensory needs. All the things that had suddenly taken over our lives. There was a whiteboard at the front, printed PowerPoint handouts and homework we were supposed to do each week. Coffee, tea and a tin of biscuits.

There were around ten other families in the group, all with children recently diagnosed. On paper, it should have been exactly what we needed. A place to ask questions, to learn more and, crucially, to meet other parents going through the same experience.

But I found it hard.

Most weeks simply getting to the course was a challenge.

Jude would sleep for three or four hours a night, leaving us both exhausted. The venue was an hour's drive away, and some weeks when it was time to go, Charlotte and Jude would both still be asleep. So I'd leave them to it and set off alone. I'd try to make as many notes as I could, bring back the worksheets and try to explain what I'd learned. If I could remember any of it. I was shattered, physically and emotionally. Fragile. Trying to listen, trying to learn but also trying not to fall apart.

When it came to the group discussions, I barely said a word. It wasn't that I didn't care, I just couldn't do it. I wasn't ready. Every time I opened my mouth, I felt like I was seconds away from tears, even if it was to share something happy or positive. So I stayed quiet unless someone asked me something directly and instead I listened, to the stories, the emotions, the exhaustion in other people's voices that echoed something I couldn't yet say out loud. Some parents did the same, others couldn't wait to let it all out and tell everyone all about their child. I could sense how much they just wanted somebody to listen to them.

Most of the other children were older than Jude by at least a year, and I remember them all seeming surprised that he'd been diagnosed so young. It had taken them much longer to get to that stage. This scared me; what did that mean for us?

I still remember three of the families from that course. There was a mum whose son was five and obsessed with *Top Gear*. She'd watched every episode on repeat, rewinding the same scenes over and over so her son could watch certain cars race along the track. *Top Gear* had become the soundtrack to their lives. She joked that maybe her son was actually obsessed with Jeremy Clarkson. She laughed as she told the story, but you could hear the tiredness behind it. How she now knew everything about cars but longed for a day when she'd never have to see *Top Gear* again.

Then there was the mum whose son was obsessed with water, always trying to turn on the taps in the kitchen and bathroom, determined to flick it everywhere. They'd already sustained major water damage to their house. But he was also verbal and loved repeating lines from his favourite shows, quoting entire conversations. That was the first time I heard anyone talk about scripting. It stuck with me. Scripting (also called echolalia) means repeating familiar lines, like quoting part of a favourite TV episode word for word, lines from a song or even a conversation they've previously heard. It's often how our kids communicate, calm themselves or process what's going on. It's meaningful, even when it doesn't sound 'conversational' and can help a person make sense of what is happening. It made me wonder if one day Jude would be talking like that, reciting his favourite parts of *Mickey Mouse Clubhouse*.

And then there was the couple with four-year-old twins. I could feel the exhaustion in their words, even when they were smiling. One of their boys was an escape artist. They had baby gates in every doorway, some with two stacked on top of each other, yet still he managed to climb them. The dad described how his son would scale them barefoot and then rest, perched on the bar like a gymnast, his toes gripping the top. A few weeks later, while their boys were in the respite play session run by the course team, a staff member rushed in. Their son had scaled the fence outside, and the staff were trying to coax him down. The parents seemed completely worn out. They openly admitted they were struggling to cope. They didn't know what to do next.

We were already struggling with just one child. I couldn't imagine what it must be like raising two non-speaking autistic boys. Little did I know, I would soon find out.

Even though I didn't say much during the course, something had started to shift in terms of my need to connect with others. I wasn't ready to talk out loud, but I found myself searching for connection in other places. Late at night, sitting in the dark beside Jude while I waited for him to fall asleep, I'd scroll on my laptop. At first, it was all the usual stuff, NHS pages, autism charity websites, medical articles. But as the years passed, I started finding blogs, YouTube videos, Facebook pages, posts written by parents who were living lives that looked a lot like ours. Some of the stories mirrored our days exactly. The meltdowns. The exhaustion. The joy in tiny moments that no one else seemed to notice. I'd read a post and feel the knot in my stomach loosen slightly. *Yes*, I'd think. *That's us. That's how it feels.*

These accounts weren't like medical journals or information leaflets, they were raw and honest, filled with the kind of details only someone living it would know. And somehow, even though I'd never met these people, I felt like they were speaking directly to me.

I didn't comment. I didn't introduce myself or share anything about Jude or Tommy. I just read. Quietly. Absorbed it all. Stories shared by families in America, Scotland, Australia, all around the world. These families didn't have all the answers either, but they made me feel like what we were going through made sense. Like we weren't the only ones.

I started following a few pages. Parents who were further along in their journey. Stories from autistic adults who shared insights I'd never considered, describing what a meltdown felt like from the inside, what sensory overload really meant and why stimming brought them comfort and joy. I wasn't participating, not yet. I was still just quietly observing. But I was learning more than I had from any of the professionals we'd met up to that point.

It felt like I was seeing autism through a new lens. For so long, I'd only seen the struggles. The things Jude and Tommy weren't doing. The milestones they weren't reaching. But now, I was seeing something different. Families who celebrated their children exactly as they were. Life wasn't easy, far from it, but they'd stopped measuring progress by anyone else's standards. They were cheering on the inchstones. The things that might go unnoticed in other families but meant the world in theirs. A new sound. Trying a new food. Sitting at the table for five minutes. Brushing their teeth without a fight. A happy moment at the park. They still shared the hard stuff, meltdowns, sleepless nights, judgement from others but alongside it was joy and presence and pride. Each night, I'd scroll through my feed and find myself smiling at their updates, feeling a jolt of hope when something went well and a lump in my throat when things were tough.

Reading those posts didn't make our challenges go away. But they helped me stop feeling like we were doing it wrong. Like *I* was doing it wrong. They reminded me that this life, this messy, complicated, beautiful life, could still be filled with love and meaning, even when it looked different to everyone else's.

Over time, I started to engage more. I joined private Facebook groups for parents, which felt like safer spaces than the wider internet. Sometimes I'd ask questions. Other times I'd scroll through posts, reading comments from people who just got it and, occasionally, I joined in, when I felt confident enough that our experience might help somebody else. And in return, I got advice from people who actually understood. Parents who reassured me that they'd been there too, that I wasn't failing, that I wasn't alone. People from all over the world, with all different kinds of backgrounds. Sharing their wins and their worries. And from that I started to see and feel the power of community. For so many parents like me, stuck at home, exhausted and isolated, social media became more than a distraction, it became a lifeline. A place to connect when the outside world felt impossible to reach. These were more than just fleeting interactions. Some of the people I met online became part of my everyday life. These were real friendships, offering real support. That changed everything.

Then, one day, I decided to do more than just read other people's stories. I started sharing my own.

Like most good ideas, it came about after a trip to the pub. It was the summer of 2015 and my cousin Tom's birthday. I had met up with him and some of our friends one Friday after work. We were sitting around two large tables, and the conversations went back and forth. By then most of our group had begun to have kids, so while there was plenty of the usual football chat, tales of nights out were starting to be replaced by anecdotes of park trips, soft play and first words. Back then, those conversations still used to bring a lump to my throat. So whenever the conversation came round to me, when I was asked, 'How are the boys?' I'd usually keep it short and sweet. 'We're all good, thanks, you know, the usual ups and downs but we're good.' And try to steer the conversation onto something else.

But for some reason, that night, I didn't give my stock answer. I opened up, just a little and admitted it had been a tough few weeks. Fuelled with Dutch courage, a couple of friends started asking questions, admitting they didn't know much about autism and asking what it meant for Jude and for Tommy. And I started to try to explain. I stumbled over my words, choked down the urge to cry and did my best to describe what autism is. At least, what I understood about it anyway. I talked about Jude and Tommy, what they liked doing, what was hard for them, why they found it difficult to go to birthday parties and why I couldn't just bring them to all the meet-ups they'd been having. As the conversation went back and forth, I realised everyone else at the table had stopped talking and were listening too. The ice had been broken. I explained the best I could, and they asked me questions, wanting to know more. I shared more with them about Jude and Tommy in those twenty minutes than I had in the previous five years.

When I sat on the train home that night, I thought a lot about those conversations. I agonised over everything I'd said, worried I hadn't explained things well enough, that my words hadn't done Jude and Tommy justice. But I also thought about how interested my mates had been. The beer had made them honest enough to admit that at times they didn't know what to say or what to ask. They didn't want to say the wrong thing, so didn't really say anything at all. When I'd been answering

'Yeah, we're all good, thanks', they had taken it to mean that I didn't really want to talk about what was going on either (which I guess I didn't).

Men are notoriously great at this, at not wanting to have the uncomfortable conversations, to talk about feelings or anything deeper than surface level. We can spend hours talking about who Arsenal need to buy to try to win the league – but what's going on in our lives, in our minds? No thanks. Certainly not back then anyway. I would never talk much about how I felt, what I was scared of or the pressure I was under. I love my mates dearly, most of them I've known for over thirty-five years now but even being that close, none of us really knew what was going on in each other's heads. Men just didn't talk about that kind of stuff. We weren't brought up to discuss those things nor were we encouraged by society to do so. It's much better now than it used to be and speaking about your mental health and what's going on in your life is actively encouraged. I've changed so much in the last ten years and talk more openly about how these things affect me. And I also want to know what's going on with my friends and how I can help them. But even with all the progress we've made, I know most of them still carry their struggles in private.

On that train journey home I started to think about writing down what I wanted to say. That way I could make sure I covered everything I wanted my friends and family to know about Jude and Tommy and ensure I didn't leave anything out. I could take the time to think about the questions they'd asked and give them the best possible answers. It popped into my mind that I could write my own blog. I could tell our stories, just like those of all the other families I'd been reading.

I could even add some photos of Jude and Tommy, like an online diary. I could share it to Facebook and then my friends and family would see it and could read it in their own time. I wouldn't have to worry about stumbling over my words, and they wouldn't have to feel nervous about asking me how Tommy and Jude are.

And from that thought, Stories About Autism was born. It wasn't some grand idea to build a community or a platform. I didn't set out to be an advocate or to help other parents. It was just a way to get my thoughts out, because I couldn't seem to say them out loud.

I had always loved writing as a kid. It was one of the things I really enjoyed in school. But somewhere along the way, I had lost that passion. Now, it was back but for a completely different reason. I needed a way to process everything that was happening. I wanted my friends and family to understand what life was really like for us. And more than anything, I needed to feel like someone else out there might get it.

I decided to write a blog, a place I could send people to if they wanted to read more and a place where I could just write freely. I bought the domain name for Stories About Autism and that made it real. A commitment to myself to follow through with this idea. For two months I wrote, deleted and rewrote the first post. Trying to figure out what I'd share, what I wanted people to know about Jude and Tommy. I came up with excuses each week as to why I wasn't ready to go live, too scared to hit the 'publish' button. What if people judged me? What if they thought I was complaining? What if I sounded like I didn't love my boys for exactly who they were?

But after many a conversation with Charlotte about it, I

plucked up the courage. I hit the button, shared it to my Facebook profile, then shut my laptop, instantly regretting my decision.

I didn't expect much of a reaction. Maybe a couple of polite likes from family and friends. But within minutes, comments started to appear. People were reading the blog post. They wanted to know more. The site had a page about Jude, a page about Tommy and my first blog post, a story about how jealousy creeps in sometimes. I described how I'd gone with some friends to watch Arsenal in the FA Cup final. Some of them had brought their kids to the game and seeing them have so much fun together it hit me that this was something I'd never experience. Something I'd done so often with my dad and assumed I'd do with my boys too. How one moment I'd been celebrating, having a great day and the next I was completely distracted, spiralling into all the things we'd never get to do as a family. I spoke about those feelings, how they'd interrupted my day but also how I shook them off and that those feelings were only natural. They were feelings that I'd found difficult to ever express out loud but felt more able to do so typing onto a webpage.

Over the next twenty-four hours I received lots of lovely comments and messages, some from people I hadn't spoken to in years, who wanted to say hello and thank me for sharing. I received some questions that I was only too happy to answer. And then, I started to get comments from people I didn't know. Friends of friends. Friends of friends of friends. Some told me how my story about jealousy, my insights into Tommy and Jude, had resonated with them and reminded them of their own family. They felt less alone reading it.

This inspired me and gave me the confidence to write more. At first, it was only the occasional update: a funny moment or a little insight into our everyday life. But the more I wrote, the more people responded. So I started sharing the hard stuff too, the meltdowns, the exhaustion and the worries over the future. I was honest in a way I had never been able to be in real life. And instead of pity or awkward silences, I was met with empathy and people who understood.

As the months passed, I started connecting with other parents from all over the world, receiving messages from people who were reading our stories in America, Australia, India, the Philippines and South Africa. Many were letting me know they felt less alone, some were even asking me for advice. Me! The dad who for so many years had felt like he was a failure was now being asked advice on being a parent. From people who believed I was doing a good job. That I was a good parent. It caused a big shift in how I saw myself and gave me more confidence when I was with Tommy and Jude. Made me feel like I was doing the best I could and that that was enough. In talking about our lives I started to feel like I could do this. I started to feel like maybe I was the dad that my boys needed.

And then, there were the friendships that formed. There were a handful of parents I started talking to regularly, people I never would have met if it wasn't for Stories About Autism. What started as comments on posts turned into direct messages that turned into phone calls and text messages. And for some of the ones who live in the UK, they became friends I actually met in person.

Even though we were from different towns, different countries, with very different backgrounds, we were connected in a way that was deeper than some of my oldest friendships. There was no awkward small talk, no need to explain every little thing. We just got it.

We knew what it was like to watch our kids struggle and feel powerless to help. How exhausting it can be to have to fight for everything your child needs. We knew what it was like to love them fiercely but still sometimes grieve the life we once imagined. We knew what it was like to feel alone and misunderstood.

But now, we had each other. A community. People who I could moan to, blow off steam with, ask for advice at 1 a.m. and bounce ideas off. People who made me feel like I never had to pretend or sugar-coat things. I had started Stories About Autism because I wanted the people in my life to understand. What I didn't expect was how many strangers would see themselves in our story too. And suddenly, we didn't feel like strangers anymore.

For the longest time, I felt like I had to do this alone. They say it takes a village to raise a child but sometimes autism means we lose that village – at the very moment when we need it more than ever. And if the village you expected to be a part of has disappeared, you have to go out and find a new one. Finding your people doesn't have to mean forcing yourself into support groups if that's not your thing. It doesn't have to mean sharing your deepest thoughts with a room full of strangers. It can be finding that one person, online or in real life, who reminds you that you're not alone.

Maybe they're another parent at your child's school, someone you've never spoken to but who stands at the school gates with the same tired eyes you recognise in yourself. Maybe they're in a Facebook group, someone whose comment made you stop and think, *That sounds exactly like my life.* Maybe they're already in your life, quietly waiting for you to open up so they can say, *'I'm here, I get it, I want to help'.*

They're out there waiting for you.

You are not alone, and you never have to be. One conversation can change everything. One connection can pull you out of the loneliness. One person who truly understands can make all the difference.

When I started writing Stories About Autism, I had no idea where it would lead. I wasn't looking for friendships. I wasn't expecting to find a community. I definitely wasn't expecting to become an advocate who others look to for advice. But somewhere along the way, that's exactly what happened.

And looking back, I don't know how I ever thought we could do this without it. Because if those of us with a voice don't talk about it, especially when our kids can't, how will anything change? How will the world ever see what it's really like or know how to do better? For thirty years I knew nothing about autism; how can I expect the rest of the world to understand what I didn't know if we don't talk about it? How will other families realise there are so many others out there living a similar life, who get it, who live differently to what they imagined?

I've come to realise over the years that not everyone agrees with sharing parts of our lives online. Autism parents often get criticised for it, told we're oversharing, that our children's lives should stay private. And I get it. These are personal moments. And technically, I don't have my boys' consent. They have no understanding of what social media is and probably never will. But I'm more than willing to stand up and take on those critics, because when the world doesn't see families like ours, doesn't hear our stories, then we stay invisible. And nothing changes. I'm not sharing for attention or sympathy. I'm sharing because it helps others feel seen. Because it helped me feel seen. And to make the world a better and more accepting place for my kids. Because while our children can't always speak for themselves, their stories still deserve to be heard. And I will always tell those stories with love, honesty and respect. If we don't talk about our lives, who will? If we don't tell our stories, nothing changes. And our kids, our lives, should never be invisible.

12

Co-parenting

There was a mattress on the living room floor. There had been for months now. Not because we were redecorating or because anyone was sleeping in there. But because bouncing on it together, Jude and Tommy side by side, was one of the only ways they could safely play in the same space. It was one of the few activities they seemed to be able to share happily and which met their sensory needs.

That Friday night, things were going well. Charlotte was at work, an evening shift at her restaurant, while I was home with the boys. Six months earlier, in the middle of all the chaos and the rollercoaster our lives seemed to be on, Charlotte had been offered the chance to take over a local restaurant – realising a dream she'd had for years. We had talked it through and decided to go for it. I wanted Charlotte to follow that passion, I could see how much it meant to her, and we vowed to make sure that, with the right support, we would juggle it all. It would be a good thing for her and for our family. In hindsight, perhaps it wasn't the smartest idea. Other families might be able to juggle two careers with two young children but Tommy's and Jude's needs were different. I don't think either of us appreciated just how difficult it would be to put in the long hours and hard work a busy restaurant demands, and mixed in with the long sleepless nights, therapies and meltdowns it would soon prove impossible. We wanted it to work. We wanted to believe we could be the family who juggled it all. And the dream was nice while it lasted, but like so many other things in our lives, the expectations didn't match up to our reality.

On that particular Friday, however, everything felt calm for once. Tommy had gone to bed without a fuss. Jude was still on the mattress, bouncing and giggling. For a few rare moments, I felt like I had everything under control.

Then it all changed. Jude's mood shifted. Fast. I never knew what might tip the balance, maybe it was the wrong episode on YouTube, maybe the excitement of the evening just got too much, but suddenly he was spiralling. A huge meltdown followed, where he began hitting himself, hard. I tried to calm him, but he lashed out, at me, at himself, unable to process the overwhelm any other way.

I was exhausted, running on empty. Just as I was about to call Charlotte and see if there was any way she could come home early, something clicked. Jude started to settle. He climbed up on the sofa, wrapped himself in his blanket, sucked on his dummy and closed his eyes. Within minutes, he was asleep. Burnt out. I carried him upstairs, tucked him in, then went and sat on the garden step in the dark. And sobbed. I let it all out.

Not just for that night but for all the nights like it. For how hard life felt and how helpless I felt. For how painful it was to watch Jude struggle like that and not know how to fix it. For feeling like it was somehow all my fault. When she got home, I didn't tell Charlotte what had happened. Not fully, anyway. She was shattered from her shift, and we both knew we only had a few hours before the next wake-up. And, if I'm honest, I didn't want her to know how much I was struggling.

I don't think any parent is truly prepared for how much life changes when they have a child. You hear people talk about it and you see it happening to others, but living it is something else entirely. It's overwhelming, exhilarating and exhausting, all at once. I thought being a dad would be easy. I thought being a husband would be too. Before your baby arrives, you imagine growing closer to your partner, united by the joy, watching this tiny person reshape your lives in the best possible way. And that does happen, but so does everything else. The sleepless nights. The uncertainty. The arguments because you're both stressed and overtired. The invisible pressure of suddenly being responsible for this tiny, fragile human. Even the strongest relationships are tested.

When Charlotte and I got married, Jude was two and Tommy wasn't yet born. At the time I still had an idealised view of what relationships looked like. I thought love would be enough to get us through. But when life becomes survival mode, when the sleepless nights keep stacking up, when meltdowns become daily occurrences, when the financial pressure builds and your world shrinks down to just getting through the day, you realise it takes far more than love to hold things together. It takes communication. It takes honesty. It takes being able to adapt to a life that looks nothing like what you expected. And sometimes, no matter how much you love someone, no matter how much you both try, the life you're living changes you in ways you never saw coming.

Parenthood forces you to adapt, to stretch into roles you can never be quite ready for. And when you add autism into the mix, the changes you expected expand into something more than you could have ever imagined. And a lot of those early challenges, the exhaustion, the uncertainty and the pressure to get it right, don't fade with time. Instead, they intensify. Even after Jude's autism diagnosis, I held onto the idea that once we got through the toddler years, once we found the right support, things would get easier. The sleepless nights would pass, the words would come and we'd settle into something closer to the life we imagined.

But life wasn't getting easier. The adjustments weren't temporary, like people kept telling us they would be. They weren't just a phase. They were becoming permanent shifts in the way we had to live. And, for a while at least, I struggled with the reality of that.

Parents often process an autism diagnosis at different speeds, which can cause a rift between them. It's not unusual for one parent to feel like they are carrying the weight of parenting alone, while their partner withdraws. I hear this all the time from parents I've met over the years, in conversations and messages. That was never the case for me and Charlotte. We always parented as a team. We both went to pretty much every appointment and were on the same page. But we handled the emotions of it all differently. Charlotte was instinctive, quick to act. If a strategy or therapy was suggested, she was all in. I was methodical, cautious. I needed to research every option, weigh up every possibility. Sometimes to the point of paralysis.

CO-PARENTING

One example of this was the suggestion that we try a gluten-free, casein-free diet for Jude. This became very popular in the early 2010s, with parents sharing online the wonders a change in diet had made for their autistic kids: they had begun to speak, be happier, more able to cope with the world around them. Hollywood actress Jenny McCarthy famously claimed this was one of the things that helped her son recover from autism. I'm ashamed to say that back then, the word 'cure' didn't raise alarm bells in the way it does today. We were desperate, our son was miserable every day, and when you see that over and over again, it's easy to look for anything that might make life better. Maybe even 'cure' him.

Somehow, we had been told about the diet, and I started to do what I do best, research and procrastinate. For a couple of weeks I read and reread every article I could find, weighing up the evidence, scared to make the wrong decision. Then I came home to a house that was full of gluten- and casein-free food, Charlotte having bought everything our local supermarket had to offer that Jude and Tommy might even attempt to eat. We were all in. Despite how much it pained me to give up my obsession with fresh, crusty bread, we followed the rules for six months, before ditching the diet, having seen little to no difference.

Neither of us were right or wrong in our approach, we just always handled decision making differently. We soon realised that we reacted to the new challenges in different ways, but we always put Tommy and Jude first. We always did everything we could for them and adjusted our lives to better meet their needs. But this also meant that there was precious little time left over for us.

When you're the parent of an autistic child (or two), you soon realise you're not going to get many moments to just be with your partner. The job is never done. There's no clocking off at the end of the day. There are few moments where you can collapse onto the sofa together, binge a box set and switch off for a few hours. And as much as we tried, there was never enough time or energy left to be us.

I know this is a struggle many parents battle with, regardless of autism or disability. But it generally gets a little easier as your kids develop and grow and become more independent. But when your child has a high level of support needs, you often find yourself doing as much, if not more, when they're twelve as you did when they were two.

For seven years, Charlotte and I rarely slept in the same bed. Most nights, I'd sleep alongside Jude, while Charlotte shared with Tommy. Then, as Jude found it increasingly difficult to be around Tommy, we started separating them for most of the day as well: one of us upstairs with Jude, the other downstairs with Tommy; one in the garden, the other in the kitchen; taking it in turns to go to the park or out for a walk. We were very rarely all four of us together. Upstairs and downstairs. Garden and kitchen. One at the park, one in the car. We were already living apart, we just hadn't admitted it yet.

We adapted because we had to. But with every new adjustment, the distance between us grew. Some days, it felt like we were flatmates, passing ships in the night. And as we tried to adjust to how different our marriage was looking compared to what we had expected, we struggled. There were so many nights like the meltdown that left me sitting outside crying.

CO-PARENTING

Moments where I felt like I was falling apart, but I tried to keep it all in.

I didn't know how to say 'I'm not coping'. Didn't know how to admit I was scared, or exhausted, or completely out of my depth. I didn't know when to bring it up, in between the meltdowns and lack of sleep. I thought I needed to be strong for Charlotte and the boys. I needed to be the man of the house and look after everyone. Life was already hard enough for Charlotte, I didn't want to be another weight for her to carry.

I think part of me didn't know how to say I was struggling because I'd never really seen other men in my life admit to this. I grew up in a working-class family where men just got on with it. You worked hard, you provided, you didn't complain. I never saw the men around me talk about feelings or fear, never saw anyone admit to struggling. It wasn't the type of conversation me and my mates ever had. So when life got hard and when I couldn't fix things or protect my family from the difficulties, I felt like I'd failed. Shame crept in. And shame, I've since learned, can be deadly.

I kept telling myself it was just a phase. That eventually we'd get through it. But the longer I stayed silent and avoided the conversations with Charlotte, the further apart we grew.

A couple of years later, as our relationship faltered, we made the decision to separate. And with that came a whole new layer of worry: how would this affect Jude and Tommy? Most parents going through a break-up worry about how their children will cope emotionally. Will they be upset? Angry? Confused? Will they blame themselves? But that wasn't what kept us up at night. Jude and Tommy didn't have a concept of what a 'typical' family looked like. They wouldn't be heartbroken that their mum and dad weren't together anymore. There wouldn't be questions or accusations. But change? That was something they both struggled with. How would they cope with two homes? Two routines? Would they understand that we weren't going back to the house they'd always known? Would everything unravel?

That was our fear. And for months, it ate away at me.

Our separation took around nine months to finalise, as we went through the process of selling our home. During that time we still lived under the same roof, trying to navigate the awkwardness of the situation. Some nights I'd take one of the boys to my parents' house, and occasionally I'd stay there by myself, as we tried to give each other some space to process the changes that were happening.

That year, Jude struggled more than ever. I don't actually think it was related to the separation, because we made sure not to let that affect the home environment. When you have two boys who are so affected by sounds and pick up on vibes like mind readers, we always had to make sure home was a calm space for them, whatever the situation. The truth was, Jude had been on a downward spiral for quite a while. The last two years at school had been the worst yet, and we were close to pulling him out and keeping him at home for a while. At home, the presence of Tommy was a trigger that we worked hard to avoid.

I don't remember the exact moment when Charlotte and I admitted to each other that splitting them up might be the best option. One boy with each parent. I do remember how much I hated the idea. Parents don't separate their children.

CO-PARENTING

Families are supposed to live together. That's just how it's meant to be, right? But deep down, I knew that this made sense. We had already been living this way for years, dividing the house, splitting our time as parents, and we wouldn't be doing Jude or Tommy any favours by clinging to some image of what family life was *supposed* to look like.

There was one selfish thought that made it all feel more palatable. A small, gnawing fear that I hated to acknowledge. If we split them up like this, I'd never be alone. I didn't want to be the kind of dad who didn't see his kids every day. The idea of a typical custody arrangement, 50:50, or alternate weekends, made me feel sick. At least this way I'd get to see one of them every single day. And that was something I held onto amid the strangeness of it all. Even so, it was the hardest decision I'd ever have to make.

We agreed that initially, for the first few days, Jude would come with me and Tommy would stay with Charlotte. As moving day approached, I lived in a constant state of dread. I had no idea how Jude or Tommy would react. Would they fight against the change? Would they be confused? Would the meltdowns escalate? Would our new neighbours be kind and understanding or would they complain about the noise? And though I didn't say it out loud, I was scared for myself too, of parenting alone, being on my own each night.

The only house I could find nearby was a small rental on the same road as our old home. Part of me dreamed of a fresh start somewhere new, but moving too far would mean not having my parents close by and losing our support network. And it would be an even bigger change for the boys. So I stayed.

LOVE NEEDS NO WORDS

The new house was smaller, quieter. Just enough for two. Once it was ready, I took Jude there for our first night together. I felt sick with fear the entire way, preparing myself for how I'd handle his first meltdown in our new space. But I didn't need to. Jude stepped through the door and paused. He stood completely still, taking everything in. Then, silently, he started to pace. Upstairs. Downstairs. From one room to the next. His fingers trailing along the doorframes. His eyes checking and noticing each familiar object. There was his beanbag, his blankets, his bed.

I held my breath. Would he cry? Ask to leave? Refuse to stay? Instead, something shifted. His shoulders dropped. His breath steadied. His whole body softened. It was as if someone had turned the volume down on his world. And for the first time in months, I saw it: relief.

For the first few weeks, Jude repeated the same routine every time he arrived. He'd walk through the house slowly, checking every room, scanning the corners, brushing his fingers along the walls. At first, I thought he was just getting familiar with his new surroundings. But then I realised what he was really doing. He was looking for Tommy.

Each time, he moved from room to room, quietly checking. Not for furniture. Not for toys. But for his brother. For Tommy. He needed to be sure it was just the two of us. And once he knew he had the space to be himself, he relaxed.

That summer, everything started to change for Jude. His anxiety eased, and while the meltdowns didn't vanish, they became less frequent and less intense. The tension that had lived in his body for so long began to loosen its grip.

It wasn't the outcome I expected, and it didn't make the

heartbreak of splitting them up disappear. But for the first time in a long time, Jude seemed at peace and so much happier. Maybe, one day, I would be too.

When I talk online about being a single parent I often get asked if autism caused our break-up. People have a tendency to ask you things by message that they'd never ask you face to face. Some are looking for validation, a reflection on what might be going on for them. Some are just curious, nosey even. Either way, I give them the same answer.

No, autism didn't break our marriage.

But it was part of the story. It's shaped everything and still does, so how could it not? It is a part of how we lived, how we coped, how we adjusted and how, over time, those adaptations changed us.

I've spoken to so many parents who have split up and for most, it's not as simple as saying, 'We just weren't in love anymore.' It's the exhaustion, the isolation, the way you become two people just trying to get through the day. The constant push and pull of trying to do what's best for your child while also trying to hold onto any sense of yourself.

Our marriage didn't end because of Jude and Tommy. It ended because we were living through years of exhaustion, financial strain, social isolation, advocacy battles and the emotional weight of seeing our children struggle every single day. It ended because life had put so much on our shoulders that we didn't know how to handle it.

Maybe if Jude and Tommy weren't autistic, we'd have stayed together. Maybe we'd have split up sooner. Maybe we'd have broken up years down the line, once the kids had grown up and left home. There's no way of knowing. No more than knowing what would have happened if I'd taken that job in the City instead of going to university. Or if I'd stayed longer in Australia when I was travelling and not come back home.

Jude and Tommy have taught me time and time again that life isn't about looking back at all the what ifs. It's about learning to accept where you are now. And making the best of it.

Even in those early days of separation, when the emotions were still raw, we both knew we had to do everything we could to stay friendly. Our boys needed us. Unlike many separated parents, there was no option for us to retreat into our own lives, only dealing with each other through strained handovers or occasional messages about schedules.

With both Jude and Tommy being non-speaking, communication between us wasn't just important, it was essential. We had to be each other's eyes and ears. If one of us noticed a shift in their behaviour, a new trigger, a slight change in their routine that helped or hindered them, we had to share it. We had to talk to each other about toileting, the food they'd eaten and if anything had upset them that day. There was no room for resentment, no space for bitterness. Our children couldn't tell us what they needed, so we had to continue to figure it out together.

That forced communication helped us through the hard days in the beginning. It meant we still checked in on each other, still supported each other, still cared about how the other was coping, not just for the boys but as people. We still had to attend regular school meetings, social worker meetings and meetings with Child and Adolescent Mental Health

CO-PARENTING

Services (CAMHS). Sitting in those rooms, advocating for Jude and Tommy together, was a reminder that whatever had happened between us as a couple, we were still a team.

We helped each other where we could. If one of us needed a night off, the other would take both boys, although this was rare, because taking care of both of them alone was difficult. But we did it anyway. Because we wanted each other's lives to be good ones.

A couple of years after we separated, Charlotte would go on to have twin girls with her new partner. It was another shift, another big change to adjust to, not just for Jude and Tommy but for me too.

The pregnancy itself was a strange, emotional time, surreal in so many ways. We were still seeing each other most days, at handovers, at the school bus drop-off outside her house or sitting side by side in meetings about Jude and Tommy. And as the months went on and her pregnancy progressed, it brought about a great many awkward moments. For me at least. Every meeting we had about Tommy and Jude, everywhere we went, people would congratulate Charlotte, ask her questions about her pregnancy and look at me too, assuming we were still together. One day we went to school for their Christmas plays. Charlotte was due to give birth any day, so I drove us both there. Tommy's was in the morning, then Jude's in the afternoon, so we went to get some lunch in between. The waitress who served us was thoroughly overexcited, congratulating us both enthusiastically. I found myself smiling along and nodding, dying inside.

Moments like that happened all the time, even after the girls were born. And while I was genuinely happy for Charlotte and knew she would be a brilliant mum to her girls, it still hit me hard some days. I guess it was a kind of grief, for the life we didn't get to have and the family I thought we'd be together. Once again, it felt as though life was moving on around me, while I was still desperately treading water.

Those early months after the twins were born were full of adjustment for all of us, especially for the boys. Tommy handled it all quite well. Already more independent than Jude, he seemed to enjoy helping with bottles and food when the girls were tiny. But just like when Tommy came along, there was no way of preparing Jude for the huge changes that were about to enter his life. At nine years old, he didn't understand what being pregnant meant, didn't understand the changes to Charlotte and definitely didn't get why these two little babies were now in his house every day. Luckily, Charlotte lived in a three-storey house, so Jude had some space to try to get away from it all. But her life was soon back to how ours had been before the separation: Jude staying away from the noise on the top floor and Charlotte trying to split herself in too many directions. That challenge of meeting everyone's needs would cause Charlotte to move house within eighteen months, searching for one with a ready-made annexe. After their first choice fell through at the last minute and with her house ready to sell, there was one more perfect option on the market, with a tiny catch. It was directly opposite my parents' house. It could have felt awkward but little did we know how much easier it would make life in years to come.

Despite all the emotions and adjustments of the first couple of years, over time we've become a truly blended family. Charlotte and I are as good friends now as we've ever been,

CO-PARENTING

probably even better in fact. When we make decisions it's always while thinking about how it would work for all of us. In recent years, as we've started trying to reintegrate Tommy and Jude, we've done more things as a four. Last Christmas we even had a day out as a seven: me, Charlotte, her partner Carl, Tommy, Jude and the twins Francesca and Seren.

We work as a team, doing whatever we can to make life better for our children. And I know how rare that is and how lucky we are. Not every separated couple gets to co-parent this way. I don't take it for granted. Because despite everything, despite the heartbreak, the detours, the unexpected turns, the life that looks so different from what I once pictured, one thing has never changed: Jude and Tommy have always had two parents who love them. Who show up. Who put them first. Who want the best for each other, not just as parents but as people. And that will never change. Not now, not ever.

13

Brothers

It was a Sunday afternoon and all four of us were at home together. Tommy was on the sofa, barely six months old, and Charlotte was helping him sit upright. He was watching the world around him, captivated by the whirl of movement zipping past him. His big brother.

Jude was happy. Rarely still, he was galloping up and down the length of the room, lost in the rhythm of his movement. I joined in, running the opposite way, our paths crossing in the middle, ending up at opposite sides of the room before setting off again. It was a game we'd played countless times before, a way of connecting without words, letting Jude lead and matching his energy.

And then out of nowhere I heard it. A giggle.

Tommy was laughing, proper, full-bellied baby laughter. His whole body shook with it, his face alight with excitement. Jude noticed too. He glanced over, taking in Tommy's reaction and, to my surprise, he smiled. Not just any smile, one of those deep, eyes-lit-up grins. The kind that told me he was having just as much fun as Tommy was.

So I ran again, Jude right behind me, and Tommy laughed

even louder. His eyes widened in delight, waiting, willing us to do it again. Jude let out a squeal of his own, his flapping hands bursting into motion, his body bouncing with excitement. He was watching Tommy, properly watching him, not just tolerating him in the background. And he was loving it.

I kept running, back and forth, matching Jude's movements. After a while, I stopped, stepping to the side to catch my breath and fight back the tears in my eyes. I looked over at Charlotte and she was smiling too. For a moment, everything felt easy. Simple. This was it. They were bonding. This was what I had hoped for. Jude was getting used to his brother; all he'd needed was some time. And Tommy was looking up to his big brother, just like younger siblings do.

In that moment I could see it: years from now, the two boys chasing each other around the house, best mates causing chaos together. Tommy looking up to Jude, Jude pulling him into his world. I thought of all the things I wanted for them, brotherly adventures, inside jokes, an unbreakable bond.

It was such a simple moment, one that fourteen years later I can still remember vividly. For the first time, I let myself believe that it was all going to be OK. Autism wasn't that scary, it would mean life might be a little bit different, that Jude would develop more slowly than most. But it would all be OK. We'd get there in the end. He'd make friends, he'd speak, he and Tommy would get along. And Tommy would love his big brother. He'd see how much fun he could be, and they'd bring out the best in each other. The four of us would still have the best times together. My little family.

I didn't know at the time how rare moments like this would turn out to be. How, as Tommy grew, as he became more mobile, more vocal, more eager to interact, Jude would start to struggle. That the easy laughter would be replaced with screams and tears. But in that moment, I wasn't thinking about any of that. In that moment, I was just a dad watching his two boys connect and allowing myself to believe they always would.

Before Tommy was born, I had built up this picture in my head of what having a second child would mean for Jude and for our family as a whole. I hoped that having a sibling would turn out to be the best thing that could happen to him. That it would help to bring him out of his world, encourage him to play, interact with other kids and maybe even help him learn to talk. I imagined the way Tommy would look up to Jude, how they'd share toys, play silly games together, whisper to each other when they were supposed to be asleep. They'd argue, fight but also be the best of friends.

I thought about my own childhood, the way friendships had come naturally. How playing with other kids had been instinctive. I thought about the close bond I had with my cousins, the memories of all the adventures we'd shared. I wanted that for my boys. Oh how I wanted that for them. The thought of Tommy and Jude growing up without that bond never really crossed my mind.

I knew that social interactions weren't easy for Jude but felt that surely having a younger brother would help? I'd seen glimmers of hope in how he was coping at nursery each day, and with school now on the horizon, maybe a sibling would help him realise how much fun being around other kids could be.

Even in the moments of doubt, while we were still learning

what Jude's autism diagnosis really meant for him, I still believed that Jude would learn from Tommy, copy his sounds, follow his lead. That Tommy would be a constant presence in his life, the person who would always be there, who would navigate the world alongside him.

When Charlotte was pregnant, there were fears, of course there were. What if it was too much for Jude? What if having a new baby in the house upset him? What if our new baby was autistic too? We weren't sure how much Jude understood about what was happening. We'd tried to explain, told him stories, showed him visuals, talked about the baby that was on the way, but it was impossible to know how much of it he truly took in. Getting him to stay still long enough to explain anything was hard enough, let alone trying to help him understand all the changes that were about to happen. But any worries that I had were quickly buried under the excitement of what was to come.

And then Tommy arrived, and slowly, the dream started to unravel.

At first, it was subtle. Jude didn't pay much attention to Tommy but that was fine, he was still so little. I brought Jude to the hospital the day after Tommy was born, to meet his baby brother for the first time. We managed some staged photos of them lying side by side, even caught a couple of smiles, but Jude wasn't interested in Tommy. Not really. He was far more focused on the corridor just outside the ward. He kept trying to escape, pulling at the door, desperate to gallop up and down, in that rhythm that helped him feel calm. Every time someone opened one of the ward doors, I'd have to spring into action, stopping him before he slipped out.

BROTHERS

We were there for a couple of hours, but Jude spent maybe fifteen minutes in the room with Tommy. And even then, he barely looked at him. He didn't point at him or stroke his head. He didn't seem to notice the tiny person who was now part of our lives or have any understanding that he would be coming home with us.

I told myself it didn't matter. That it was too soon. That it would all come in time. But looking back, it's almost funny, the way we were juggling them both, keeping them apart from the moment they first met. Not realising that, in the years to come, that would become our normal.

I often wonder what Jude thought the first day we walked through the front door of the house with Tommy. A baby who never left. Who was there every morning when he woke up, crying every now and again throughout the day and still there every night when he went to bed. At first, he continued to show little acknowledgement of Tommy's presence. Then, as Tommy became more active, started making more noise, started existing in Jude's space, things began to change and become more difficult.

I had imagined them playing side by side. Instead, Jude would leave the room when Tommy entered it. I had imagined Tommy looking up to his big brother, following him everywhere. Instead, Tommy was happy playing alone, not particularly drawn to Jude at all. I had imagined Jude adapting, learning from Tommy's presence. Instead, he became more anxious, more unsettled, more desperate to escape. As Tommy raced around the house with his walker, Jude would climb up onto the back of the sofa out of his way, realising Tommy couldn't reach him up there.

Tommy didn't seem to mind the lack of interaction. He didn't seem to be seeking any kind of brotherly bond either. He had a strong desire to be independent, happy in his own world, often playing alone or alongside adults, where he could control the interactions.

The problem we had was a clash of personalities. Tommy was loud and unpredictable, everything Jude found hardest about the world. He was never trying to upset his brother, he was just being himself. But Jude wanted space, quiet and predictability, and Tommy was never going to be able to give him that. His movements, his sounds, his inquisitive nature, they were all triggers for Jude. And when Jude would get upset, cry, scream and eventually start to self-injure, it scared Tommy. Who would then also cry, scream and even start to head-bang. Which only made things even worse.

In the early years, it wasn't like that every day. There were still plenty of happy moments, times when the four of us laughed and played together; we even managed a couple of UK holidays in those first couple of years. But more often than not, those moments came when the boys were apart. Joy was easier in twos: me with Jude and Charlotte with Tommy or vice versa. That way, we weren't walking on eggshells, constantly anticipating a clash or trying to avoid a meltdown.

At some point, I had to start accepting that the sibling bond I'd imagined wasn't going to happen. At least not in the way I'd hoped.

By the time Jude was six and Tommy was three, the reality of their relationship had become painfully clear. Spending time together was less about creating memories and more about preventing meltdowns. We weren't living as a family in the way I had once imagined. We were living in two separate worlds under one roof, constantly trying to stop those worlds from colliding.

Our days were largely structured around keeping the boys apart. During the day it happened naturally with Jude at school, Tommy at home. But evenings and weekends? School holidays? They were difficult. When Jude got home from school he had already used up every ounce of tolerance handling the sensory overload he'd been faced with all day long: the noise, the colours, the smells and, most importantly, all the other children. At home he wanted to decompress and recover from all that stimulation – but now he had the whirlwind of Tommy to deal with.

I understand it better now, watching how they both want to decompress after school. They crave peace and quiet. Well, maybe not quiet as such but sounds that they have control over. The clash of music and cartoons that Jude watches mixed in with his humming. Tommy turning the TV up and down again as he leaps from the sofa, hopping loudly around the room. They crave control. And back then, Jude couldn't understand why his little brother kept disrupting that for him.

So we adapted. We spent a lot of our time in separate rooms, often on different floors. Sometimes one of us would take Jude out for a drive to regulate while the other stayed back with Tommy. Even at my parents' house, where we had extra support, the boys naturally drifted to opposite ends of the house. We didn't even have to plan it, it just happened.

Around this time, Jude's meltdowns were also becoming more frequent and more intense. The world seemed to be too overwhelming for him, too much to handle, and at home Tommy was either the trigger or caught in the middle while we tried to manage them.

Jude loved having control over his environment, the volume, the routine, the order of things. He was far from quiet himself – being non-speaking does not mean our house is a quiet one. But the sounds Jude made were his own. Predictable and in his own control. He knew what to expect. Tommy, on the other hand, was full of unpredictable energy. He wasn't seeking attention from Jude, he didn't need a playmate. He was just being Tommy: curious, loud, constantly on the move. But for Jude, Tommy's presence could feel like a threat.

Jude would be standing in front of the TV, flapping to his favourite cartoons, completely absorbed. Then Tommy would rush in, excited by the colours and music. Jude would back away instantly, his eyebrows furrowing, his whole body stiffening.

You could feel the tension in the air, the anxiety rising. Tommy would get louder, bouncing and squealing. And that was enough. Jude would drop to his knees, start bouncing, slapping his legs and crying out. And we'd find ourselves right back in crisis mode.

When we were both there, one of us would rush to help Jude regulate while the other comforted Tommy. If only one of us was there, that's when the real problems began. Because when Jude was distressed, when he started hurting himself or crying uncontrollably, it frightened Tommy. And that fear would spiral too. Sometimes Tommy would cry, sometimes he'd head-bang, sometimes he'd just freeze, wide-eyed and lost.

Tommy didn't understand why Jude reacted the way he

did. He couldn't possibly understand at that age why him simply being near his brother could lead to such distress. To be honest, I didn't understand it either. I just knew I had to try to protect them both.

And then there was my own guilt.

As much as I adored Tommy, as much as I wanted to be fully present for him, I struggled to connect in those early years. Not because of him, but because I felt like Jude needed me more. When Jude was in distress, I had to be there. When he was hurting himself, I had to be the one beside him. It wasn't a choice. It was instinct. But that meant Tommy got less of me. Less time. Less attention.

And it wasn't until years later, when the boys were living apart, that I truly realised how much I'd missed in dividing myself like this. Without the constant pressure of splitting my focus, I started to feel that bond with Tommy grow stronger. We had space to just be together, without the tension, without the fear I held that what we were doing might upset Jude.

But at the time, separating them wasn't some master plan. There was no one moment that made us say, *'We can't keep living like this.'* It was more a slow wearing down. A realisation, bit by bit, that the vision we'd once held of our family, living together under one roof, growing up side by side, simply wasn't working. So when the conversation came, the one where Charlotte and I admitted to each other that our marriage was over, there was a deeper, even harder conversation beneath it. How could we give them the care that they need, if every day was the two of them and only one of us?

And eventually we came to a realisation. What if we separated the boys too?

And that idea? That was as hard to accept as our marriage ending.

Because everything we're taught, everything we grow up believing about family, tells us the opposite. Siblings are meant to be together. That's the constant through childhood. The shared bedrooms, shared holidays, shared memories. Siblings will argue, fall out, compete for attention. But ultimately, they're each other's people. That's the story we all carry.

So the idea that *our* sons might not grow up side by side, that we might *choose* to separate them, felt like we were breaking some unspoken rule. It felt wrong. Like we were failing them or taking something away they'd never get back.

And yet . . . trying to keep them together wasn't working. They weren't just brothers bickering, going through a rough patch. It was relentless distress. Screaming. Self-injury. Constant crisis. Day after day. One child in meltdown, the other terrified or pushed into a meltdown because of it. And in the middle of it all, Charlotte and me, trying to keep the house from falling apart and feeling like we were failing everyone.

We never chose to give up on the sibling bond. We chose to stop forcing a version of it that was hurting them both. It went against everything we'd believed about what a family should look like, but deep down, we knew: the dream had to change, if we were going to give them both a chance to feel safe, to feel calm, to feel loved. To be happy.

Not everyone understood. Some people close to us were shocked or even against it. To them, it sounded extreme, unnatural. Brothers should be together. But they weren't seeing what we were living through every day. They weren't feeling the weight of trying to hold everything together when

BROTHERS

simply being in the same space was making life so much harder for both of them.

Around that time I remember sitting at the Maudsley Hospital in London, exhausted and desperate, explaining Jude's meltdowns to his paediatrician, describing what day-to-day life was like for him at school and at home, discussing medication options and hoping for a strategy that would fix it all. She listened carefully, offered advice – and then said something that stuck with me.

'Some families,' she said gently, 'are just never together.'

She went on to explain how there were some families she'd worked with who rarely spent time all together; the challenges of anxiety and the meltdowns they triggered were simply too much. We weren't the only ones out there who were having to spend so much time splitting their kids up.

It landed like a punch to the stomach. No matter what we did, Jude might *always* find being around Tommy challenging. But it also felt like permission. Permission to choose what was right for *our* children, not what looked right from the outside.

It didn't erase the guilt. It didn't quiet the voices in my head saying, *'Brothers should be together.'* That would take years. But it did give us the courage to take the steps that we needed and to understand this wasn't failure. This wasn't giving up. It was love, in its hardest, most complicated form. It was choosing what was best for Tommy and for Jude, even if it went against everything I longed for. And it was the beginning of giving them both what they really needed: space, support and the chance to be happy, in their own way.

*

Even though we chose to separate Tommy and Jude, the goal was never to keep them apart forever. We hoped that it would be a temporary thing. It would allow them both to develop and grow better, allow us to find our feet as single parents, and in time, when life was more stable for them both, the hope was that they'd spend more time together. We set no timeline and decided Tommy and Jude would show us the way.

Within weeks, our decision seemed justified. Over the summer Jude's anxiety reduced massively and when he went back to school in September, he was much happier to be there. He went on to have the best school year. His teachers couldn't believe the difference in him.

Tommy also thrived. He and I spent more time together than we ever had before, and over those first few months our bond deepened. For most of his life up to that point I'd missed his weeknight bedtimes, as I was usually still on the way home from work. Now, on the nights he was with me, I was always home and it brought us closer.

It was working. It was unconventional, heartbreaking at times and brought up a lot of emotions each day, but it was working. And with that realisation came something else: relief. With the pressure to force a bond gone, we could focus on meeting their individual needs, and ironically, over time, that would give them the best chance of eventually coming together.

For years, I carried the weight of that decision like a quiet shame. Had we tried hard enough? Did we give up too soon? I'd dread explaining it to people. Especially to new people I met. Not only would I have to explain that both my boys are autistic and non-speaking but also that they live apart. The automatic assumption was often that I had children with two different mums, and I'd find myself rambling through an explanation, usually met with confused looks. But I felt like I had to explain. I worried what people would think of me.

But with each passing month more and more changes started to show, confirming to us that we'd made the right choice for both boys. They were calmer, happier, more settled. At school, they were making progress, and at home, the constant stress had lifted. When one of them was struggling, we could give them our full attention without worrying how it would ripple out to the other. We could manage the meltdowns more effectively, help them regulate and recover more easily.

And with that peace came space. Space to try again, this time, on their terms.

In 2019, we had our first meetings with their school about helping them spend small amounts of time together in a structured way. The goal wasn't to force a relationship. It wasn't about pushing them into being close. It was simply to try to create positive experiences, moments where they could be in the same space, enjoy something side by side and maybe even start to associate each other with having fun.

The school was brilliant. The staff understood the history, the sensitivity. They knew it wasn't just about what we wanted as parents, it had to be right for Jude and Tommy. It started small: a few minutes in the sensory room, a short music therapy session, some time outdoors together, bouncing on trampolines. The school created these sessions gently, always with an option to pause if needed. If Jude showed any signs of distress, the session could end immediately and both boys would slot back into their separate routines. If either of the boys had been having a difficult day leading up to the session, it was moved to another day. There was no pressure, no forced interactions, they were just sharing the same space. The idea was to let them see each other in a different context, one that wasn't tied to all the history and tension of home.

And then, just as things were starting to take shape and we could see real positive signs of breakthrough, the world shut down.

The pandemic put everything on hold. For almost two years we lost the structure, the sessions, the little bits of progress we had been making. It felt like we'd been knocked right back to square one. Jude and Tommy had a lot to adjust to during that period, as they struggled with the world changing so much. But when the world reopened and both boys had found their rhythm again at school, we picked up where we left off. Only this time, things moved faster than I could ever have imagined.

We started with the things that had worked before: sensory sessions, music therapy, outdoor play. But it wasn't long before the school introduced something new: shared lunchtimes.

It might not sound like much but for us, this was huge. For years, Jude had eaten his lunch in the quiet safety of his classroom. The dining hall was too loud, too bright, too unpredictable, too much. But now, not only had he progressed to being able to eat in there each day but he did so sitting opposite his brother. A space that had once been overwhelming had become somewhere they could share time together.

Then they tried swimming. It worked. Then horse riding.

Which was so far outside Jude's comfort zone I nearly turned the suggestion down. Before the pandemic, I'd taken Tommy for a few one-to-one lessons at a local stables and he seemed to enjoy it. But Jude? I thought it would be way too much for him, with or without Tommy. Understanding what was being asked of him, being brave enough to climb onto a horse and sit there, even the act of physically holding on, it seemed too much to ask. I was worried for him.

And yet . . . that worked too. And so each week they travelled there together on the school bus, along with a small group of learners. The reports and photos we got back were full of smiles. Two brothers, side by side, taking part in the same activity. Not just tolerating it but enjoying it.

Each small win built on the last. And the moments kept coming. Tommy making Jude a Christmas card and taking it to him in class. Art sessions where they'd sit and paint together. Even a special end of term party with both of their classes – and special guests Spider-Man and Elsa.

Slowly, it stopped being all small steps and anxiety management. There was still structure, still support, but it didn't feel so tense anymore. The expectation became that it would go well. And that's when it turned into simply being about having fun together.

Outside of school, we kept looking for chances to bring them together. Occasionally it would be when we had to but mainly when it felt right. There were trips to McDonald's, SEN trampolining sessions, ice creams, afternoons at the park. Each time we approached it with cautious optimism and a lot of planning. If either of the boys was already struggling that day, we'd postpone. If it went well, we'd try to build on it.

It hasn't all been smooth. There have been setbacks, times when one of them found it too hard and we had to pull back. Jude, in particular, seems to hold onto difficult experiences. One stressful moment can linger for months, meaning he'd associate Tommy with that memory. Which is why we've always been so careful to manage their time together, knowing one tough moment could set back months of progress. But as they've both grown and matured they have learned to be together. Not just to be physically in the same space but to feel emotionally safe and at ease in it too.

The same brothers who couldn't share a living room can now share lunch in a crowded dining hall. The same boys who once had to be kept apart to protect them both now go riding together. And even at Charlotte's house, they're beginning to build a kind of rhythm. For the first few years after our separation, when I needed a night off, Tommy would stay with my parents. As my parents' health declined that was no longer an option, so they both started staying at Charlotte's. And it has worked. There's enough space there that most of the time their paths don't even cross, but some mornings Tommy will go out to Jude in the annexe, curious to see what he's up to. He'll see what Jude is watching on TV or his iPad and try to get involved. At first Jude was shocked and would retreat, but as time has gone on he's become more comfortable with Tommy being in his space. They might not chat or play like other siblings, but they'll sit near each other, watching TV for ten or twenty minutes. Until, of course, the temptation becomes too much and Tommy tries to take Jude's iPad. Which leaves poor old passive Jude confused and watching on anxiously, never once getting aggressive or trying to take it back like most older brothers would.

Jude is a watcher at school too, happy on the edges, observing his classmates and what they're getting up to, joining in for fleeting moments. And that's what he seems to do with Tommy now. He watches Tommy bounce his ball, flapping alongside him with a smile. Jude doesn't just tolerate being around his brother now, I can see that he actually enjoys it.

The change isn't only in their relationship, it's a reflection of how much they've both grown individually. Jude is more confident now, more adaptable, more open to connection than I've ever seen him. His bond with Tommy reflects that shift, just like his growing bonds with his peers at school. After years of feedback from school of how much Jude prefers to stay separate to the class, he's begun to make friends, a couple of his classmates that he feels close to and relaxed around; other teens who interact with him and make him smile, even bringing out a cheeky side to him that we rarely see at home.

And Tommy's growing too, becoming more independent, more aware of the world around him, more comfortable in who he is. He understands pretty much everything you say to him. He knows what it means when I hold a finger to my lips and ask him to be quiet, even if he doesn't always comply!

This past Christmas, we went to Marsh Farm together, a children's animal adventure park, not far from us. Not just me, Jude and Tommy but their sisters, Charlotte and Carl too, along with ten other families we'd invited from our local community, all of whom are raising autistic kids. We know first hand how difficult it can be for our kids to access days out, so we wanted to do something special. We arranged with the farm that they would open an hour earlier just for our group, meaning we had the whole place to ourselves for a while. We spent an hour and a half at their Christmas experience, taking part in the different activities. Tommy got involved; Jude mainly watched, a little unsure of what was going on but relaxed, with music playing through his headphones to help him regulate. We even managed some family photos. Me, Jude and Tommy. Then, a photo of all seven of us, to capture the first time we've ever all been in the same space together.

We finished up on the large bouncing pillows outside, the part that all of our kids loved way more than anything Santa had to offer. I led both boys out there, helped Jude get on next to me and started bouncing. Tommy, a regular at Marsh Farm, raced around, in his element. Jude hung next to me, still wary of the younger kids and the erratic bouncing of his brother, keeping an eye on everyone to make sure they didn't come too close – but happy and coping better than we could ever have hoped. And so I bounced more, the three of us, in the same space, having fun. I had a huge grin on my face as I tried my hardest to fight back the happy tears.

A few years ago, I wouldn't have even let myself dream of a day like that. It would've felt too far out of reach. Too painful. But here we were. And it was perfect. A Christmas miracle, at a time of year that usually does nothing but highlight all the differences in the life we lead. But that day, it made those differences feel all the more special.

I don't know how much Jude and Tommy understand about the fact that they're brothers or whether they really grasp the connection they share. But I do know they *have* one now. I used to believe that if they couldn't live together, if they weren't side by side every day, maybe they wouldn't have a relationship at all. Now I know that's not true.

Sibling relationships don't have to look like they do in the movies. They don't need similar personalities or interests or constant time together — or even words. They can be built on patience, acceptance and gentle progress over years. Quiet joy in small wins that nobody else would even notice but that you'll never forget.

Maybe my boys will never live together under the same roof again. Maybe that's not what they need. Maybe that's not how *their* relationship is meant to be. But if we can keep having these moments, keep finding ways to be together, keep building on what they have now, then that will always be more than enough.

14

The Most Wonderful Time of the Year

I'd always loved Christmas Eve growing up. It was one of those days filled with excitement and tradition. Every year my dad would drive me and my mum to Oxford Street in London's West End, Christmas songs playing on the radio, for some last-minute shopping. We'd be surrounded by festive lights and the buzz of everyone rushing around. On the way home, we'd stop at the off-licence and stock up for the next few days: bottles of Coke, snacks, crisps, chocolates, drinks for all the family and friends who'd be visiting. Then we'd head home to a house full of people dropping in, laughter, noise, excitement. We'd go to church in the evening for a carol service, then come home and watch some Christmas TV before bed. Some of my favourite memories are of childhood Christmas Eves, and I always thought that when I became a dad, this would be one of the most exciting nights of the year.

But Christmas Eve 2013 was nothing like that.

Jude was five and Tommy had just turned two. The run-up to Christmas had been brutal and after a week of no sleep, relentless meltdowns, I was running on empty. Charlotte had to be at work at the restaurant early the next morning, serving Christmas dinner to seventy guests. The contrast between the happy, family experience she'd be helping to create for her customers and what we were experiencing at home wasn't lost on me.

And so, that Christmas Eve, Jude went to stay with Charlotte's dad for the night. The first and only time he ever stayed there. That's how bad things were. Charlotte's dad lived just down the road and he and his wife were prepared to take Jude on long drives through the night if that's what it took to calm him down and get him to sleep. I think they knew we were close to breaking point. And though I hated the idea of spending Christmas Eve without my son, I didn't argue. I didn't have the energy to. I hate to admit it, but I needed a break, just a few hours where we weren't in full crisis mode.

Every Christmas Eve, Santa came to visit our town, his sleigh on the back of a truck, and families would tumble from their front doors to come and see him. That year, we did the same, holding Tommy in my arms, posing for a photo with Father Christmas, but all I could feel was the absence of Jude. For the last couple of years, he'd been there too, uninterested in Santa but wide-eyed at the chocolate buttons he was handing out. This time, he was in someone else's house, wrapped in a blanket, dummy in his mouth, clinging to his muslin. It was what we needed, but it still broke my heart. Letting your child go on Christmas Eve, even when it's the right thing, felt like giving up, admitting defeat. I told myself that Jude wouldn't even notice, that he didn't understand what day it was. But *I* did.

THE MOST WONDERFUL TIME OF THE YEAR

That night, once Tommy was asleep, I collapsed onto the sofa under a blanket. *Wreck-It Ralph* was on the TV. I'm not sure why that's stuck with me. Maybe because it was the kind of movie you're supposed to sit down as a family and watch together. I wasn't really following the film, I just needed something to stop the stream of thoughts running through my head. Jude was missing. Charlotte was out delivering some last-minute presents. And Christmas was nothing like I had imagined it would be.

Christmas is a season full of expectations. The onslaught comes from every direction: the adverts, the movies, the social media posts. Even the stories passed down from our own childhoods. It's supposed to be *the most wonderful time of the year*.

I had so many expectations of how this would play out once I became a dad. I'd imagined it all. Writing letters to Santa. The countdown to Christmas morning. That excited dash downstairs, diving into presents, wrapping paper everywhere. A house filled with noise, with chaos, with laughter. Building Lego sets, assembling new toys. Taking their first bikes for a ride in the park before Christmas dinner and a house full of family and friends. Then, tired but happy, cuddling up together on the sofa watching *Elf* or *Santa Claus: The Movie*.

But for us, Christmas has never looked like that. It wasn't that the dream faded, it was that it never even materialised. None of it. No excitement about Santa, no stories, no early wake-ups to rush downstairs and open presents. Well, we had the early wake-ups. But no matching pyjamas or leaving out carrots and mince pies for Santa and his reindeer.

And it's not just the day itself. It's the build-up. The parties we couldn't go to. The family gatherings that we had to leave early or skip altogether. The pantomimes, the Christmas shows, the trips to see the lights in London or going to meet Father Christmas. Even putting the tree and decorations up have been non-events most years. All of those things I thought we'd do, the things I thought you're *meant* to do, just haven't been our reality. And when we did try to make them happen, they usually went horribly wrong.

Even now, Jude shows no signs of understanding Christmas at all. He's never cared about the tree, the decorations or the date. He doesn't want to open presents, in fact most years he never even touches them. We learned early on that presents just weren't his thing. Tommy has always been more into presents – maybe too into them! He'll open all of his as quickly as he can. Then he'll open mine, Jude's, anyone's he can get his hands on. For Tommy it's all about the excitement of finding out what's inside. I still can't put any presents under the tree before Christmas morning, as no matter how often I explain to Tommy that it's not yet time, there'll come a point when he just won't be able to resist the pull to find out what's inside.

So why is Christmas, this time of year that's meant to be filled with joy and magic, so difficult for so many autistic children and their families? Well, because it's everything that makes the world harder for us, all at once. The change in routine. The sensory overload. The unpredictability. The pressure. The social expectations.

For Jude and Tommy and for so many other autistic kids, they find comfort in knowing what to expect: from routine,

THE MOST WONDERFUL TIME OF THE YEAR

familiarity, sameness. That's where they feel safe. But Christmas turns all of that on its head. One day the house looks a certain way and the next it's full of flashing lights, new decorations and different smells. At school, the daily routine is disrupted by rehearsals and new activities. Decorations go up, the timetable shifts, classrooms are full of glitter and noise. Then the holidays arrive and with them come changes to childcare, support and everything that usually keeps life calm.

At home, the calendar fills with events. People visit, often people you haven't seen since last year or worse, people you've never met before. They ask questions. Get too close. Expect hugs. Give presents that need to be opened on the spot, with the right facial expression and a big, visible thank you.

On Christmas Day itself, everything is different again. The morning is filled with presents and mess. There are more visitors, more noise. A special meal, at a different time, in a different place, with different food. A crowded table. Loud voices. Music in the background. The pressure to sit, stay, smile, eat. To be like everybody else.

The things that are supposed to be fun – the songs, the outings, the traditions – can simply be too much. And the pressure to enjoy them can be just as intense as the events themselves. And if you're the parent, you carry that pressure too, sometimes more so. Because the messaging is that this is what joy looks like. And that if you're not having fun at Christmas – or worse, if your child isn't – then you must be doing something wrong. But the truth is that Christmas isn't hard because we've failed. It's hard because it asks too much, of our children and of us. And some years, the bravest thing we can do is stop pretending it has to be magical or match the version of Christmas we've held onto for years and start building one that actually works for our family.

A few days later, during that 2013 Christmas period, in the early hours of the morning, I found myself lying next to Jude in bed, the blue glow of his iPad lighting up the room.

It was 2.30 a.m. He'd woken up again, unsettled and anxious. The Christmas Eve night off had been a brief respite in what had otherwise been a pretty miserable Christmas. I'd spent most of it walking the streets of Burnham-on-Crouch with Jude in his buggy or driving around late at night, as motion seemed to be the only thing that helped him to regulate. Now, here we were again, with another long night ahead. I was exhausted – mentally, emotionally and physically – but also wide awake. Because even in the middle of the night, I couldn't switch off. I needed to *understand*. I needed answers. I needed something that might help me help him.

That year, I'd been given a book for Christmas, *The Reason I Jump* by Naoki Higashida. Naoki is a non-speaking Japanese autistic person who uses a letterboard to communicate. The fact that he is non-speaking and had written a book blew my mind. The book, written when Naoki was a teenager, was filled with short, question-and-answer reflections about life as an autistic child. I'd started reading it earlier that day and now, lying beside Jude in the semi-dark, I picked it up again. One question jumped out at me.

Q57: What causes panic attacks and meltdowns?

THE MOST WONDERFUL TIME OF THE YEAR

I'll never forget the way Naoki ended his answer.

> When this is happening to us, please just let us cry, or yell, and get it all out. Stay close by and keep a gentle eye on us, and while we're swept up in our torment, please stop us hurting ourselves or others.

It felt like Jude was speaking directly to me, offering a glimmer of understanding in the chaos. I took a photo of the page right there and then, just to make sure I wouldn't forget it in the fog of sleep deprivation and information overload.

I lay there for a long time after that, watching him. Watching his breathing slow. His body relax. The dummy still in his mouth. The iPad glowing. His hand clinging to the corner of his muslin cloth. He seemed relaxed, far more so than he had been at any point over the last few days. And for the first time in a while, I didn't feel completely lost. I still didn't know how to make Christmas work for Jude, but I knew I never wanted a repeat of the one we'd just had. It was the start of a shift, and from that night on, doing what would work for Jude, and for Tommy, became the focus.

It's not just Christmas. So many of the seasons and periods that other families look forward to can feel impossible when you're raising an autistic child. They spark the opposite reaction, and you start to fear them instead.

Halloween sounds great in theory. Dressing up, sweets, neighbours being friendly. But for Tommy and Jude, none of it makes any sense. Why would they want to dress up in a costume? They're uncomfortable and out of the usual routine.

As for any kind of face paint or mask, don't even think about it. We've never been trick or treating. When Tommy was younger, he liked trying to run into other people's houses whenever we were out for a walk; spending a night knocking on people's doors and being given sweets and chocolate in return would make things even more difficult. I know how his brain works, he'd be thinking, *Why would they give me sweets last time I went to their house but not today?*

Easter is another time of year that should work in theory. Like most kids, Jude and Tommy have always loved chocolate, so Easter eggs have always been a hit. But trying to do anything social around it just hasn't worked. When Tommy was five I took him to my cousin's house for an Easter party. There were lots of friends and family there, with all their children rushing around and playing, but Tommy was more comfortable in social occasions than Jude was at that age, so I wasn't as worried about him being overwhelmed. So I was a combination of anxious and hopeful when we arrived. My parents were with me too, so there were three of us who knew Tommy inside out, and we hoped that by tag-teaming throughout the day I might get some time to actually socialise, rather than constantly chasing Tommy from room to room.

We walked through the front door to a wall of noise and happy, excited voices. I started saying hello, and Tommy seemed content in my arms, smiling away – until he saw a huge tower of Easter eggs on the table. There were games planned for all the kids and the eggs were prizes to be given out over the course of the day. But of course Tommy didn't understand that. He scrambled out of my arms and made his way through the crowd, straight to the tower. He had to check them out, then and there. I reached him just as he started to grab for them, trying to explain that he'd get an egg very soon. It was no use. My cousin quickly offered him one – much to the surprise of some of the other kids, who had obviously been told they couldn't have one yet! Tommy ripped it open, took a look inside, pulled out the egg, and made a beeline for another box. You see, while Tommy loves chocolate, he also loves opening things. If there were thirty eggs on that table, he was going to try to open every single one.

A stressful few minutes followed. I tried to distract Tommy while the eggs were moved and hidden, but it was a bumpy start and made the next hour a difficult one. We didn't quite reach a meltdown but we were very close, and Tommy spent the rest of the party roaming from room to room, never still for more than a few seconds. It seemed so easy for everyone else. Their kids understood the social expectations, even if they didn't always agree with them. They understood the games that had been organised, they socialised and played together. Their parents kept a watchful eye but were also able to sit, eat, drink and chat. I couldn't relax for a second. In the few hours we were there I must have sat down for a total of ten minutes. By the time I decided to take Tommy and my parents home, I was exhausted. Parties, it turns out, are just too much.

After a few tough experiences, we gave up on throwing the boys birthday parties too. Jude's last proper party was his fourth birthday. Since then, his birthdays have been quiet. There are no piles of presents, as he's never shown any interest in them. We keep it calm. We do the things he loves: a drive, his favourite songs, his favourite foods. We have a birthday cake but he's not going to blow the candles out, he never has. There's no singing 'Happy Birthday', no fuss. Just a day that feels safe for him. And that's enough. After all, it's his birthday, his day and it's his way.

Tommy's a little different. He loves birthdays. I'm still not 100 per cent sure if he understands what it actually means, but he definitely knows what happens on that day. Since he loves presents so much, I have to make sure anything I've bought him is well hidden so that he doesn't find it before the big day. I've lost count of the number of gifts that have been found and opened ahead of time, a trail of torn wrapping paper on the floor. We'll have a cake, and in recent years he's figured out how to blow out the candles. It's rare the cake stays in one piece, as the temptation to dig his fingers into the icing is too much to resist, but it's his cake, so that's OK. We'll get some helium balloons for him, usually Mickey Mouse ones, and that'll keep him happily occupied for most of the night. He'll flap with them, bash them around the room, over and over again. And then, when he's decided he's had enough, he'll take them into the garden, pull off the weights holding them down and let them go up and away into the sky.

And then there are the school holidays. When you're raising autistic children, school holidays can be some of the hardest weeks of the year. Every summer, the structure that is such an important part of Tommy's and Jude's lives disappears for six weeks. Their routines disappear. And what's left can leave you feeling like you're in survival mode. Holiday clubs aren't an option for us, as most of them are too unpredictable, too loud, too busy, and there are no alternatives locally that meet Jude's and Tommy's needs. Their school used to run holiday clubs for the first couple of weeks of the summer holidays and over Easter, which was a huge help. But they closed during the Covid pandemic and the first lockdown and they've never come back, due to lack of funding and staff issues.

It's a similar story when it comes to visiting attractions. Everywhere is full of people, noise and queues. Jude can't handle the overwhelm, so we end up more or less housebound with him for the duration of the holidays. Even though the town we live in is pretty quiet and the park is never very busy, there have been months when even that is just too much for him. Tommy is much better at coping around others, and now, thanks to the support of his carers, he enjoys going to a number of places locally, as long as it's not *too* busy, of course.

For us, the holidays can feel like the loneliest time, confined mainly to home, managing anxiety and meltdowns. But in between all of that, we've found our way. A sense of rhythm and routines that work for Tommy and Jude. Simple moments. Park mornings, supermarket trips and the odd day out with Tommy, adapting to his mood and his expectations. Drives with Jude and quiet days at home with lots of screentime and music. Then, this past summer, with Jude seemingly in a good place, I decided it was time to try our river walks again. He is now more accepting of wearing wireless headphones, and I thought these might make a difference, helping him to feel more relaxed and blocking out some of the overwhelm that floods his senses. I had his Spotify playlist already playing through the headphones and put them straight over his ears when I picked him up from Charlotte's house. As we made our way down her drive, he automatically turned towards my house, but I gestured for him to follow me along the path and out onto the street. He seemed reluctant at first and a bit surprised but he followed.

It only takes a couple of minutes to reach the river from our house, then we followed the river as it runs alongside the park. As we reached the first empty bench Jude marched over to it and sat down. I thought this meant he'd had enough and assumed we would soon be turning for home. I sat at the other end of the bench, giving him plenty of space, expecting him to get straight back up again. But he didn't. He sat gazing out at the river, and we stayed.

For the next hour Jude rocked back and forth to the music in his headphones, flapping his hands, enjoying watching the birds fly past. He watched dogs running in the park, fascinated by them, as long as they didn't come too close. As the time continued ticking by, I couldn't believe it. We'd never sat anywhere for this long. Not even in the house, let alone out in the world. Jude was calm, relaxed, happy and as the time passed, so was I. A little shocked, perhaps and still watching for potential triggers, not to mention holding back the happy tears that threatened to come streaming out. Eventually Jude stood up, and we made our way back home. We repeated that same little trip seven or eight times over the summer holidays, and I loved every minute of them. It wouldn't be much to most people, sitting on a bench, watching the world go by, but for us it was huge. There were no conversations but lots of smiles. From both of us.

For other families, the holidays might be a time for more exotic travel and adventure. When I was a kid we'd usually go away for a week or two. Some years it would be to Tenerife, Lanzarote or Portugal, others it was the Isle of Wight. It didn't matter where, it was always exciting. I always thought this wasn't an option for my boys. But then, in October 2023, Tommy took a huge step and went abroad with Charlotte, Carl and their girls. When Charlotte first told me her plans for taking him abroad, I was so scared that the change of routine would be too much for him, convinced that he wouldn't understand and would want to come home, because on Mondays he's supposed to be with me. That's before you take into account the whole airport and plane experience. What if he had a meltdown on the plane? What if he wouldn't sit in his seat? What if there was a delay and they had to wait too long? It would ruin their holiday before it had even started. But, as always, Charlotte was more willing to stretch their boundaries and go for it. And sometimes she has to. She has her girls to think about too and the life that she wants to give them. Since I am unable to have both boys to stay with me for a whole week, if the girls were going to experience a holiday abroad, we would have to find ways to make it work for Tommy too. So we agreed to give it a try.

We prepared Tommy as best we could. His school helped create social stories and visual schedules for us to use and even did some work in class on planes and airports. Tommy took a trip to Southend airport to see the planes close up. Charlotte showed him photos of the villa they would be staying in, including the pool and did a countdown of how many days until they were going away. They chose a villa to help create a safe space, away from the potential overwhelm of a busy hotel or apartment block. It would also make it easier to ensure they had Tommy's safe foods on hand, and the private pool meant they didn't have to worry about how much he splashed or his tendency to jump in the pool naked.

In the build-up to their departure I felt sick with nerves. But I needn't have worried. Tommy did brilliantly. Armed with his social story in his hands, I walked him to Charlotte's car, said an emotional goodbye and off they went. Prepared. Excited. Charlotte told me he flapped and bounced his way through the airport to the plane. He handled the flight better than I could have ever imagined. And as soon as they arrived at the villa he couldn't wait to get into the pool.

They had a lovely week away. There were a few tricky moments, of course, but with the reassurance of his visual schedule and a clear understanding of when he'd be coming home to me, he soon relaxed and had the best time. So much so, they went back to the exact same villa a year later, and it worked even better. The familiarity seemed to help Tommy enjoy it even more.

I felt incredibly proud of Tommy for managing both trips and was happy that they'd all managed to have such a lovely holiday. It fills me with hope too that one day soon Tommy and I will get to do the same. When things are more settled at home, I'd love to take him away and get some sun. I know it's still a step too far for Jude. I don't think we'll ever manage a foreign holiday together and that's OK. When the time is right we'll do something in the UK instead. Just like everything else in our world, we'll do it differently. But it'll be ours.

*

THE MOST WONDERFUL TIME OF THE YEAR

For most of my life as a parent, holidays have felt like a constant reminder of everything we were missing. The milestones that never happened. The memories that didn't get made. But as with so many other aspects of our lives, these moments have also been filled with a joy and magic unique to us.

Four years ago, something incredible happened. After years of Christmas being something Tommy barely engaged with, apart from tearing open his presents, something shifted. We'd just got home one evening in November and as I was parking the car Tommy spotted the Christmas lights outside our neighbour's house. He stared for a moment, then grabbed his AAC device and typed out: 'Christmas tree'. I laughed and told him how clever he was. 'You're right Tom, Christmas tree.' And he smiled back at me.

When we got inside, he ran straight to the cupboard under the stairs, where some of the decorations were kept. I watched in disbelief as he kept pointing at the cupboard and pressed 'Christmas'. For the first time ever, it felt as though Christmas was something he was looking forward to. This was confirmed later that evening when, after his bath, he picked up his AAC device again and said: 'Dad, I would like Christmas.'

That was all I needed to hear. I'm not usually someone who puts up decorations in November but how could I say no? I rummaged through the cupboard, where luckily I had a small tree and some Mickey Mouse baubles that I'd bought a couple of years before, hoping the Disney connection would spark something in Tommy or Jude. Tommy grabbed them off me and got to work straight away, cramming all the decorations onto a tiny section of the tree, just how he liked it.

Then he pointed to our Alexa. I wasn't sure what he wanted at first but eventually I worked it out: he wanted Christmas music. The second it started, he began bouncing around the living room, flapping with excitement, a huge smile on his face as his little tree lit up the corner.

It was one of those rare moments where time slows down. I felt like this was some kind of strange dream. After years of Christmas being a source of stress, overwhelm and heartache, there we were, dancing in the living room, the lights twinkling, Mickey baubles swinging and Mariah Carey blaring out of the speaker on repeat.

Ever since that night, Tommy's little Christmas tree has gone up every year. At some random date in November or December, whenever Tommy has decided it's time to get into the Christmas spirit, he goes searching for that tree. He decorates it himself and then our festive season can begin. And every year he does it, I find myself thinking back to that first night. The magic of it. The pride I felt. The unexpected joy.

Christmas and other holidays are not about recreating the past. They're not about keeping up with other families. They're about finding what makes *our* family smile and building our traditions from there. Our holidays and celebrations don't look like anyone else's but they're ours.

15

Finding my Voice

We dropped my mum off for a hospital appointment, and with time to kill, I took Tommy to a McDonald's we'd never been to before. One of the great things about McDonald's (and one of the reasons many autistic kids have a favourite fast food chain where they will eat over and over again) is that, no matter where you go, the food will always taste the same. And for someone like Tommy, who has a limited and rigid diet, chicken nuggets and fries always go down well. It was busy but as we had time, I gave the drive-thru a miss and we went inside. Tommy has always been pretty comfortable going inside; the free balloons and the chance to do some colouring are good motivations for him. Whereas for Jude, a busy McDonald's in the summer holidays would be his idea of hell. We always eat in the car. His safe space.

Tommy and I made our way to the self-serve machines and I placed our order. As a visual learner, their interactive screens have always been a great way to encourage Tommy to make choices and work on his communication. I held his hand tightly as he tried to run off. I knew from previous experience letting go would not be a good idea, as nobody else's chips would be safe. I've lost track of the number of times I've apologised to people over the years as Tommy or Jude tried to take their chips or their ice cream.

I'm sure most families could easily wait in line. I'm sure most seven-year-olds, the age Tommy was at the time, could have sat at the table and happily waited while I collected our food. But not Tommy, so I spent the next few minutes trying to distract him, always with one hand holding him tight, wishing our food would hurry up.

Eventually, we were able to sit down with one chicken nugget Happy Meal with fries and a Fruit Shoot. And an unspoken promise that an ice cream was to follow, just like every other McDonald's trip of the last three years. Only, when Tommy had finished his food and leapt from his chair, racing back towards the self-serve counter, we discovered there were no ice creams available. No milkshakes either. My stomach sank. This was not going to go down well. How was I going to get Tommy to understand this?

I tried to explain, 'Tommy, today we're going to the shop to get ice cream.' This was met by a loud scream in protest. 'It's OK, Tom. First, Daddy's car, then shop, then ice cream.' He screamed again, broke away from me and headed for the counter. He ran, he stomped, he screamed. Everyone turned around to see what was going on. I could feel the stares, hear the tuts.

Tommy pushed to the front of the queue, trying to get to where the ice cream machine was. Maybe in his mind, unable to say it out loud, he wasn't communicating to me well enough what it was he wanted. He was trying to show me, as loud as he could. I asked the member of staff if there was any ice cream, hoping somehow the self-serve machine had been wrong. It wasn't; the milkshake and ice cream machine was out of service. They apologised, there was nothing they could do. I tried to explain to Tommy again, reassuring him we could still get an ice cream, just not here. But he scrambled up onto the counter, and I had to grab him before he disappeared into the kitchen. I could feel all eyes in the restaurant locking onto us. This struggling dad and his naughty child. I found myself blurting out, 'I'm sorry, he's autistic, and he has an ice cream every time we're here. He doesn't understand it's not working.'

I tried to carry Tommy out to the car, and he fought me the whole way. Grabbing onto anything he could, the counter, the doorframe, spitting at me and screaming. Eventually, we made it. I put him in his car seat, put his seat belt on while dodging and blocking the blows that rained down on me and closed the door. As I took a few deep breaths and fought back the tears, I realised there was a petrol station on the other side of the road. I got into the car, told Tommy where we were going and quickly drove over there. Two minutes later, he had a Strawberry Cornetto in his hand and the screaming had stopped. A wave of emotions swept over me. I was relieved that Tommy was calming down, while also anxious about the impact this would have on the rest of our day. I was also embarrassed at what had just happened, with everyone staring and judging us and yet at the same time I felt guilty for feeling like that. I somehow wished I'd done more. Said more to the people giving us dirty looks and mumbling their disapproval. Made them realise that Tommy was the one struggling and having a hard time, it wasn't his fault . . .

Most people don't understand what they're seeing in moments like that. They don't understand hidden disability. They see a screaming child and assume bad behaviour. They see a meltdown and call it a tantrum. They don't understand the invisible effort it takes for Jude or Tommy even to step inside a busy place like that. They don't see how hard they work just to exist in a world that isn't designed for them. That's the thing about hidden disabilities, they're invisible, and as a result they're often judged. This is where the role of the advocate comes in.

In the simplest terms, advocacy means speaking up for our children when they can't speak up for themselves. It's not as easy as it might sound. The truth is that people can be rude and unkind. They stare, they whisper, they pass judgement, all because they don't understand and because difference scares them. That part hurts. But it also gives you a fire in your chest, a fierce determination to protect your child from that cruelty and shield them from a world that's so quick to make assumptions. To show them, with every word and every action, that they are worthy. That they belong. That you'll never stop fighting for them.

And one of the most important ways we do this is by believing in them. Over time I have learned to presume competence; to believe that just because Jude or Tommy can't say something, doesn't mean they don't know it. To believe that they understand what someone is saying, even if they can't reply. And that presumed competence changes how you speak to your kids and how you support them. And it can change how others treat them too. But you have to lead the way – and that can be hard.

One of the hardest parts of advocacy is when you have to do it in public, out in the world, surrounded by people who don't understand. It's one thing to explain your child's needs to family members or professionals, but it's something else entirely to try to do so when all eyes are on you and you can feel the judgement in every glance. Advocacy in public settings can feel like a constant balancing act: managing your child's needs, shielding them from judgement, and trying to keep your own emotions in check. In those moments, it's easy to feel overwhelmed, embarrassed even and wonder if you're doing the right thing.

It's OK to feel nervous about advocating in public. It's hard. And it takes time to build confidence. But the more you do it, the easier it becomes. Of course, there's a balance to be struck. Advocating in public can feel exhausting and over time I have learned how to manage that and to protect myself. You can't educate everyone, and it's not your job to be a walking autism encyclopaedia. Some days, you just won't have the energy, the patience or the desire to have a conversation. Some days, your child's wellbeing (or your own) needs to come first.

And that's fine. Not every comment needs a response. Not every sideways glance needs correcting. It's important to recognise your limits and conserve your energy for the moments that matter most. Because when you *do* have the energy, those moments of education can be powerful.

One Saturday morning, when Tommy was six, we had gone to the park nice and early to ensure we were there before it got too busy. Everything was going to plan and we had the whole place to ourselves. Tommy moved from the roundabout to the sandpit, crouched down onto his haunches and started flicking the sand, moving all the way across the sandpit. Even when we're on our own, I still try to redirect him a little and encourage him to keep it controlled, in the hope that he'll follow those same guidelines on the days when it's busier. But I have to admit, that day some of the sand was escaping the sandpit and scattering on the path around it. The groundsman was passing and came rushing over, shouting at Tommy to stop, complaining about the mess he was making and how he'd just swept it all up. I was taken aback. We'd seen this man a few times over the months of coming there and always said hello and sometimes chatted briefly. A mixture of sadness and anger swept over me. I fought back the urge to let rip, conscious of Tommy and the need to keep him calm. But I couldn't let it slide, so I said firmly, 'My son Tommy is autistic, and he's not going to understand you shouting at him. And if you've got something to say, then talk to me.' Within seconds he was apologising, clearly embarrassed and quickly went on his way. My adrenaline was pumping. Those moments stay with you. The way people misinterpret what they see. It's made me self-conscious at times, and I know many families who avoid public places as much as possible as a result. Not because of their child's behaviour but because of how cruel strangers can be.

There have been so many times I've felt the urge to snap at someone staring, to fire back at a whispered comment. And believe me, there are things I've wanted to say. But I've learned, mostly through trial and error, that reacting like that rarely helps. It just makes things harder. Jude and Tommy are incredibly tuned in to tone. The last thing they need when they're already struggling is to feel my stress on top of theirs, to hear my raised voice or feel the anger in it. They might think it's directed towards them.

So instead, they become my focus. I try to tune out everyone else and do what they need in that moment. It's not always easy. And I still replay some of the worst moments in my head afterwards, sometimes even years later, thinking of what I *should* have said. But over time, I've learned that the most powerful kind of advocacy isn't always being loud and proud or being right. Sometimes it's just showing up for your child, putting their needs first and blocking out the rest.

Public advocacy isn't just about managing meltdowns, though those are often the most intense and visible moments we face. It's also about navigating spaces that weren't designed with our children in mind and having the confidence to ask for adjustments that might help them feel safe and supported. Like the time I asked the trampoline park to turn the music down because it was too loud for Jude. Or when I asked a theme park attendant if Tommy could skip the queue for a ride because he was struggling to wait.

These moments don't always go to plan. Sometimes people are kind and understanding. Other times you're met with blank stares, dismissiveness or worse. A big part of it comes down to autism being an invisible disability. You can't always *see* what my boys are navigating, and without a visible marker, people don't adjust their expectations. I've noticed that whenever Jude or Tommy have worn ear defenders or when Jude was in a buggy, we've often been treated differently. They act as visual cues, and suddenly, people were more understanding and less judgemental. Not always of course, but often. And while those tools were essential for my boys, lifelines that helped them manage the world around them, it also struck me how much we rely on appearances to dictate how compassionate we are.

When it comes to the buggy, it's gone both ways. Up until Jude was nine, the buggy was essential every time we went out. For Jude it wasn't just a way to get from A to B, it was a shield. A safe space from the noise, the crowds, the chaos of the world. It also kept him safe, especially near roads, where he had no sense of danger. Back in 2016, I took Jude to Suffolk for a week, just the two of us. I was waiting to get a place of my own after Charlotte and I had separated and with Jude having a hard time at school I thought the break would do us both good. We spent most of the week walking from our rental down to the beachfront and along the pier.

Jude loved the walks. He'd leap out of the buggy and run to the end of the pier, spinning in circles, flapping with joy, humming with delight, completely captivated by the wind and the waves. But people didn't see what often came next. The sudden switch. The overwhelm. The tears. The frantic running. The moment when he'd climb back into the buggy, desperate to escape it all.

And when they saw us walking along, this tall, physically able eight-year-old, in a buggy, they stared. Maybe they thought I was being lazy. Maybe they thought he was spoiled. I could hear and feel the 'He's too big for a pram' comments. What they didn't see was the bigger picture, that the buggy wasn't for my convenience, it was the reason we could get outside and have those joyful moments on the pier in the first place.

I've noticed something else over the years too, which is

how differently mums are treated, both online and in person. They'll be handling the same behaviours and the same meltdowns, using the same tools like buggies or iPads, yet for some reason, mums are judged more harshly than dads. It's unfair, it's awful to watch and it makes public advocacy even harder for so many families. The bar for what makes a good parent seems to be set so much lower when it comes to dads. I don't have to do much to be hailed as some kind of superhero, while mums who do the same or even more than me, are constantly criticised for their parenting choices.

I've seen it in the supermarket, in the online comments section, in the way strangers offer sympathy to me but side-eye a mum going through exactly the same thing. Some of it is pure sexism and misogyny but then a lot of the comments and judgements I see come from other women too. I don't get it. It shouldn't be that way. But it is.

Advocacy happens closer to home too. It's often about gently educating the people in your life, friends, extended family, even close relatives, on how to create an environment where your child can feel safe, included and understood. Whether it's explaining to a grandparent why your child doesn't want a hug, helping a teacher understand why transitions are so hard or asking family not to overwhelm your child with questions or noise, these conversations are a crucial part of advocacy. They're no easier than advocating in public. In fact, they can be repetitive, exhausting and emotionally draining. But over time, they can make a huge difference.

One Christmas gathering showed me just how powerful those conversations can be.

When Jude was ten, my aunt and cousins were having a Christmas get-together at my aunt's house. I really wanted to see them all and wanted to be able to take my mum and dad to see them too but also knew it would likely be difficult for Jude to cope. So I spoke to my aunt and cousins beforehand; we talked about what we could do to make it work and together we decided to give it a go. They prepared a bedroom to be a quiet space for Jude, with a TV in there so he could watch his favourite programmes and agreed to keep the other children (and the cats!) downstairs when Jude was up there. We made sure everyone knew not to be too loud or make a fuss when we arrived and to keep the music turned down. Everyone knew not to thrust Christmas presents upon Jude or try to force any interactions. They had made a Christmas buffet for everyone but had some of Jude's favourite foods ready too. When I brought him downstairs after an hour to try the buffet, he sat on a chair next to me and demolished some sausage rolls. He even tried some different foods with a huge smile on his face. When he'd had enough, I showed him the way back to the bedroom, and he was very content.

My family gave Jude the space and time that he needed to settle into a strange, new environment. They also trusted in what I was telling them, and didn't try to force their own parenting beliefs on the situation. Because of that we managed to stay for four hours, when there was every chance we could have been out of there after just ten minutes. Over the next couple of years, that one good experience and the lessons it taught me and my wider family led to us being able to go to three family barbecues, and enjoy two weekends away with my cousins and their children. Each time was another small step out of Jude's comfort zone, each time we saw a little more interaction. Without those initial conversations and adaptations, none of this would have been possible.

That's the power of advocacy, when it's met with understanding of what the advocate is trying to achieve. I wasn't demanding special treatment; I was helping my family see the world through Jude's eyes. Then we worked together to create an environment where he could feel safe and supported. And it showed me what's possible when people are willing to listen and make room for difference.

Educating others about your child's needs doesn't just make their world easier to navigate, it helps change how people see autism altogether. It challenges the idea that autistic children are 'naughty', 'difficult' or 'disobedient'. It breaks down the assumptions and stereotypes that so often get in the way of empathy. Every explanation, every one of those moments where you choose to say, 'Here's what's really going on', is an opportunity to shift someone's perspective. Sometimes that means explaining why your child doesn't like loud noises. Why they struggle with crowds. Why they need routine, repetition or sensory tools to help regulate. And while it may not feel like much at the time, over weeks, months and years, all those small moments can make a big difference. Educating others can feel like an uphill battle at times, especially when the same misconceptions come up again and again. But every time you explain, you're planting a seed of understanding that hopefully will grow into something bigger.

Advocacy isn't one grand gesture. It's a collection of moments, big and small, where you step up for your child and help others see them as you do. It's easy to feel like the smaller moments don't count, but these small acts of advocacy matter because they help shape the world around your child. They build understanding, create connections and pave the way for bigger changes. And sometimes, they make the difference between your child feeling like they don't fit in and feeling safe and supported.

When I became a dad, I thought I'd be teaching my kids about the world. But as it turns out, I've spent most of my time teaching the world about my kids.

One of the most effective ways I've found to educate others is through sharing stories. Personal examples can make abstract concepts relatable. Explaining how Tommy manages transitions, describing Jude's sensory preferences or sharing how Tommy communicates with an AAC device helps paint a fuller picture. I've seen this impact not just with family and friends but also through Stories About Autism and the connections I've made on social media. Over the years, the stories I've read and the moments I've watched on other accounts have brought me so much comfort and helped me better understand my own boys too. Sharing Jude's and Tommy's experiences has been a way for me to pay that forward. Since starting Stories About Autism, I've had thousands of messages from people saying it's helped them to better understand their own child, their student or even themselves, through the sharing of stories. They give people a chance to see your child for who they really are. To look beyond the behaviour or the meltdown and begin to understand the human underneath. To learn a little. And sometimes, those are the moments that stay with people the most. Through stories, we're able to reach those who have no direct connection to autism and little knowledge about it. And one day that might help them be a bit more considerate and a bit more understanding when they meet families like ours in the park, at a restaurant, at school, in a supermarket or at work. All the places where we need people to better understand.

Stories also bridge that gap between what people think they know and what they need to understand. When it comes to autism, people often have a narrow viewpoint. They base their understanding on the one autistic person they've met or on stories they've heard second-hand from a friend of a friend. We've all heard the 'My neighbours' grandson is autistic and he . . .'

People simply don't see the full picture. They rarely understand just how vast the autism spectrum is or how different each autistic person can be. To be honest, I didn't either, before Jude and Tommy. And I get it. It can be confusing. How can Jude and Tommy be autistic and non-speaking, while someone else is autistic, has been to university, holds down a job, is married with kids? How can that be the same diagnosis?

I understand the confusion. I understand how hard it can be for the public to get their heads around what the spectrum really means. Even now, all these years later, I'm still learning – and still unlearning things I thought I knew. I'm still listening, still growing, still trying to do better. And I think that's what makes the biggest difference, for us as parents and for people in general: being open to learning. Not just once but over and over again.

Since I first started on this journey with Jude and Tommy,

there's been an incredible amount to learn. Advocacy doesn't end after the first meeting, the first diagnosis or even the first big win. It's not a task you tick off a list. It's a journey, a lifelong commitment that evolves with your child's needs. Every stage of their life brings new challenges, new systems to navigate and new lessons to learn. Some of it came easily, some of it took time to sink in.

When Jude was first diagnosed it felt like we'd been dropped into a foreign country where we didn't speak the language. Suddenly, our lives were filled with all these unfamiliar terms and acronyms to remember. Autism, Autism Spectrum Disorder, ASD, ASC, GDD, ADHD, One Plans, DLA, the list went on and on. Then there was a revolving door of professionals: occupational therapists, speech and language therapists, behaviour specialists, the learning disabilities team and social care. Some were helpful, some just made things more confusing and frustrating. Each meeting felt like we were trying to decode a new system while juggling sleepless nights, fear for the future and the everyday stresses of life. How were we supposed to know which forms to fill out, which services to apply for or even where to begin?

Even thinking back to those days while typing that out is overwhelming. If you're feeling the same way, let me reassure you: it's OK not to know everything right away. None of us start out as experts. Advocacy, being an advocate, is a role you grow into, one meeting, one form and one conversation at a time. I remember sitting in our first meeting, frantically scribbling down notes and Googling things afterwards, trying to make sense of what had just happened. It took time, plenty of mistakes and moments of frustration, but slowly I began to understand the language of professionals. And with that understanding came the confidence to communicate Jude's and Tommy's needs more effectively, while also knowing what they were entitled to – and, when necessary, fighting to ensure they got it.

Here's what helped me in those early days:

Ask questions

If a professional uses a term you don't understand, don't hesitate to ask them to explain it. You might feel awkward at first but remember: you're not expected to know everything. Asking questions shows that you're engaged and trying your best to meet your child's needs.

Keep a notebook

Bring a notebook to every meeting or keep notes on your phone. Write down the key points, terms and names and what their role is. Have a list of questions you want to ask, all those things that keep you up at night. It's impossible to remember everything in the moment and having notes to refer back to can make a huge difference.

Do your research

Spend time researching about autism and the systems you're navigating. Read books, listen to audiobooks or podcasts, watch documentaries or videos on social media. Whatever is the best form for you to consume. Some information might go over your head initially, it certainly did mine, but everything that you learn will help build your confidence.

Find allies

One of the most helpful things I did was connect with other parents, some of whom were further down the road than us. They were like translators, explaining what to expect, who to turn to and even which questions to ask. They're the ones who helped me feel less alone and more able to advocate for my boys.

The truth is, you'll never know everything and that's fine. Advocacy is about progress, not perfection. Even now, seventeen years in, knowing all that I've learned along the way, I still rely on a network of people I can turn to for advice on how to get Tommy and Jude what they need. And I still get nervous walking into certain meetings. But I also know that I can do this. And so can you.

And all that advocacy in the small moments – with friends, family, strangers in the street, educating others, educating myself – all of this also enables you to make the bigger stands when needed, to stand up to the systems that fail our children and push for what they need, what they deserve. Advocacy in this guise is refusing to let a broken system stand in the way of their future. It's about pushing past the red tape, the long waits, the dismissals and misunderstandings. It's doing whatever it takes to make sure their needs are understood and met.

When Jude was four he was assigned a disability social worker. I was against it at first. In my mind, social workers were for families who had real problems, those struggling with parenting or safety concerns, who were in crisis. Not ours. Maybe it was because I'd only ever seen the term in the newspaper headlines after family tragedies. There's a lot of stigma still around the term social worker, and it made me feel uncomfortable. I felt uneasy about someone coming into our home, picking us apart and judging our parenting ability. But I couldn't have been more wrong. A good social worker is worth their weight in gold, and Jude's soon became an important part of our support network.

She helped us navigate school meetings, provided evidence for other professionals and applications and even put us forward for Direct Payments, a lifeline that allowed us to employ a carer for a few hours each week. She took Jude out, enabling Charlotte to spend some one-to-one time with Tommy or even to give us a much-needed break every now and again. I came to see just how much of a difference a good social worker could make for families like ours. A social worker was not someone to fear but someone who could help us access the available support out there.

Seeing what a difference it made for Jude, we applied for the same support for Tommy a couple of years later. Only this time, we were turned down. The assessor claimed he didn't meet the criteria, which didn't make any sense. Tommy's and Jude's needs were so similar, even Jude's social worker agreed Tommy needed one.

At first, I was prepared to just accept it. They were the professionals, right? They knew the system, they'd seen hundreds of families like ours, surely they knew best? And maybe if we hadn't already been through everything with

Jude, if we hadn't already started to understand our role as advocates for our children, we *would* have accepted it. Maybe if that had been our first ever assessment, we would have walked away thinking there was nothing more we could do. But we knew better by then. We knew how important this support could be, not just for Tommy but for our whole family. Why should Tommy miss out on the same level of support Jude was getting?

So we appealed. We filled out the forms again. Gathered more evidence outlining exactly why Tommy needed the support. We wrote, rewrote and relived the hardest parts of our lives, again and again. It was frustrating and emotionally draining, as it always is when you're listing the challenges and difficulties over and over again. What makes it harder is knowing that, to get any support, you can't talk about what they're good at, what they love to do or what makes them happy. You have to list everything they can't do. You have to reduce the child you love into a form of tick boxes and worst moments, again and again. And every time you do it, it chips away at you a little more. I've spoken to so many parents who really struggle with their feelings after completing paperwork, so I know I'm not the only one.

But, it worked. With someone else looking over Tommy's case, we had a different outcome. He was awarded a social worker, and now we could access the support our whole family needed. Over the years this has made a huge difference to Tommy's life. I see it every Saturday when Tommy goes out for the day with his carer. They go bowling, to the cinema, the beach, the funfair, the farm and every single time, he has the *best* day. And over time, those good days have added up, all of these experiences helping him mature and develop in ways I never could have imagined. They've given him a greater understanding of the world and all the little social expectations that come with it.

I used to find it really difficult to take Tommy out anywhere. He'd try to run off constantly. It was a battle just to keep him safe, and by the end of the trip I'd come home wondering why we bothered. But all the time he's spent with his carers in these places has changed that. He knows what to expect now and what's expected of him. And he's much more able to enjoy our days out together.

A huge part of that has been down to the relationships he's developed with his carer's children. They've become the friends – and the role models – that Tommy never had. They've stepped into a position that Jude could never fill. And Tommy has thrived because of it. He watches them and follows their lead. Whether it's trying new things like ice skating, rollercoasters or slides, they're right there beside him, and he copies them. They've shown him patience, love and understanding. And he absolutely loves being around them.

With every photo and video his carers send me, I get to see his huge smile. His giggle. In places I never thought possible. All of that growth, all of those experiences, all of those joyful days, they've only been possible because we appealed social care's original decision. Because all those years ago and at every review since we've fought for him to access the funding for that support. That's what advocacy does. It creates opportunities. It opens doors.

It wouldn't be the last time we'd have to appeal a decision. Social care panels, DLA applications, EHCPs, CAMHS referrals,

ADHD assessments, almost every step forward has come with an automatic 'no'. And it wears you down. It feels like the system is built to test your resilience, to make you give up. It can feel as though they're quietly hoping you'll stop chasing, stop asking, stop pushing and that will solve their budget problems. Because when you're already exhausted, overwhelmed and doing everything you can to hold your family together, adding more barriers can be enough to break you.

But we've learned that persistence pays off. If we hadn't questioned that first 'no' for Tommy, he wouldn't have the support he has now. If we'd accepted every knock-back along the way, Jude and Tommy wouldn't have half of what they're entitled to. Advocacy isn't just about speaking up, it's about refusing to be dismissed when the barriers are inevitably put in your way. Refusing to let a broken system impact your child's needs.

These battles aren't unique to our family, they're happening to parents everywhere, up and down the country. I receive countless messages each week from people sharing their own stories of the battles they're facing trying to access any support, how they are stuck on waiting lists, rejected from services, told their child 'doesn't meet criteria'. Messages full of worry, fear and exhaustion.

And it's not just social media that's telling me this. The news is finally catching on too. Every week, I see reports about how the system is failing families like ours. About the shortage of specialist school places. The postcode lottery of diagnosis timelines. The impossible hoops parents are expected to jump through just to get basic support. It's heartbreaking. It's infuriating. And it's why we keep going. Because every time we fight back, appeal a decision, challenge the system and push for what our kids deserve, we're not just doing it for our own children. We're doing it for the families who'll come after us. Advocacy is exhausting, but it's also one of the most powerful ways we can make a difference.

As I learned more about the systems and language of advocacy, I started to realise something else: no matter how much I knew or didn't know, my instincts as a parent were just as important. You know your child. You see the things no one else sees. You feel the things no one else feels. Understanding the jargon and processes gave me the tools to advocate, but it was my gut feeling, my knowledge of Jude and Tommy as individuals, that guided me. Over time, I learned to trust those instincts, even when others didn't see what I saw. So while the system might be set up to make you doubt yourself, to question whether you're 'qualified' to speak up, I promise you, you are.

There's something incredibly empowering about seeing the difference your advocacy can make. Whether it's securing the right therapy, getting a teacher to understand your child's needs or watching your child thrive because of a change you fought for, those moments remind you why you do this. And in the process, you realise something important: you can do the hard things and have the hard conversations. Not because you want to. Not because it's easy. But because your child needs you to. And slowly, almost without noticing, you grow into someone who can stand their ground. Someone who can walk into a meeting with their head held high. Someone who knows what their child needs and won't settle for less.

If there's one thing I've learned through all of this, it's that advocacy changes you. It challenges you, pushes you and forces you to grow in ways you never expected. It empowers you, showing you how much of a difference you can make, not just for your child but also for yourself. It's taught me to be more patient, more compassionate and more determined. It's shown me that I'm capable of doing hard things, not just for them but for myself too. And it's given me a sense of purpose that I didn't have before. Advocacy isn't just about helping my boys navigate the world, it's about growing alongside them, becoming the best version of myself so I can help them become the best versions of themselves.

Looking back, it's hard to recognise the person I was before Jude's and Tommy's diagnoses; it's almost like looking at a stranger. I was quieter, less confident and much more comfortable staying in the background. I didn't see myself as someone who could speak up, challenge authority or take charge of difficult situations. I avoided any type of confrontation. But advocacy has a way of pushing you out of your comfort zone. It forces you to step into roles you never imagined – negotiator, teacher, therapist – and in the process, shows you strength and resilience you never knew you had.

At the same time, advocating day in and day out can be exhausting. There have been moments where I've felt completely drained, mentally, emotionally, physically. When I've felt like I haven't got another battle in me. Because when you're the one holding it all together, managing the meetings, chasing the calls, writing the emails, prepping for the next review, it's easy to become overwhelmed. What's helped me in those moments is learning to take a step back. To zoom out. To notice the small victories. The inchstones. The steps forward that Jude and Tommy have made.

Advocacy isn't about fixing everything all at once. We have to be in it for the long haul. So it's important we remember this too: *you can't pour from an empty cup.* Taking care of yourself matters. Not instead of your child but because of them. Because advocacy isn't a sprint. It's a marathon. It's lifelong. It's about persistence and sustainability. And you matter in this story too.

Sometimes, that means letting other people step up to share the load – or even letting the boys step up. As my boys have grown older, I've started to think more about what advocacy will look like for them in the future. As much as I try to keep my mind rooted firmly in the present, the question lingers in the back of my mind: what will happen when I'm no longer here to advocate for them? For families like ours the future looks very different. We're not just thinking about the next school term or the following year, we're thinking about the next forty-plus years, while also having to plan and worry about the twenty-plus years after we're gone and who will look after them.

The weight of that can feel heavy at times. The pressure to try to build something sustainable that will outlast us. It's something I know many other parents experience too. For some families this means teaching their kids how to advocate for themselves, how to explain to teachers, work colleagues and friends what accommodations they may need. For others, for families like ours where communication is mainly non-verbal, it's about putting systems in place now, so that when we're not around, someone else is. Someone who understands their needs. Someone who cares. Someone who will keep fighting for them like we always have.

And so, one of the most important parts of my role now is helping my boys find their own voices. For Jude, that might mean finding ways to show me what he needs and communicating in ways that others will understand too. For Tommy, it's using his AAC device to express his preferences and tell us what he needs in social situations.

Every child's journey with self-advocacy will look different. It might not be a TED Talk or a big speech. It might be a tap on the shoulder. A symbol tapped on a screen. A firm 'no'. But the goal is the same: to help them speak up in whatever way works for them and make sure the world is ready to listen. And our job is to ensure that we put systems in place to advocate for them for the rest of their lives, even if we are not there to do so in person.

16

Carer, Son, Dad

It was around 7.30 in the morning when Jude finally fell asleep. Sprawled across his bed, head at the bottom, feet up by his headboard. I crept in, took his iPad from under his body and put it on charge, made sure his curtain was fully closed and tiptoed back out. It had been a long night. A mixture of pacing, stimming, anger, dancing and aggression, with Jude unable to regulate, unable to wind down. While I tried simultaneously to keep out of his way to avoid triggering a meltdown, yet remain close enough to do whatever he needed me to do within five seconds before the delay triggered a meltdown too. I had dozed on and off, fifteen minutes here, twenty minutes there, my sleep interrupted by Jude constantly getting up again. I never thought that when my sixteen-year-old started pulling all-nighters I'd be right by his side. But then these weren't the kind of all-nighters I thought he'd be having either.

And then, just as I lay back down on my sofa bed, my body about to collapse, the bell went. My dad was awake and needing help to get out of bed. I dragged myself through the house, my limbs aching, barely able to see straight and helped him get out of bed, washed and dressed. I prepared his breakfast, gave him his morning medication, made sure he was steady on his feet.

All while Jude finally slept.

The summer holidays had been brutal. Jude was struggling with big, physical meltdowns, chronic sleep disruption and an anxiety that seemed to sit just under the surface all day long. Every need, every demand, every transition became a trigger. We went weeks without a full night's sleep. Most nights he didn't fall asleep before 4 a.m., night blurring into morning.

That was my life last summer. No buffer. No space. No recovery. Nights of meltdowns and anxiety, followed by mornings of medication routines and fall prevention. Days full of constant hypervigilance, trying to keep Jude calm, having fun with Tommy, doing everything for my dad and somehow trying to work around it all. There were few moments to breathe. I'd often realise it was midday before I'd had a drink of water, let alone breakfast. Some days there was no time for a shower.

Because I had a job to do.

It's a job I've been doing for years now but which I've only recently given a name to.

Caring.

Not parenting. Not helping. Not just being there when needed. Caring. Full-time, unpaid, around the clock. For my boys. For my dad. For my family. It's not a job I applied for, definitely not one I trained for or one I ever imagined doing. But it's a role I've had to shape my whole life around.

For a long time, I didn't use the word. It felt clinical, too formal, like it belonged to professionals who got paid to do this work. I thought it didn't apply when the people you were looking after were your children or your parents, as though calling myself a carer would somehow strip away the love and the connection, the years of history we share. I wasn't a carer, I was just a dad. Doing what dads are supposed to do.

But as time passed, as I became more submerged in our online world, learning more about the many families who live similar lives to ours, I came to realise that what I do each day goes far beyond what most people would recognise as parenting. It's attending to personal care. Navigating meltdowns. Being the calm during chaos. Managing routines down to the minute. Communicating through AAC, gestures, expression. Carrying out risk assessments before and during every outing. Going to meetings. So many meetings. Medical appointments and daily medications. More paperwork than I ever imagined parenthood could involve.

And it's not just for the boys anymore. Now it's for my dad too. Now in his eighties, he's had Parkinson's for over fifteen years, which means he needs a lot of support each day. I help him get out of bed, get washed and dressed and prepare all of his meals. Throughout the day I need to be there in case he falls. I track his medication and give it to him four times a day. I arrange his health appointments and take him to and from them. I take him to have his hair cut or to his feet appointments. I handle all the bills, all the letters, all the admin. And a lot of that is actually the easy stuff. The middle of the night wake-ups, helping him back into bed, dealing with the confusion, the hallucinations and the constant threat of falls. That's the draining part.

My day often starts before I've even had a chance to recover from the one before. Jude and Tommy are usually up late into the night. Then my dad will normally wake up in the middle of the night, sometimes before I've even got into bed. Then Jude wakes up early. Tommy wants to lie in, and so when Jude is at Charlotte's and it's just Tommy and me I will try to sleep in, but my dad often has other ideas. And so the day starts all over again. There's no time to ease into it. No moment to think, *I'll just sit for five minutes first.* You get up. You move. You start juggling. And all day long, the plates keep spinning.

I'm bouncing between completely different kinds of care, teenage and elderly, autism and Parkinson's, each with its own needs, rhythms and risks. My day consists of trying to anticipate who will need me next or who needs me the most. Trying to prevent the boys from becoming overwhelmed, while also worrying whether my dad will be safe in the kitchen on his own. I often have to decide in the moment who to turn to first.

Some days, it feels like I'm being pulled in too many directions at once. Especially if Jude or Tommy is struggling. When that happens I just want an empty house and to be alone with them. And on the days when my dad is struggling, I find it hard trying to get myself into the calm and positive mood that the boys need.

There's no chance to pause. It's a constant back and forth. It's not that I'm being dramatic. It's just that right now, there is no back-up.

For me, as for many, this crept up slowly. Around 2017, my role with my parents started to shift. It began with small things. My dad stopped driving, so I started driving them to appointments and helping with food shopping. Then I was taking over bits of admin here and there. I noticed my mum starting to repeat herself. Little signs. Easy to brush off. But deep down, I knew something was changing.

In some ways, it felt like going through Jude's and Tommy's diagnoses all over again. I could see it, feel it but other people told me not to worry, that I was imagining it, that there were other explanations. But I knew. I knew my mum needed to see a doctor, and I knew it wasn't going to be a simple conversation. Because how do you tell someone you love that you think they're losing parts of themselves? Or that you're worried it might be dementia, while they think everything is OK? I thought my experience with medical appointments, with advocating for Jude and Tommy, might have helped. But this was different. With the boys, Charlotte and I were the ones making the decisions. With my mum, it was still her choice. It was her health, her body and her mind. Her life. And I needed to tread carefully.

I tried raising it gently, mentioning her memory slips and encouraging her to talk to someone. Eventually, in early 2020, I managed to persuade her to go to the GP. She promised she would bring up the memory issues and we even rehearsed what she was going to say. I remember feeling so relieved, hoping this might finally be the start of getting some help. She came home from the appointment full of smiles. 'Everything's fine,' she said. She'd talked about her B12 levels, mentioned some tiredness but nothing else. She hadn't said a word about the memory concerns and hadn't asked a single question we'd prepared. She'd bluffed her way through the whole thing.

Not long after that, the pandemic hit. Schools closed. My

parents isolated. Support disappeared. We all went into survival mode. I always had one of the boys with me, swapping back and forth with Charlotte, while trying to check in with my parents and trying to stay calm while everything felt completely out of my control.

It took until November of that year, the day before my fortieth birthday, for my mum to receive her diagnosis. A video call with a dementia nurse confirmed what I'd feared for so long. Just like with Jude's and Tommy's diagnoses, I already knew. It wasn't a shock. But it still hit differently. Because this time, there was no hope of answers. No roadmap for support or education or therapy. No unknown future full of possibilities. Having seen what dementia had done to my nan twenty years before, I knew exactly what was coming: further regression, more decline. We spoke about medication that would try to slow things down, we spoke about what the future might look like. And that future arrived more quickly than I could ever have imagined.

The confusion my mum had been experiencing while waiting for her diagnosis was soon happening more and more often. She'd forget who people were, in particular my dad, lose track of time and become upset or agitated over things that didn't make sense to her. She'd call me in a panic multiple times a day and I'd try to calm her, talk her down, while also trying to manage Tommy or Jude in the next room. I'd spend most of the school day round at theirs and would often try to bring the boys there for a while after school. But the safe space that Tommy and Jude had always enjoyed at their house was changing. It was no longer the calm, relaxed place they'd love spending time at and was instead becoming stressful and unpredictable. And the whole thing was made harder by not being able to explain it to the boys. First, I couldn't take them to their grandparents' house because of Covid, which was a huge change to their routine that they struggled to cope with. Then, when we were able to go back there, Nanny wasn't the same. She didn't interact with them in the way she used to and didn't understand their needs as well as she used to. She could be loud and unpredictable, even angry. Nanny was changing, and they didn't understand that. So while I wanted to be there more, Tommy and Jude didn't. But even as we were at my parents' house more often and for longer, within fifteen minutes of leaving, when I'd take Tommy for a drive to kickstart his evening routine, I'd receive a phone call from my mum, asking where I was and why I hadn't been round there to see her that day.

My dad, too, was declining slowly. Physically he was becoming more and more dependent and could no longer rely on my mum to help him. And emotionally, he was overwhelmed too. He couldn't care for her alone, but I couldn't always be there either. I was constantly being pulled from one emotional emergency to the next, having to make decisions as to whether to answer the phone and try to deal with whatever crisis my mum and dad were having or to let the phone ring and focus on helping Jude calm down from a meltdown. I had one foot in each world, trying not to let either fall apart.

Every day became a cycle of juggling appointments, answering crisis calls, trying to prevent meltdowns, handling transitions and feeling like I was barely holding everything together. All I looked forward to each day was when I knew my mum was in bed asleep, thankful that at least then I could just concentrate on Tommy or Jude.

I didn't even have time to be upset about what was happening to my parents. I couldn't grieve or be angry. I coped the only way I knew how: I shut down emotionally and got on with it. I did the school runs. I took calls. I calmed my mum. I wiped away the tears, answered questions, dealt with challenging behaviour.

But when my dad was hospitalised multiple times in the summer of 2022, it all came crashing down. Suddenly, I was trying to be in three different places at once. At home looking after my boys, visiting my dad in hospital and trying to get to the bottom of what was wrong and trying to look after my mum too. Unable to do it all, I arranged for my mum to go into respite care temporarily. When my dad finally came home he was weaker, more dependent than before and with it being the summer holidays too, I extended my mum's stay, to give us some breathing space and a chance for him to recover.

At this point, something unexpected happened. My mum settled in the care home, becoming calmer and much happier than she had been at home. The agitation that had taken over her for months seemed to ease. Within a couple of weeks, she was referring to the care home as 'home', as if she'd always lived there. I think she'd already started to lose the concept of who I was to her. She knew I was connected to her but not that I was her son. The memories and connections had already started to fade, but she was happy.

It went so well that we turned the temporary stay into a permanent one. It was an incredibly difficult decision but being at home simply wasn't safe anymore, for her or for my dad. And as painful as it was, I knew I couldn't care for everyone. Something had to give. For a while, the guilt was crushing but I knew deep down it was the right choice, and three years later I can look back and say it was 100 per cent the right decision for everyone.

Once my mum was settled, it soon became clear that my dad couldn't be left alone either. He was struggling physically, needing more and more support each day. And going back and forth between the two houses, even though only a few minutes apart, wasn't going to work. I couldn't leave Tommy or Jude at home alone as I raced round there multiple times a day, and I couldn't get them to simply come with me if it wasn't a part of their routine visits. The combination of autism and my dad's support needs made these moments almost impossible to navigate.

So we made another huge change. We built an annexe in the garden of my parents' house, a space for me and the boys to sleep in, close enough that I could care for my dad properly but separate enough that the boys could have their own space. It was a massive undertaking – the logistics, the stress, the worry about how Jude and Tommy would handle it all. For three months I managed the build, juggled all the usual responsibilities and braced myself for how it might affect the boys.

We'd moved before and they'd coped well, but this was different. This wasn't a new house, it was an old house in a new set-up. A place they'd been visiting for years but would always leave after a few hours, going back to their own space. Would they understand that we were staying? I did everything

I could to prepare them. We used social stories. I added a bath to the main house, something I knew they both loved and would help them feel more at home. I tried to make it as predictable and comforting as possible.

Then, one Friday at the start of December, we went for it. It was Tommy's turn first. He got off the school bus curious and excited. School had gone over the social story we'd prepared for him before he left that day, and he clearly had an understanding of what was happening. He went straight to the annexe and explored, walking back and forth between the two buildings. As the night wore on, we did our usual trip to the shop, then came back to the annexe, and he let us work through his night-time routines without a fuss. The next day it was Jude's turn. Less able to communicate than Tommy, to make his thoughts known, I wondered what he must be thinking. He smiled when he recognised his bed, his TV. His iPad was working, his favourite songs playing on his Alexa, the wifi was strong. He had everything he needed. He adjusted in his own way, realising that he now had the best of both worlds, all the comforts of Nanny and Grandad's house but with his own designated space too.

As the days passed, I started to breathe a little easier. We'd found a solution. A set-up that met everyone's needs and that worked for now. But for me, even three years later, for some reason it still doesn't feel like home. It's comfortable, yes. It functions. But it's not the life I pictured.

My mum, now in full-time care, no longer knows who I am. My dad needs more and more support with each passing month. And I live in a house that feels like a constant reminder of this. I sleep on a sofa bed each night outside Jude and

Tommy's room; I spend my days shuffling between the house and the annexe, trying to hold it all together. It was the right decision, but it still feels like a loss – of independence, of space, of freedom. Of how life might have looked. And maybe, on some days, a loss of myself.

People don't often see what carers give up. The things we slowly let go of, not because we wanted to but because life didn't give us much choice: careers, independence, social lives, freedom. The ability to say yes to things without weeks of planning or the anxiety of what might go wrong when you finally get some free time. The freedom to choose where you live, what job you take, how you spend your weekend, all of it ends up shaped around someone else's needs.

This is the long-term reality of being a carer. Always tired, with no real chance to recover. Always busy, because you're always needed. Not just a parent but a carer too. And the longer it goes on, the harder it becomes to separate where one role ends and the other begins.

Over time, being a carer leaves its mark, on your body and on your sense of self. It's not just the exhaustion you feel in your bones after another night of broken sleep. It's not just the anxiety that comes from being constantly on. It's how you slowly start to lose sight of the person you used to be. You still turn up each day, still do everything that's needed but something shifts. You stop making plans. Stop looking forward. You become so focused on getting through the day, on doing what has to be done, that you forget what it felt like to live for yourself too. It doesn't happen all at once. It creeps in slowly, quietly. Until one day you realise you don't feel much like *you* anymore. When you're living day to day with those feelings and responsibilities and trying to meet the daily routines and demands you shift into survival mode.

It's not dramatic. It's not even obvious. From the outside, it probably looks like you're doing OK. Still showing up. Still smiling. Still functioning. But inside, you're stretched thin, just trying to stay afloat. And the longer you stay in that place, the harder it becomes to feel much of anything. You stop letting yourself fully enjoy the good days, just in case something bad is around the corner. You keep your guard up. You protect yourself. But you also disconnect from a lot of the joy too.

For me, this emotional toll also came with a financial one. I was too embarrassed to talk about it at the time but it feels important to mention. There was a period where I couldn't juggle everything, the care for Jude and Tommy, supporting my mum and dad, the endless appointments and sleepless nights – working full-time on top of all this just didn't fit anymore. And so for a couple of years, I claimed benefits. Which I felt really uncomfortable about. I was in my late-thirties, relying on the government to keep a roof over our heads and eating most of my dinners at my parents' house because there wasn't enough money left some months to buy groceries and still pay the rent. The embarrassment I felt over this was tied in with my preconceived ideas of what a dad, a provider, should be. It wasn't about the benefits themselves. Caring is work, and it is often unpaid and incompatible with a regular job. Many families like ours depend on that safety net at some point. It just wasn't the life I saw my friends living or that I had imagined for myself. I'm not embarrassed

CARER, SON, DAD

about it now. I'm grateful it was there, and I see it for what it is: support we're entitled to while we do the work of caring.

For years we were just lurching from one crisis to the next. No sleep, meltdowns, confusion, phone calls, hospitals, appointments. There wasn't time to think, let alone *feel*. But eventually, things began to settle and the chaos eased, just a little. Jude and Tommy were more comfortable and happy in their new home. My mum was safe and no longer someone I had to worry about 24/7. My dad needed increasing levels of support, but we were figuring out new routines and getting by. For the first time in a long time, we weren't in full-blown crisis mode.

And that's actually when I struggled. When you're not fighting fires, when everyone's doing OK, that's when you're finally left with your own thoughts. And it was only then that I realised I wasn't enjoying the happy moments as much as I thought I would. As much as I should. I'd spent so long hoping for a time of quiet, for a chance to breathe, but when it came, I didn't know how to. I'd been in survival mode for so long I didn't know how to come out of it.

I was so used to scanning for danger. Watching for the next meltdown. The next call. The next fall. Never really relaxing. Never fully present. Even in the good moments, I felt detached. Like I was there but slightly removed, always one step ahead, always waiting for something to go wrong. That's what long-term caring can do. You get so used to coping that you forget how to live. You forget what excitement feels like. What joy feels like. You know it's there, that you *should* be feeling it but for some reason you don't.

I slowly realised that I didn't feel much of anything anymore. Even in the good moments, I'd smile without really feeling it. All my energy went into trying to meet everyone's needs, every day: Tommy, Jude, my mum, my dad. There was no room for mine. I was exhausted in a way that no amount of sleep could ever fix. After a lot of self-reflection, I've realised that becoming emotionally 'numb' is how I've coped with things. It's what gets me through the days filled with big aggressive meltdowns, when my heart feels like it might shatter. It got me through the hardest days after my marriage ended and we went through the divorce. It gets me through the loneliness I often feel, being a full-time single parent and carer, when I long to be more social and have more adult connection. And it's got me through the last five years of watching my mum and dad change dramatically in front of me and needing my support.

While the last few years have been pretty difficult emotionally, there have also been plenty of happy memories and many days where both Tommy and Jude are simply living their best life. And those days make me smile, I enjoy them but too often I struggle to feel much more than that. I seem to keep to a happy medium. It's a coping mechanism, sacrificing the highs, the buzz and excitement of life, in return for not getting too low on the harder days.

I first noticed it in the little things. Arsenal matches that used to leave me buzzing or gutted now barely register. I'll watch if I can. I'll smile if we win. But that deep emotional connection just isn't there anymore. It's the same with Stories About Autism and all that's brought into my life. I've had incredible experiences, awards, collaborations, messages from celebrities and met some amazing people. These are all things I know I should feel proud of and I *am* proud, but it's almost an uncomfortable pride. One that doesn't come with much feeling. I never quite celebrate or pause to take in the accomplishment, I just move on to the next thing that needs my attention.

As I sit writing this, I'm about to go to Sydney to deliver two talks for the charity Autism Awareness Australia. Me. They want *me* to go to the other side of the world and share our story because that's how much it resonates with other families. I'll be in Sydney for a week, exploring a city that I last visited over twenty years ago and never thought I'd get to see again. I'll get to sleep in a bed for a week, with no interruptions, which, after nearly three years on a sofa is quite an upgrade! Am I excited about all this? I wish I could say yes. In truth, I'm more worried about how Tommy is going to cope with me being away and the break from his regular routines and how my dad will manage without me.

Or take this book. Something I've wanted to write for years. I finally found the courage to write and share it. And it turned out multiple publishers wanted it; I got to *choose* who published my book. And I'm glad, of course I am. But even that has felt . . . a little flat. Because my brain is already somewhere else, worrying about Tommy or Jude or planning my dad's meds or wondering how we'll juggle next week.

It's not that I don't care. I care deeply, maybe even too much, especially about those I'm responsible for. But caring is different from feeling and I want to feel more. I want to come out of this fog. Even if that means facing more of the harder feelings too. Because I don't want to just get through life, I want to actually live it.

The first step to addressing this has been recognising it and sharing it. We talk a lot about masking in the autism community, how our kids learn to hide their feelings at school and how draining it can be. But I've realised as parents and carers, we do this too. We smile through the hard days, we say we're fine, we keep going – all while carrying more than we ever thought we could. I'll be honest, some days I am falling apart. But I don't have the option to stop. If I don't show up, if I don't stay calm, everyone else will suffer.

It took me years to realise how much this was affecting me. When you're in it, when your day often starts before you've recovered from the last, when you're running on caffeine and autopilot, you don't always notice what it's doing to you. You can live that way so long it starts to feel normal. You forget how much you're holding, how much tension you're carrying, until something tiny pushes you over the edge. It might be a broken washing machine, a cancelled appointment or someone making a comment when you're out with your kids. Something that shouldn't matter, but it does. When you've been stretched for so long, emotionally, mentally, physically, the little things can hit hard because you've got nothing left in reserve. You're already at capacity, already running on fumes. And suddenly, something so small feels like too much to carry.

That's when the tears come or the frustration spills out. And then the guilt follows, because you *know* it wasn't a big deal but it tipped the balance anyway. Those are the moments that remind me I need to pay attention. It isn't a sign that you've failed, it's a reminder that staying in survival mode just isn't sustainable and that something needs to change. Your body and mind are asking you to pay attention, telling you that you need rest, support, space to feel like *you* again. Because we can't care for others the way we want to if we're falling apart inside. And we can't be the parents or children we want to be if we've got nothing left to give.

And this is why realising and acknowledging that I'm a carer matters. Why talking about it matters. Because unless we name it and recognise it as that, no one else will. And if no one else sees the role and sees the realities of our day-to-day lives, then no one sees the need for help. For respite. For space. For support. If we want to be able to provide all that we do for our kids, for our families, we need to realise we need support too.

In recent years 'self-care' has become a bit of a buzzword. It used to be seen as spa days, pampering, a holiday, a bit of luxury – something not necessary but desirable. Now it's recognised as something we all need, something we *deserve*, in order to live fuller, healthier, more balanced lives. We recognise how important it is to meet our own needs, to discover what lights us up and brings us joy. And I fully support this. But when you're a full-time carer, self-care often becomes a lot more basic than that. It's not a yoga session and a green smoothie, it might just be eating a meal while it's still warm. The number of times I've longed to just sit down and eat my dinner without being interrupted five times by Jude. Or to be able to have a shower. There have been many days, especially during the school holidays, where that's just not been an option. I can't leave Tommy or Jude alone, unattended, and by the time they finally fall asleep, I'm too exhausted and too worried the noise of the shower might wake them up. And as for sleep, every time I open up my phone it feels like I'm bombarded with facts about how important it is. How if we want to stay healthy we need at least seven hours' sleep a night. But for many of us, this part of our lives is completely out of our control. I can't go to bed before Jude or Tommy do, no matter how tired I am. Most evenings, I'm battling sleep, trying to stay awake until they finally settle. And when they do, I have to force my body to shift from 'on' to 'off' as quickly as possible, to squeeze in as many hours as I can before they, or now my dad too, wake up again.

In a schedule like this, self-care is hard to come by. One of the biggest challenges in full-time caring is the realisation that the rest of your world doesn't just stop because you've reached full capacity. Your responsibilities don't pause. The world doesn't slow down. There's no allowance made for the fact you're looking after a child who needs you every waking moment or an elderly parent whose health is in decline. And often as parents and carers we feel like we have to do everything ourselves. That no one else will understand or be able to look after our kids the way that we do. That our kids won't be comfortable with anybody else during the weekends or the school holidays. Especially when they're non-speaking. How could they tell us if something was wrong? Or if they didn't like the person who we'd entrusted their care to? Our kids are quite vulnerable, so we're often too scared to take the risk.

There's also an element of guilt. Somewhere inside we feel that we should be the one looking after them 24/7. We chose to be parents, so we have to be the ones who go through everything with them. But the reality is, most other parents have support. Their kids go on playdates, sleepovers, stay with grandparents and aunts and uncles. During school holidays they go to camps and clubs. It's something most children want to do, so it's seen as a normal part of their childhood. But it also gives the parents a break, a chance to do things as a couple, go and meet friends, have an early night or even go away for a weekend. A chance to do all the regular things that adults do, without the guilt or judgement.

I'd argue we carers need a break just as much, if not more. The problem is we don't often have many realistic options. Whether that's family who can help or camps and clubs that would actually work for our kids. So we have to look elsewhere.

We've had carers involved with Tommy and Jude since Jude was four and Tommy one. At first, we found someone locally who had worked in a nursery and who was keen to learn about working with kids with additional needs. While I was at work, Victoria helped Charlotte with the boys, who absolutely loved her, and for a few years she became part of our family. When Tommy was ready to start school she moved on, and we found various people who helped out here and there after school or at weekends, gradually taking over the role that my mum and dad had been filling as they were increasingly physically unable to look after the boys. Then we found two incredible carers for Tommy. First came Caz and then Jody, both teaching assistants from school who had worked in his class. Each Saturday he spends the day with them and their families, enabling him to access social opportunities he might never have had. He's become close friends with their daughters, who've helped guide him and who he's been happy to learn from. They've helped lead him outside of his comfort zone, as he goes ice skating, on rollercoasters, visits farms, goes to the cinema, bowling, trampolining. He can't wait to spend time with them every Saturday, and I'm more than happy for him to go with them. They've given me, and Charlotte, some breathing space to keep juggling everything that we do, whether that's for me to work or visit my mum or for Charlotte to do things with her girls. We'd truly be lost without them.

So I know first hand how important support is and how much we need to extend that circle of care so that it's not always falling on our shoulders. But when it comes to my parents I've been more reluctant to do so. It took me a long time to seek or accept any support for my mum. In fact, we'd only just started having carers come into their house to help and my mum had just started attending a day centre a couple of times a week, when my dad got ill and everything changed again. Since then, for a while I had some support one or two mornings a week for my dad, but I ended up cancelling it. It felt as though it wasn't making much difference, as I was at home a lot of the times they'd come, and I was having to cancel them throughout the school holidays as Jude and Tommy were unsettled by the presence of unfamiliar carers in the house. But I know deep down that this is something I need to address. I can't keep doing it all by myself. And caring for my dad is only going to get harder, more physically demanding, more emotionally draining.

The decline is hard to watch. The way I can see my dad's memory, his grasp of reality, starting to fade, just like it did with my mum. Some days he's sharp and with it, and other days he forgets what time it is, forgets what we've just said or imagines things that aren't really there. He's started repeating himself more often. I know where this is heading and that knowledge sits heavy. It also makes me angry that I don't have the space to process any of it properly. There's always something to do, someone to support. If I start to feel emotional, I have to put those feelings back in a box. There's no time to fall apart.

This inability to process what's going on with my dad is a part no one sees. One that's hard to explain and that I avoid talking about. Sometimes I worry that all this stress, the anxiety, the exhaustion of the last few years, will be what I remember most about him. Not the holidays we went on when I was a kid. Not the Sunday dinners. Not the years of love, laughter and everything they did for me. Just this. The slow fading away. Moments that are so surreal it doesn't feel possible that they're the same people. I hate that thought. Because they gave me so much. They loved me so well. And I don't want the last few years to eclipse all of that. It's a fear I carry quietly. The thought that maybe, by doing everything I can to care for everyone, I've started to lose sight of everything that came before.

I've seen for myself when I was caring for my mum how close I came to breaking point. Trying to wrestle with all the emotions, combined with a lack of sleep and never being able to fully relax. There have been times over the last year where I've felt that familiar tension, known that I'm pushing myself to the very limit. I keep telling myself it will be OK, to keep going, but I know one day it won't be. Maybe I'm burying my head in the sand a little. But some days I feel like I don't have it in me to go through this all over again, this time with my dad. To explain to various professionals, social care and carers all that he needs, all the different challenges he faces each day, all against the backdrop of Tommy, Jude and their needs. I don't want more people in our lives, even though I know how special and important those who have helped Tommy and Jude are. I want it to be manageable for just a little bit longer. But I know that at some point I need to let other people in, let them shoulder some of the care.

A few years ago I heard a quote that's stuck with me ever since.

> Taking care of yourself doesn't mean me first.
> It means me too.

It sounds simple, obvious even. But when you're a carer, especially a parent too, it's one of the hardest things to believe. Because when someone you love needs you, it's easy to feel like everything else can wait. Your meals. Your sleep. Your exercise. Your social life. Your dreams. Your health. Your happiness.

But I've come to understand that if I don't make space for myself, even in small ways, there won't be much left to give. The oxygen mask analogy is regularly used in the parent/carer world. When you're on a plane and they go through the safety guidelines, talking you through what to do if the oxygen masks come down in the cabin, they tell you to put your own mask on first before helping others. You're no help to others if you run out of oxygen yourself. Which also rings true of caring. If we don't put our own masks on, we're going to burn out, we're going to get sick, and we're not going to be able to look after those we love and care about so much.

Of course, while I'm good at saying this to others and reminding fellow parents how important it is to look after themselves, actually doing it myself is a different story. I can manage four people's medications, appointments, routines and daily needs but forget to take a multivitamin for myself. I can make sure everyone's where they need to be, that the house is stocked with everyone's particular food preferences, the iPads are charged and the school uniforms ready each morning and still forget to drink enough water most days.

So now I try to make a point of doing something for myself every day, even if it's tiny. No matter how hard our day has been, no matter how little sleep I've had, I commit to doing something for myself. It might be scrolling on my phone for twenty minutes, going for a walk along the river while the boys are at school, reading a few pages of a book with my breakfast or watching an episode of a box set late at night, once everyone's finally settled. Anything to give my brain a chance to switch off.

Sometimes, that's all there's room for. It's not much, but it helps me reset and reminds me I still exist outside of my responsibilities and makes me feel like I'm doing something for my life too. Meeting up with my oldest friends always helps as well. I sometimes only manage it a couple of times a year, but it makes the world of difference. In those moments I let down my barriers, I no longer feel numb.

And when I can, I prioritise exercise. Going to the gym clears my head and makes me feel stronger, physically and mentally. It's one of the only things I do where I feel like

I'm investing in my future, not just reacting to what's going on each day. With what I've seen my parents go through in the last few years, as well as other family members, the fear of dementia weighs heavy on my mind. Not just because of what it would mean for me but because I know how much Jude and Tommy will always need me. Sleep and exercise are two things that are important to our general health but have specifically been linked to decreased risks of dementia too. And so, when I lose control of both sleep and exercise, it stresses me out even more. When I make time for sleep or go to the gym or try to eat better, I'm not doing it to chase six-pack abs, I'm doing it because I need to be here, in good health, for as long as I possibly can. Looking after myself is one of the few ways I can hold that fear at bay.

But I'm also learning that self-care isn't a magical fix. There's no one night off that's going to make things better. What we need more of in this space isn't another inspirational quote or a list of things we should be doing. We need sustainable support and realistic tools. Along with permission to be human, to rest and to step away for a moment without feeling guilty. To be able to say 'this is too much' without feeling like we've failed.

And finally, I know that I have made this sound hard – because it is. But I also know how easy it is for people to look in from the outside and see only the challenges and miss the joy, and I am aware how damaging it can be when all people hear are the hard parts. I never want anyone to pity Jude or Tommy – or me. I never want people to think our life is sad. I want them to see what I see: the love that fills our home, the laughter, the beauty in the small moments. But to understand that this doesn't mean it's easy. Both things can be true. This life can be full of happiness *and* full of hard moments. Caring can be challenging, exhausting and the most rewarding, fulfilling thing I'll ever do. I can want to do it all *and* still need help. I can love my boys with every part of me *and* still need a break.

We're not meant to do this alone. There are thousands of families out there just like mine. Just like yours. We need support. We need community. We need people who understand the realities of this life, not just the pretty parts we manage to post online on the better days. We need a way to care for ourselves without feeling like we've let anyone down.

So here's what I want you to know – and what I need myself to remember too. If you're tired, it doesn't mean you're weak. If you're overwhelmed, it doesn't mean you're failing. If you've lost touch with who you are outside of caring, you're not alone in feeling that way.

You're doing more than most people could ever imagine. And you deserve to be supported on this journey too. If we're going to make this life sustainable, we can't do it alone. We need rest. We need help. We need space for joy. Because caring isn't just what we do for others. It's something we have to learn to do for ourselves too.

17

Becoming an Adult

There's something surreal about standing next to your son and realising he's now the same height as you. I feel like I closed my eyes for the merest moment and Jude has transformed into this large teenager. One minute I was crouched beside him, teaching him to walk or carrying him up the stairs after he'd fallen asleep in the car. The next, we're shoulder to shoulder in the kitchen, as I try to guide him away from the fridge for the tenth time that day. I notice it every time I open the door of his school bus and we walk side by side back into the house. Every time he gets out of the shower and I wrap a towel around him, press my face against his and start to pat him dry. We now stand eye to eye.

His voice, though still limited to non-verbal sounds, is much deeper. His frame bigger. His presence heavier. It still shocks me when I help him get dressed for the day. He's wearing the same size clothes as me now, sometimes wearing my T-shirts, hoodies or shorts when I can't find one of his. He's not my little boy anymore. He's growing into a man.

But then, almost in the same breath, I see him struggle to communicate a basic need. See the look on his face when he doesn't understand the world around him. See how much he still needs support. That contrast lands hard.

Jude isn't a little boy anymore, not physically. But in many ways his needs haven't changed in the way most people expect them to. That's one of the most difficult parts of this stage of parenting. The outside world sees a young man who should be gaining independence, becoming more self-aware, figuring out who they are. Someone in the process of becoming an adult, with all that entails. But autism doesn't always follow that timeline. Jude still needs the same level of support he did when he was much younger. In some ways, he needs even more.

And that contrast, between appearance and ability, between expectation and reality, can be hard to carry. It's a new phase of life, and as with all the previous stages, we're learning to negotiate it as we go. As I write this we're right in the thick of puberty, which is confusing for any teenager. But for autistic teens, who already struggle with sensory overload, communication barriers and emotional regulation, it can feel like a full-blown storm.

The last year with Jude has been one of the most challenging. The mood swings. The outbursts. The growing intensity of his emotions. His body has been changing rapidly, and so has his strength. We have tried to explain to him what is happening, but I'm not sure how successful it's been. He's really struggled emotionally, at times he's been all over the place, and you can see he doesn't understand why.

After some blood tests, we also had to go through a medication change. This seemed to spark a surge in testosterone, and life changed very quickly. When Jude is struggling I seem

BECOMING AN ADULT

to take the brunt of his frustrations. One day, completely out of the blue, he had a huge meltdown and became really aggressive towards me as we were driving home. I had to pull over to the side of the road three times during a twenty-minute journey to try to escape his fury and keep us safe. By the time we got home we were both emotional wrecks. It was a switchover day, and he was going to Charlotte's house after our drive. I had to go and ask her to come and get him out of the car, knowing he'd be much calmer for her.

As he went across the road with her, sobbing but calming down, my heart shattered. Again. My left arm was covered in blood from the scratches he had made as he leaned forward into the front of the car. My neck and cheek were bleeding too. I couldn't understand it. We'd had such a lovely twenty-four hours, and he'd been so happy, dancing to the music as we began our drive home. Then, everything had turned. We hadn't had a moment anything like that for nearly two years. As I shuffled off home, waiting for Tommy to come over, I tried to piece together what might have triggered it but was left none the wiser. My arm stung, but my heart was what was really hurting.

I hoped it was just a blip, a one-off, and that we would get back on track. Instead, over the next six months it got worse and worse. I seemed to become a trigger for Jude. Every interaction was tense, and I was constantly walking on eggshells, just hoping he wouldn't explode. He'd go to school happy, spend time at his mum's house happy, a little more tense than usual but happy and then let it all out with me.

The shift in Jude's size and power had also changed the dynamic. Now, there were moments when the physical side of caregiving became intimidating. I'm not proud to admit it, but I became afraid around him. At the same time, my heart broke for him, that he was going through all of these emotions he couldn't control. Because Jude still has such a high level of support needs, it made life incredibly difficult. He wanted to just be left alone, but he also needed me multiple times a day. Tasks that he needs support with, such as teeth brushing or hair washing, became near impossible. Every interaction would be tense, him trying to keep it together, me trying to meet his needs as quickly and quietly as I possibly could. He would bubble over multiple times a day, the meltdowns returning to a level we hadn't seen for many years.

We tried to spend more time apart, Charlotte stepping in and even coming across the road at times, to take me out of the firing line. But with Tommy expecting to stick to his regular routines and not wanting to risk ruining all the progress we'd made with their relationship, we tried to keep to our usual set-up as much as possible.

That summer, things got even worse. Sleep disintegrated and Jude would be awake until 4 a.m. most nights, running on four or five hours of broken sleep. Walks became too much and drives felt too risky, so we became housebound. Even Charlotte's house, which had always been a safe haven, became a place of stress. The bond Jude and I had spent years building felt like it was slipping through my fingers. And I didn't know how to stop it. From April to September it felt like the clock had rewound eight years. Only this time, Jude was my size and that made everything harder.

It's not a subject that's easy to talk about, but how do you cope when your child is repeatedly physical towards you? Not just once, during a meltdown where the trigger was obvious but over and over again. And you have to keep putting yourself in that situation multiple times a day, because they're your child and you're the one who looks after them. This was difficult enough when Jude was six, nine, twelve but is a whole different ball game now he's becoming a man who's the same size as me. And when your child is struggling, when they're upset multiple times a day, physically lashing out at you or themselves, it's incredibly difficult to find the joy. I found myself slipping that summer, dark thoughts circling my mind, blaming myself, even though deep down, after all these years and experiences we'd been through, I knew it wasn't my fault.

And the hardest part? Jude couldn't tell us what was going on. That's one of the most painful parts of caring deeply for someone who can't communicate their inner world. You're left guessing, wondering, worrying. People around you might say it's puberty, hormones, a surge in testosterone. And maybe they're right. But that doesn't make it easier. Because then what? You just wait and hope it passes? How long do you wait? Six months? A year? What if it doesn't pass?

What if this is the new normal?

After five months of outbursts, we could wait no longer and demanded a new solution from CAMHS. Jude's medication plan was clearly not working, and puberty or not, we needed to do something before he hurt himself. And, after multiple emergency meetings, a change in medication was decided. The removal of risperidone, which had been for health reasons, clearly hadn't been adequately replaced. Finally, they reached an agreement and we began a combination of aripiprazole and sertraline. Within a couple of weeks, once the medications had reached the required dose within his body, there was a huge change. The meltdowns reduced, the intensity dropped and slowly his anxiety began to fade. Jude began to trust me again and our bond started to improve once more.

As we pushed for support that summer, as we sat in meetings and demanded a change in Jude's medication, there was a profound fear quietly haunting me, one I was too scared to say out loud at the time.

What if they decided we couldn't cope?

Because I've read the stories. I've spoken to the families this has happened to. I know what can happen when the professionals decide they need to take over. When a young person in crisis is sectioned under the Mental Health Act 'for their safety'. When they're placed in an inpatient setting designed for containment, not care. Somewhere that doesn't fully understand autism and learning disabilities and where these adults often deteriorate and have traumatic experiences.

There are thousands of autistic adults in inpatient settings in the UK right now. Many of them with learning disabilities. Many of them have been locked away for five years or more. And their parents, people just like me, with stories just like ours, are still fighting to bring them home.

That's the worst-case scenario for families like ours. That fear of asking for support and instead having your child taken away. That fear that someone will misinterpret your cry for help as a sign you've failed. That someone will see aggression or self-harm and make a decision without understanding what's really going on.

BECOMING AN ADULT

Last summer, as I sat with my darkest thoughts, that was the outcome that scared me most. That I might lose Jude. Not because I'd given up or walked away. Not because I didn't care. But because I'd cared so much, fought so hard and then finally admitted we needed help, only to be misunderstood. That's not something I ever thought I'd have to worry about when I became a parent.

Thankfully, that wasn't our story. The change in medication quickly brought about a sense of calm and Jude began to settle. As the red mist started to clear, we began to connect again. Jude returned to looking me in the eye and wanting to communicate with me, and the sense of trust started to come back. We rebuilt slowly, without pressure or expectation. It was in the small things, being able to help him get dressed without incident, walking with me to the car, letting me sit next to him for a few moments, listening to me reciting some of his favourite lines from *Mickey Mouse Clubhouse*. These were all tiny signs that the storm had passed. For now.

We're not quite back to where we once were, but maybe we're not supposed to be. Jude's older now. Different. More independent in some ways, more withdrawn in others. He wants me and his mum around less than before, which I guess is true of most teenagers when they reach this age. It's a hard balance to get right when he has such high support needs, but we try to give him as much space as he needs and step in only when necessary. Our relationship has shifted. It's not always playful or light anymore, sometimes it's quiet, practical, even distant. Some days our relationship feels more carer than parent. It hurts to write that. But most days, we find the warmth again and our days are happy once more.

Jude communicates lovingly with his eyes again, and my mental health is improving too.

For a while I was worried we might not find our way back, but now there's trust again and safety. And after all that we've been through, that's enough right now.

One of the scariest shifts in adolescence is realising that the people around you don't always see your child in the same way anymore. I still see Jude and Tommy as my boys, childlike, innocent, full of love and joy. The rest of the world doesn't see that. They see size, movement and behaviours. They see young men and all the expectations they have of them. And they judge.

I've lost count of the number of times I've been out in public with one of the boys, trying to help them regulate, trying to keep them safe and felt everyone looking at us with a mixture of confusion and judgement. They don't see autism or overwhelm, they see a teenager being loud, moving awkwardly, different to what they'd expect and assume something's wrong. When your child is big and visibly distressed, people don't ask questions, they stare, they cross the street, they judge. Some might think you're being forceful and a bad parent. Some might think your child is dangerous.

It was hard enough when the boys were younger, but when that sweet, innocent little autistic boy becomes a big, out-of-control autistic man, that can be dangerous. I've heard too many stories, of the police being called, of situations escalating because someone assumed a grown autistic adult was being 'aggressive' or 'disruptive', when really they were just scared or dysregulated. Stories of restraint, of trauma, of being misunderstood in ways that leave scars, both physical and mental. My American followers have shared stories with me of autistic adults being shot by police due to those misunderstandings, and I'm grateful we don't face the same risks here.

But there are other dangers. During the summer holidays a few years ago, Tommy and I were on our regular river walk, about to follow the route we'd been taking for the last four years, when he suddenly pulled away in a different direction. Intrigued, I went with it, trying to understand where he wanted to go. He went the other way through town, and I assumed he wanted to go to the supermarket, but he kept going past it. We crossed the railway bridge (I realised later that this was the first time we'd ever done that) and continued, Tommy giggling all the way. He wanted to go faster, further, and I quickly saw that what had initially seemed fun was at risk of spiralling out of control. We reached the main road, and I tried to hold his hand a little more firmly. At this he dropped to the floor, rolled, leapt up and started running. I caught him up, my heart pounding, worried about the busy road and the cars zooming past. I tried to convince him to go back with me the other way, but he wouldn't have it. We were at a crossroads in more ways than one.

What do you do in a situation like this? Your twelve-year-old, with very little safety awareness, has become dysregulated and wants to run along a busy road. What I wanted to do was scoop him up and carry him to somewhere safe, where he could run as much as he liked. But at twelve Tommy was far too big and strong for that to be an option.

My attempts to convince him to turn back were met by

him lashing out at me, so I decided it was safest to keep going. I positioned myself between him and the road, on red alert, hoping I'd be fast enough if he veered towards the cars. All I kept thinking was that if I could just give him a sense of control, help him to regulate, we might make our way back to our normal route and safety. And it worked. Eventually. By the time we made it home our usual forty-five-minute walk had taken nearly three hours. There had been tears, screaming, long periods of lying on the pavement, climbing, jumping, running and lots of hitting. We were both exhausted. I don't think I'd ever felt so scared, my brain constantly scanning through all the worst possible outcomes. My nervous system was shot to bits. My tears came once he was in the shower, and I thought they might never stop.

Once our day was back on track and the adrenaline had worn off, my mind replayed the morning over and over, trying to figure out what had happened, what I could have done better. I had been too scared to take my eyes off Tommy for a second to even take my phone out of my pocket and call for help. But who would I have called?

And I thought of what anyone passing us had seen that morning and what they might have thought. I was actually surprised nobody had got involved, either through a desire to help or a fear of what was going on. At some points I must have looked like a man trying to kidnap a terrified child. At others it must have been obvious how scared I was of the passing traffic, literally lifting Tommy up and away from the road. I wondered what would have happened if someone had called the police. Would they have been understanding? Would they have had any knowledge about autism and learning disabilities? Or would they have made an incredibly stressful situation even worse?

Luckily, since then, we've had very few moments like this. Nothing even close to how stressful that day was. But I know one day it might happen again. That day has stayed at the forefront of my mind. It showed me how vulnerable we are – both our kids and us as carers – to the physical dangers but also to the misinterpretation. I'm aware of how easily my actions, born out of love, instinct and desperation, could be misread by strangers or the authorities. And how dangerous that misunderstanding could be.

As we move into adulthood, I know there might be more moments like this ahead and that fear of being misunderstood, those worries over safety out in public and of things spiralling beyond your control, becomes part of what you carry day to day. Quietly but constantly. It's yet another layer of what it means to love and protect children and adults whom the world doesn't always understand.

It's one of the hardest parts of this stage, knowing that a large chunk of the population out there don't understand autism or learning disabilities and will look at Tommy and Jude differently now they're becoming adults and are no longer cute little boys, humming and flapping excitedly.

With Jude being so dependent and spending most of his time at home, we've not felt it too much with him. But Tommy, who's out and about far more often, stands out already. He's fourteen but tall for his age, and he still loves the things most kids outgrow by six or seven. Soft play. Swings and slides. Rides at the fair designed for younger children. Places where the rest of the kids are a good head shorter than him. And even though I love seeing him happy, part of me quietly dreads the day when someone questions whether he belongs there. When someone decides his joy makes them uncomfortable. When he's aged out of places that were never built with someone like him in mind. One of his favourite places to go on a weekend is Marsh Farm, but that is specifically for kids and their parents. One day soon he's going to be too old, and I don't know how he's ever going to process that.

I've already noticed a difference in people's reactions at the supermarket. Tommy and I go together once a week, and it's one of his favourite things to do. Once upon a time a supermarket was a no-go zone: too overwhelming, too many exciting things, too many people and Tommy with no concept of not being able to take everything he wants or the social cues that people follow. He'd drop to the floor in the middle of the aisle, kick and scream. Then he'd be up and off again, racing around the supermarket as I desperately chased behind him, apologising to people we passed. We've come a long way since those days. I never would have imagined I'd find so much joy in going to a supermarket with Tommy as I do now. Over time we've developed our routines, helping Tommy understand he can choose different items (with some limits!). At first he couldn't process that I might also need to buy some things for all of us or for the house. He only wanted *his* items in the basket, he didn't want black bin bags, prawns or toilet roll. Now he happily lets me shop alongside him, carrying the basket or pushing the trolley. He understands when I tell him we need to get Grandad's dinner too and helps me get what we need. He scans the items at the self-checkout and helps me put them into the bag, which he carries back to the car. It's huge progress, but there are still the odd moments of stress or overexcitement that cause him to sprint or hop around the store. And people stare more, tut more. They see a growing teenager who 'should' know better. One day they'll see a fully grown man hopping. One who might bump into their trolley or step in front of them to grab his sausage rolls. I hope they're kind to him.

The supermarket has been an invaluable place for Tommy to gain and develop life skills and promote his independence. When we think of independence as an adult, we think of getting a job, learning to drive or moving out of the family home. But, after seventeen years of parenting my boys, my definition of it and what it means for us has changed entirely. And that doesn't make it any less meaningful. In fact, in many ways, it's even more powerful, because I know how much we've had to fight for every step. For us, independence is more about the basic life skills that make a difference to Tommy's and Jude's daily lives. And it looks different for each of them.

It's about Tommy being able to make himself his own drink. Taking the Robinson's Summer Fruits (because that's all he'll drink), pouring it into his cup, mixing it with water from the tap and screwing the lid back onto his bottle. For Jude it's about him finding his bottle and bringing it to me, letting me know he wants a drink.

It's about them learning to wash themselves in the shower, rubbing the shower gel all over their body and rinsing it off. It's about learning to dry themselves properly with a towel. This is still a work in progress.

It's Tommy being able to use the TV remote controls, navigating his favourite apps to find exactly what he wants to watch, even typing out the show names in the A–Z search. It's Jude handing me the remote control to tell me he wants the programme changed. Standing in front of the TV and tapping on the tile of the show he wants to watch as I scroll through them.

It's being able to choose what clothes they want to wear, whether they want to wear shorts or trousers, a hoodie or no hoodie. It's being able to get dressed with less assistance. Being able to use the toilet independently.

It's Tommy taking the ice cream from the freezer, getting a bowl, using a spoon to take a couple of scoops, putting the ice cream back and then putting his empty bowl and spoon into the sink. It's Jude getting the biscuits out of the cupboard and handing them to me to open.

For us, those moments have become just as big as any driving test or university offer. They're skills that are going to have a big impact on Tommy's and Jude's everyday life and ensure that their needs are being met. It also gives them the satisfaction and sense of accomplishment in being able to do these things themselves and not being reliant on me, Charlotte or others for every single thing. They are moments of celebration and connection, and they fill me with pride.

It's not the kind of independence that I once imagined for either of them as they transition into adulthood. We don't know exactly what the future holds, but we do know that Jude and Tommy will need lifelong support. They will never be fully independent – and that's OK. At some point in the journey you come to understand that and make peace with it. The goals shift to helping them become as independent and happy as possible. A goal we'll forever keep working towards. And when we see them do something new, something we once thought might never come, that's progress. That's hope.

As we move towards the next stage, the worry is knowing that support doesn't necessarily grow with your child. In fact, for some it disappears. After spending years battling the system to find the right school, the right support, for disability benefits, suddenly your child becomes an adult and everything changes.

We've started transition meetings for Jude with his teachers, his social worker and his healthcare professionals. Health and social care will both move to adult services shortly. There will be new people who will need to get to know the boys, who we will have to advocate to and trust to put the right support in place. Jude and Tommy will be at their school until they're nineteen, and then it will be time to leave. Which in itself is terrifying. By then they will have spent fifteen years of their life going to the same place, being around the same classmates and teachers, and then suddenly it will all end. I remember leaving my secondary school at sixteen after five years of being there and starting at college. I had friends going with me, and I had consciously made that choice, going to open days and choosing my subjects and that was still a nerve-wracking transition – exciting but scary too.

How do you prepare someone for that who is non-speaking and struggles with understanding language? Someone who shows no signs of understanding the future and who lives very much in the here and now? How to explain to Jude that one day, school will end and he'll never go back. He'll never see most of those familiar people again and will have to go somewhere completely new. New buildings, new support staff, new people around him. How do we help him make sense of that?

It's a question that looms large for Tommy too. So much of his world is built around routine, structure and predictability. A change that big, walking away from a school he loves, staff who know him and classmates who've grown up beside him, feels seismic.

And that's all before we even get to what comes after. From what I understand, in our area we'll receive a joint package of support from education and social care up until they're twenty-five. That might include two or three days at a specialist college, combined with access to day centres for adults with learning disabilities. Or, some of that funding can be used to support one-to-one personal assistants to take them out into the community.

These are big decisions. And right now, I honestly don't know what the best path is. We'll visit colleges, explore the options, talk with their teachers and try to make the best choice we can. But part of me wishes Jude and Tommy could help shape those decisions too. That we could sit down, talk it all through and figure out together how to help them follow their dreams. Instead, it's a stage filled with fear and uncertainty once more. One where the weight of whatever choice we make feels impossibly heavy.

When Jude and Tommy move into adult social services we will have to learn to navigate another system, another set of professionals and workers, all who have the power to make incredibly important decisions about my boys' lives. I'm well aware of how limited funding and support is, how stretched services are. I'm also aware of how quickly things can change, especially within the current financial climate. Disability support seems to be one of the areas that is the first to suffer when budgets are cut, and the decade of austerity has caused a lot of long-term damage. I've heard good stories about the transition to adulthood and what's been made available. I've also heard horror stories about the lack of support and how much a person has struggled with all of the change, even the odd horrific article that crops up every now and again about adults with disabilities being mistreated by carers or care homes. Honestly, it's terrifying to have this on our horizon.

But while I hold all this fear, I'm fortunate that I'm also exposed to a lot of positives. Firstly through some of the accounts I follow and talk to online, who share their own stories about adulthood. I can see how complex, yet how beautiful it can be. There are countless different set-ups, different experiences, but ones that show how kind and accepting other people can be. I receive DMs from followers who want to share a little about their story, about what life is like for them. I see how it can all work out.

Sometimes I let my mind drift and I start to imagine what a future like that could hold for my boys. I picture a warm afternoon. I'm sitting in the garden. Tommy is in our swimming pool splashing away (well, this is a dream, right; maybe an XL paddling pool if I'm more realistic). He's hopping on one leg, flicking the water with his hands, loving the sensory experience.

Inside the house, two different songs are playing at once, Ed Sheeran from one speaker, the *Special Agent Oso* theme tune blaring from Jude's iPad. He's standing with the iPad up against his ear, rocking from side to side.

Both boys are in and out of the house, not necessarily spending much time together but comfortable that the other one is there. Jude isn't anxious or upset when a wet Tommy goes running past. We're all together but everyone has space. Jude is smiling, humming to the music, Tommy is laughing loudly, jumping into the pool. I'm sitting back, ever watchful but more relaxed than before. Perhaps even reading a book while always keeping an eye and an ear out. I've found a happy medium somewhere between a hypervigilant state and carefree. We're home, we're safe, I can relax. Confident that we can spend this time together without it all going wrong. I'm present. Grateful.

And that vision feels possible. Hopeful but possible. Not too far out of reach. It's a version of adulthood that doesn't look like anyone else's but one that works for us. One built on love, not expectation.

And if we can get there, if we can live a version anything close to what I've just described, that will be more than enough.

18

What Comes Next?

There's a thought that creeps in every now and again. It happens when I have a quiet moment in the car or on the train to London. It might arrive in the aftermath of a meltdown or at the end of the happiest of days. It can keep me awake at night when I finally get the chance to sleep. It's a part of parenting that no one prepares you for. Not something you ever imagine. It doesn't come up in baby books. It's not written about in any leaflets you get after an autism diagnosis. And it's not something the vast majority of our friends and family will ever have to consider. Yet, it's never far from the minds of parents like us.

What's going to happen when I'm no longer here?

It's a thought that weighs heavily on my heart and my mind. I can feel my chest tighten whenever I think about it. And when those thoughts begin, it's easy for them to start to spiral:

What if I get sick?
Who will be there for them?
Who will understand them like I do?
What will Jude think? What will Tommy feel?

LOVE NEEDS NO WORDS

Will they understand I didn't choose to leave them?

I try to push it aside, tell myself to stay focused on the here and now. Tell myself that it's pointless to worry about something that's so far off in the future. But the worry doesn't care. It comes back time and time again. It's not logical, but it is natural. Because there's no guarantee; what if it's *not* far off? What if there's *not* lots of time?

Becoming a parent, especially to children like Jude and Tommy, makes you confront your own mortality in a way you never expect. You realise how fragile time is. How little control you really have. How high the stakes are when someone else depends on you for everything.

Because there's a part of me that knows I'm the one who understands their worlds best. I know the look on Jude's face when he's about to get overwhelmed and I know what I have to do in that moment, the songs that will help and how to create the safe space he needs to help him calm. I know how Tommy needs to sit in the car for five minutes before he's ready to walk into the house and how important, how critically important, his routine is for him to have a successful day; that the timing, the flow, the rhythm of his day, all of it matters. These aren't things you just write down and pass on. How could anyone absorb the thousand tiny details that make up their lives, the ones we've learned, slowly, through years of trial and error and a deep love that keeps me going on the hardest of days. And while I can plan for the logistics, put systems in place, write instructions, make lists, I can't plan for the connection. I can't pass on the feeling of knowing, deep in your gut, that something is off, that a storm is coming, that they're not OK, even before they show you they're not.

WHAT COMES NEXT?

That kind of knowing can't be taught. It comes from living it, day after day, year after year. It comes from being their person, from knowing them inside out. And when I imagine someone else stepping into that role, no matter how well meaning, no matter how highly trained or loving they might be, I wonder if they'll see what I see. Hear what I hear. Feel what I feel. Because I'm not just looking after them, I'm also translating them to the world. And the thought of someone misreading them, misunderstanding them, even with the best intentions, it breaks me.

When Jude was two, I was worried he wouldn't speak. Now, as he approaches adulthood, I still think about communication, but I also worry whether the people around him understand the ways he *does* communicate. Whether they'll know how to listen to him when I'm not there to help interpret. When Tommy was little, I worried about his sensory needs and how they'd impact his daily life. Now I think about what that will mean in adulthood. How he'll navigate public spaces when he's trying to self-regulate but is the size of a fully grown man. What will happen when he still wants to go down the slide in the kids' playground? Will the world make space for him if I'm not there to seek it out?

Most parents expect to raise their children for around eighteen years. Then slowly, gradually, their children become more independent and eventually the roles shift. They go out into the world, forging their own path. And we hope that in twenty to thirty years or so, they'll come back and help support us in the final years of our lives; a thought that's prominent in my mind as I've done exactly that for my own parents.

As parents of autistic children with high support needs,

we're not working towards letting go, we're preparing to hold on. For decades. Maybe for life. No one ever stops being a parent, but we will also be carers long past the point we expected to be.

And then, we have to plan for the years that come *after* that. We're not just raising our children for twenty or thirty years, we're also trying to imagine the twenty or thirty years that follow, when we're not here anymore or not physically able to meet their needs. When someone else will need to step into our shoes and help them carry out their daily routines, meet their needs, be their world.

For many people, retirement is something to look forward to as they get older: the daily freedom, the travel they'll get to enjoy, perhaps a chance to pursue new interests or old hobbies. For parents like us, retirement, reaching that kind of age, fills us with dread. I've spoken to so many parents who share my fear, imagining a time when they might not be there to help their child survive. It's not just about toilet training or sleep routines or EHCP reviews, it's about whether your child will be OK when you're not here to fight for them anymore. We joke with each other, half-serious, half-desperate: 'We need to live forever.'

Because for us, parenting isn't an eighteen-year chapter. It's a lifelong story. One we're still living and writing but already trying to imagine how it will continue when we're no longer a part of it. And that's what makes it so hard. It's knowing there may come a day when Jude and Tommy are still here, still needing support and I'm not going to be there to give it. It's knowing we might leave behind our children who don't understand where we've gone. Who still need our love, our patience, our connection and will one day be without all that. That's the part that breaks me.

The truth is, no one else will ever know them the way we do. No one else will ever care for them or fight for them as intensely as we do. Yet somehow we need to find people who will. Who we can rely on to care for and support our children long after we're no longer around. It's hard to talk about, even to think about. Because how do you plan for a future you don't want to imagine? And yet . . . we have to. Love isn't about pretending the hard things don't exist, it's about facing them anyway. Planning for the future is frightening but what I've reluctantly come to learn over the years, and am still working on, is that *not* planning for the future is even scarier.

For years, I assumed my boys would always live with me. It wasn't even something I questioned, it just seemed obvious. I couldn't imagine trusting anyone else to fully understand their needs or look after them when they are so vulnerable and need so much support. It's hard saying that word out loud: 'vulnerable'. But that's what Jude and Tommy are and will still be when they're adults. Vulnerable. Reliant on others for so many facets of their day-to-day life and care. I told myself that keeping them with me and with their mum was the safest, kindest thing we could do. And there's some truth in that. The depth of knowledge we have as parents, the connection, the instinct, the lived experience, the fierce desire to keep them safe, it can't just be replicated.

But over time, I also realised that the idea of them living with me forever was less about love and more about fear. Because what if I can't do it? What if my body starts to give out before they stop needing physical support? What happens if I'm seventy and still helping one of them shower or manage a meltdown? What if something suddenly happens to me and there's no plan in place? That's when that difficult shift in thinking began. Little by little, I started to realise that the 'forever' plan I'd been holding onto might not be what's best. For Jude, for Tommy, for me. For any of us. And, more importantly, it might not be sustainable.

I read a post from another parent once, talking about how they chose supported living for their son in his twenties. Not because they didn't want him at home but because they wanted to help him build a future with structure, with support, with space to grow. And they wanted to do so while they were still around to guide him through it, to keep a watchful eye and fully manage that transition. That stuck with me.

I know some people will feel deeply uncomfortable even contemplating that choice, vowing that their child will never leave their home and that they'll always look after them. I get it. A huge part of my heart feels the same way. But I also know deep down that it's not that simple. Because the alternative, that emergency move when I'm in my seventies or eighties, when I'm no longer able to manage physically or mentally, is terrifying. The thought of them going through that sudden upheaval, with no preparation and no familiar face beside them, is not one I can contemplate. My heart breaks at the thought of a fifty-five-year-old Jude or Tommy suddenly being taken into care because I can no longer look after them, having spent their whole life knowing nothing but living at home. How confusing and frightening that would be for them. Wouldn't it be better if those transitions happened with Charlotte and me by their side, rather than because we're no longer here?

WHAT COMES NEXT?

I've thought about it a lot over the last seven to eight years, especially when I've been unwell. I've had Covid, tonsilitis and the flu, and each time I've just had to carry on, because there was no alternative. I've got up and gone to the park with Tommy in order to stick to his routines. I've gone on the evening drives so that he doesn't get distressed. I've made every meal, showered them and helped them get dressed and in between lay down on the sofa to grab every minute of rest I could. I've been far from 100 per cent and just had to get on with it, which was doable for a day or two, knowing I'm going to recover. But what if it were something longer term? Because it's not just about ageing, it's about illness, injury, burnout. All the things we *don't* plan for until it's too late. Having been a carer for my own parents for the last six or seven years, I've seen first hand how quickly our health can change. Very quickly they both moved from being independent and able to help me with Tommy, to being very dependent on me to look after them. And that reality scares me. It makes me worry about my own long-term health, especially about dementia, and what that would mean.

And that's why building a support network, beyond me, beyond Charlotte, has gone from feeling optional to feeling absolutely essential. We can't do this alone. Not forever. Of course, that doesn't make it easy. Letting go of the idea of them always being under my roof isn't something I do lightly. It's not something I want to do. Saying it out loud feels wrong, even writing it here makes me worry what people will think of me.

There's a part of me that still clings to the idea that if I just stay healthy enough, strong enough, I can protect them forever. I can hold the world at bay. It's the main reason why I've been determined to improve my own mental and physical health over the last few years. I want to be as strong and fit as I can be for as long as I can be. Not just in order to get the most out of my life but largely because I want to be there for my boys.

But deep down, I know that living with me forever might not be fair on them. Or me. Because a good life for them isn't about being kept in a bubble. It's about being supported in a way that lets them feel safe, valued and understood. And one day, that might mean somewhere else. With someone else.

It's a phase of life that happens naturally for most adults in their twenties. It's a time to stand on their own two feet, leave the safety of home and make a path for themselves. And while that's not the path that lies ahead for my boys, it might make sense that their version of that journey begins in their twenties too.

I've seen other families like ours make it work. I've seen young adults in supported housing who are thriving. They still need plenty of support, the right support, it's just structured in a way that works for them. I've seen parents who were terrified of handing over the reins slowly find peace in knowing that their child has a team around them. I've listened to them talk about how they visit their kids daily or at weekends or sometimes less often depending how close by they live. How they still have a hands-on approach, are still highly involved in the decision making and the structure of their child's life; it's just that there are also others who help carry out that physical and emotional support on a daily basis.

WHAT COMES NEXT?

The right path will look different for everyone, and we're still no closer to making a definite decision. There's plenty of time, plenty of growth and change ahead of us in the years to come before we have to decide. But I know now that 'forever at home' doesn't have to be the only version of a happy life for my boys. It doesn't mean we're giving up. It's not because we want an easier life. It's about building something sustainable that lasts beyond me, beyond Charlotte. And I want to be part of that transition. I want to help Tommy and Jude feel safe, seen and supported, not handed off to a stranger in a moment of crisis.

So maybe letting go of the forever plan isn't about letting go at all. Maybe it's just about loosening the grip. Leaving space for new possibilities. And trusting that love doesn't have to mean doing everything alone. Because after seventeen years of being a dad I've realised that sometimes it's not our children who are afraid of the next step, it's us. And if I'm not careful, my fear of someone else stepping in, of someone else getting it wrong, could be the very thing that holds Tommy and Jude back from building a life that works for them. That's not the parent I want to be. I want to be brave enough to step aside if that's what helps them thrive. I see how well school supports them both; I see how much of a positive impact carers have had on their lives too. So I need to trust others, even when it scares me and not let my own fear be the reason they stay small. Because letting go of fear, just a little, can sometimes be the most loving thing we do.

This is where we're at right now. I've started to realise that loving Tommy and Jude isn't just about what I do today but also what I put in place for tomorrow – especially the tomorrows I might not be here for. It's not the fear of the unknown – that's always there – but the responsibility of preparing for it.

Charlotte and I are starting to talk about guardianship and who makes decisions if we no longer can. That alone is a huge responsibility, deciding who will speak on their behalf. Who will sit in a room and make decisions about housing, healthcare, finances, safety and support? Who will fight for them the way I do? Who will be there for the everyday things and the once-in-a-decade emergencies.

I hope when that time comes, there's family who will help. People who know Tommy and Jude already and aren't starting from scratch. I know Charlotte hopes deep down that her girls will take up the mantle when we no longer can, even if it's just overseeing their care. But she also knows that future is a long way off and a lot can happen in that time; they'll have their own lives and who knows where that will lead them. It's complex, just like all of these decisions are.

Preparing doesn't just mean choosing a person, it means creating a whole system: wills, trusts, care plans. These aren't easy conversations, and the truth is, I've avoided some of them for years. But there is help out there when it comes to navigating these systems, and we're going to be seeking professional advice. Things are a little more complicated as Charlotte and I are divorced but just like everything else we do for the boys, we'll figure it out together. We have been used to acting as lawyer, financial planner and strategist, while still being a carer, an advocate, a provider and a parent. Jude and Tommy are still going to be financially dependent on me and Charlotte

WHAT COMES NEXT?

for many years to come. While I know they will be entitled to some benefits when they become adults, I also know I'm going to have to continue to provide financially. And so in this respect too we will need a plan and a structure of what happens when one of us, and then both of us, are no longer here.

It's not easy. In fact, it's one of the hardest things I've had to think about. One that makes my stomach flip and makes me want to do anything but sort this out. Writing this chapter has made me confront a lot of thoughts and emotions I've been trying to bury deep inside. But it's also made me fully understand how important having these conversations and starting to plan really is.

For years I've written on my Stories About Autism page about the importance of staying in the present. The future is your enemy, the present is your friend. And for the most part, I really believe that. I needed to think that way, to process a lot of change. It allowed me to let go of a lot of the worries and enjoy the day-to-day moments. It helped me focus on the inchstones, the big smiles, the joy. But I realise now that we need a balance. The scary future isn't going to disappear just because I keep focusing on today. Not planning, not thinking about it, feels more irresponsible the more I consider it. I need more of a 'plan for the worst, hope for the best' approach.

Right now, there is no perfect plan. Just the slow, uncomfortable realisation that we need one, sooner rather than later. And even that, admitting that it's time, feels like a big step. We're still figuring out the questions, let alone the answers. But sharing our stories has made this feel more possible lately.

I'm not doing this completely alone. I have people in my life now who've already started walking this path. Other parents I've met through Stories About Autism, both online and locally. Families who are further ahead in the journey and willing to share what they've learned. People who've helped me see what supported living can actually look like. What guardianship really means. Who've helped me figure out what questions to ask and who to ask them to. They're helping to make the process feel less scary. Even the stories of struggle help me feel more prepared for what might lie ahead.

And through Stories About Autism, I've been lucky enough to connect with professionals too, people who can explain the legalities and the practical steps I need to take. The more I talk to others, the less overwhelming it feels. The more stories I hear, the more I realise there's no single right way but there are people willing to help you find *your* way.

The process works both ways. I'm aware that as we tread these steps, just as with every other phase and life event we go through, I'll be talking about it and sharing what I learn; discussing the processes, the deliberations and the options we have. I will share what I feel comfortable sharing about the choices we make. And that experience will help many families that are coming up behind us.

That matters. Because planning for a future like this shouldn't happen in isolation. It feels so much brighter thanks to the conversations we've had, thanks to our community and the connections we've made. It's better when we share what we're scared of, what we've learned and what we still don't know.

WHAT COMES NEXT?

A big part of this has been the launch of SAA Clothing. Since opening our SAA Clothing shop in 2024, I've also got to meet a whole new community of people and have these conversations in person. In December 2023, I launched SAA Clothing as an online brand. For years I'd wanted to create a clothing range that could help people feel more connected, that showcased positive messaging about autism and disability but that also looked cool, that you'd actually want to wear, wherever you were going. I had a dream of people seeing others wearing the brand at the park, at the school gates, on the bus or on holiday. That our designs would start conversations and help people feel less alone. In the same way that you spot someone wearing the shirt of the football team you support and realise you've got something in common, I hoped that's what we could bring our community. We launched with designs like Love Needs No Words, Neurodiverse Club and Never Alone, proud to wear our feelings on our chest. And it went crazy!

That December I worked eighteen-hour days right up to Christmas Eve, roping in friends wherever I could, desperately trying to get all our orders out in time for Christmas. By February we took the leap from an online business to opening a shop in our hometown of Burnham. The shop provided a space to wrap and ship our orders but also for connection, a space for families to visit and have conversations with me or our team. I soon got rid of the stockroom and turned it into a sensory room, wanting to make the experience more comfortable for anyone autistic who visited our store and to provide a safe space for behaviours that others might see as different. Soon I was taking on staff, all of whom are parent carers or are neurodivergent themselves, creating a working environment that suited them, whether that means adapting how we work or fitting around childcare issues or school meetings. Charlotte was our very first employee, I mean who knows our story better than her? And as we've grown we've added more from our local community. This summer we had an autistic teenager doing his work experience with us, and I hope that in the future we can provide more job opportunities for adults with learning disabilities too.

We've been to school fetes and festivals. We got a group of parent carers together for a Christmas wreath-making workshop. We've brought families together for days out and have seen them become friends. On World Autism Awareness Day we had lots of local businesses wearing our T-shirts, showing their support and desire to be allies. We did a talk at our local primary school teaching the children a little about autism and difference. And last summer we hosted our first SEND Fest, a festival specifically for families whose kids are autistic or have other additional needs. An event where you're surrounded by other people living similar lives. An event where you can relax, and not worry about being judged. Often, when companies organise anything SEN/autism-friendly they offer an hour at the beginning or end of the day. I've been to trampolining sessions like this with Jude and they were great, but it was always hit and miss because of how early they were. So we wanted to do something different. At the very end of the summer holidays, we hired Marsh Farm for the whole day and put on an event just for families like ours. Tickets sold out within a couple of hours. We had nearly 2,000 people come along, and it was a truly incredible

WHAT COMES NEXT?

day. Families travelled from all over the country, to meet other families and be in an environment where they felt accepted. Our kids flapped and splashed. Screamed and squealed. Flicked sand, hopped and bounced their way around the farm and nobody cared, nobody judged, everyone was free to be themselves. So many people shared stories with me that day, but one stood out to me more than the rest. A mum thanked me, telling me it was the only day out they'd managed in the whole of the six-week holiday. Life had been tough, isolating and now here they were having fun, feeling less alone. Not for the first time that day I choked back tears. Something so simple, so needed, just being able to feel like you're not alone. We immediately set up an event for Halloween and are making plans for a number of events next year. Maybe even across the UK.

It's only been eighteen months since SAA Clothing launched, but already it's turning into something much bigger than I could have dreamed of. That's what I'm most proud of, not the sales or numbers but the message we carry and the community we're building. A place where people feel seen. Where being neurodivergent isn't something to be hidden but embraced. A brand that celebrates difference and tells the world we belong. A brand that people are proud to wear, reaching right across the world.

Through the shop I have met autistic and disabled adults with various levels of support needs, along with their parents and their carers, and spoken about what adulthood is like for them. I've come to realise, just like everything else since Jude received his autism diagnosis, there's no one size fits all solution. Some adults live at home with their parents, some live in assisted living facilities, others in group home settings. Many of them have tried different things, fought for the support they deserve and figured out what the best possible solution is. Some adults need two-to-one support while out in the community, others live in a setting alongside other adults with similar needs and have a little support once or twice a day. And others stay at home with their parents.

One of the things that's helped over the past year is getting to know a local man called Laurence and seeing, first hand, what adulthood can look like for someone with support needs. Laurence is autistic and has Fragile X Syndrome. Since the start of 2025, he now works in our shop every Monday afternoon. He lives at home with his mum, supported by a team of brilliant personal assistants who help him access all the things he enjoys in the community. He's on a waiting list to move into a supported living facility where some of his friends already live, but for now, he's built a full, joyful life around the people and places that matter to him.

Every Monday, he walks into SAA Clothing with a huge smile. He chats to everyone, he's incredibly social and with help from his PA Ben, he unpacks deliveries, tidies the shelves, helps prepare orders for shipping and makes a perfect cup of tea for everyone on the team. Sometimes he even gets involved in our social media videos, which he loves. Followers love to see their parcel being labelled by Laurence as he loudly calls out their name and tells them their order is 'on its way'. Recently we celebrated his thirtieth birthday in the shop with a little party. After we mentioned it on our stories he got sent cards from all around the world. It seems our global community love sharing in Laurence's life too.

WHAT COMES NEXT?

Watching Laurence with Ben, seeing their relationship and the rhythm of their routine, fills me with something that all too often has been missing: *hope*. Because while it might not be the life I'd imagined for Jude or Tommy twenty years ago, it's still a good life. It's still full of meaning, connection and joy. I can see a community of people who see Laurence, value him, welcome him. And that's everything I could want for Tommy and Jude too.

I don't know whether they'll ever be interested in helping out at the shop. I don't know what their version of work or structure or contribution will look like. But spending time with Laurence has shown me that there are paths. There are options. There are people out there who get it and who are happy to support our kids in adulthood. If adulthood for Tommy and Jude is one where they're well supported and their days are filled with smiles and happy moments, then life will be good.

As I write this, I don't know exactly what the future holds. I don't have a polished plan. Maybe the shape of one will be in place by the time this book is published, but for now it's still a work in progress. Even so, I'm learning to keep moving forward without all the answers. Helped along by the community around us, a constant reminder that we don't have to do this alone.

And more than anything, I hope that whatever the future looks like, whoever is with my boys, whatever the set-up, they'll still have days full of what they love. Driving around with the music playing, feeling regulated, connected and safe. Moments of joy, moments full of laughter. Whether I'm in the driving seat or not.

19

Choosing Joy

The sound of Bruno Mars and a long, repetitive humming that could only be described as Jude's version of singing wakes me from my dreams. My mind slowly starts to stir, eyes opening as I reach for my phone. 7.30 a.m. Not bad, I must have managed six hours' sleep.

Jude's humming? That means he's happy. He's reached for his iPad and gone straight to his favourite songs on YouTube. I often wish I could wake up so full of energy and joy.

I lie there for a few moments, easing into the day. It's Sunday. No school. No rush.

I scroll to the Blink app on my phone and check the camera in my dad's bedroom. Still asleep. Last night was a successful one all round.

A few minutes later, Jude is standing over me. It's time to get up. I get off the sofa, roll up my mattress topper and put away my bedclothes. This sofa has been my bed every night for the last three years. It's more comfortable than it sounds, but it's also in Jude's living space, and he wants his TV on and breakfast made. So it's time for me to move.

I head into the house and prepare his breakfast. Cereal

poured out onto a plate: dry, no milk. That's how he likes it. I add some blueberries and a banana, get his drink ready and prepare his medication. Once he's settled, I shift gears to my next job: getting my dad up. I help him wash and dress, then get his breakfast and medication sorted too.

Just as I'm about to sit down, Jude comes back in with the TV remote in his hand, beckoning me to change the channel. Once that's done, I finally focus on making my own breakfast and getting myself ready for the day.

Sundays are the slowest days in our world. Jude is happy with his iPad, rocking back and forth to the music and watching TV. Every twenty minutes or so, he makes the short walk from the annexe to the house, sometimes for food, sometimes for a shower, sometimes to get me to change the channel for him. My dad is settled in the lounge, watching TV. I scroll my phone, reply to a few messages, grab my laptop and catch up on some work.

As lunchtime approaches, I do round two of my dad's medication, prepare his lunch and then help Jude get dressed. On Sundays we go out for a drive. It's a sunny day, but our river walks haven't been too successful lately, so we'll stick to the car instead.

I recently got a seven-seater car, with enough space for Jude to sit in the very back row. The meltdowns and aggression of last summer led to us being housebound as the car became too unsafe to be in. This new set-up seems to help. Jude likes the space. It gives him a sense of security – and it gives me one too; I can focus on driving without worrying or constantly looking in the mirror or over my shoulder.

We drive for an hour. I flick through the radio stations,

playing our version of musical roulette. Jude's music taste is eclectic, he loves everything from '60s classics to '90s R&B. Ed Sheeran to Beyoncé. I skip from station to station, waiting for the moment his eyes light up. When he smiles, when he rocks back and forth to the beat, I know we've found a winner.

I often record these drives on my phone and share them online. Our followers love to see Jude happy. They love guessing which songs he's into that week. I love watching them back too, getting to see the smiles and facial expressions I missed while driving.

We stop at McDonald's – the drive-thru of course, it's far too busy inside. I order him a large five-piece Chicken Selects meal with a Fruit Shoot. The Happy Meal days are long gone and we've graduated from nuggets to Chicken Selects now, but the Fruit Shoot has stayed. He's never been into fizzy drinks. I've offered him a sip a few times, but he always pulls a face immediately. The sensory experience is too much. He and Tommy are in a very exclusive group of teens who have never tried Coca-Cola.

Once he's eaten and accepted that there are no more chips to be had, we make the hour drive back home, same route, same radio roulette. And every now and then, when I look in the rear-view mirror and we lock eyes mid-song, my heart swells. He's happy. For so many years, this has been all I wanted. This was the dream, to have a day just like this. One where he was calm, content, connected. Where the simplest of things brought joy. Today is one of those days.

As our drive ends, we pull up outside my parents' house and begin our usual switchover. I help Jude out of the back seat and walk him across the road to Charlotte's house. We go through the back gate, straight into the annexe. Jude still struggles with being around his sisters, so we take it slow. This is the smoothest way to help him transition.

I turn the TV on and ask Alexa to play Ed Sheeran, while he takes his shoes and T-shirt off. I tap his nose, he taps mine back. I tell him I love him and say I'll see him on Wednesday. He's already focused on his iPad. I know he'll never say it back. I'm not even sure he understands what I've said. But I hope that he feels the love. I hope he knows he'll see me again soon.

I go into Charlotte's house, have a quick catch-up with her, and we exchange all the relevant info we need to know about the boys' day so far. Then I head upstairs. Tommy waits in her bedroom for the changeover, buried under the duvet. I stand at the door and call, 'Tommy! Five, four, three, two, one, time for Daddy's house!' He lifts the duvet off his head, gives me a smile and a thumbs up, then pulls it back over himself. It'll take him about half an hour to be ready, but the transition has begun.

I go back home, prep the house for Tommy and make my dad a cup of tea. I put a cake in the front seat of my car, which is part of Tommy's current transition phase. When he gets off the school bus or switches houses, he likes to sit in the car for five minutes. It's how he processes the change. It has caused a few logistical issues lately, but I go with it. Some things aren't worth pushing. I still pick my battles.

When he finally decides to come inside, he walks through the house room by room. It's like he's checking everything is still as he left it before settling into his space again. Then it's straight into the bathroom for a shower. He's always been a big sensory seeker and water continues to be an all-time favourite. He goes back and forth from the shower to the bath. I have to make sure the toilet roll and any toiletries are removed beforehand, though, as the temptation to empty them all out or put sheets and sheets of paper into the toilet, is too much for him. It brings him too much sensory joy but leaves me with a blocked toilet and an expensive toiletry bill each month. Lately, Tommy can be in there for up to two hours. And again, I go with it. It helps him regulate, helps him relax, and it gives me time to reset too. I sort out the house, check in on my dad, maybe stretch out on the sofa for a few minutes, before starting to get Tommy's dinner ready.

When Tommy finally comes out of the bathroom, it's time for dinner, which he has in the annexe. It's breaded chicken, cut into strips. Always the same. He eats that in front of the TV, watching one of his current favourites. Sometimes he scrolls YouTube, but just like the previous fourteen years, it's nearly always *Mickey Mouse Clubhouse*. He pauses, rewinds, skips forwards, watching some of the same clips over and over. Each show he watches is linked to the little routine in his head. Certain clips at certain times. He bounces around the annexe, hops and crashes to the floor. He runs into the garden, starts building a puzzle on the table, then it's back into the annexe again.

After numerous countdowns and prompts, he makes his way into the house. It's time for his chips. Exactly eight of them. He eats them in my office, sitting at my desk; his current place of choice. I say 'eight' and 'hot', and he repeats back to me the first sound of each word. Then he eats the chips. Every part of the routine has meaning. Every part helps him feel safe, in control.

An hour later, we head out for our nightly drive. What started in lockdown as something to fill time has now become a non-negotiable part of our day. Christmas Day, New Year's Eve, it doesn't matter. It's a step we don't skip. We drive around for fifteen minutes, giving ourselves a slow wind-down from the day. Then we stop at Tesco. Tommy uses his AAC device to say, 'Dad I would like . . .' and today, it's 'Dad I would like pink cake.' Tommy always chooses his cake by colour.

I go in alone while he stays in the car, and I look for a cake that's pink enough to meet his expectations. The colour can refer to the packaging or the colour of the cake itself; he seems to be happy with either. I bring it back to him and he beams. He'll try to say the words again, looking at me for reassurance: 'Dad I would like pink cake.' I hand him the cake, and his whole face lights up. There are days when this trip feels like a chore, when I'm tired and the thought of dragging myself out again feels like a lot. But then Tommy smiles. He laughs. And suddenly, it's worth it all over again.

We head for home and the start of our bedtime routines. First, I give my dad his final tablets and help him into bed. Then it's time to begin the second transition, helping Tommy move from evening to bedtime.

After some gentle prompting, we head over to the annexe. We spend ten minutes together on the sofa, Tommy flicking through the pages of his three favourite books, remote control in the other hand, scrolling to find the exact right moment in the exact right programme. It's always the same three Disney books. Always *Mickey Mouse Clubhouse* on the TV. I count down from five and then it's time for the shower.

This is non-negotiable. A sensory reset and a signal that bedtime is coming. No matter how delayed our bedtime routine is some nights, no matter how tired he is, that shower has to happen. He lets the water run over him, calming his body, helping him make sense of the time of day. When he's done, I help him into his pyjamas and we return to the sofa.

He scrolls back and forth through *Mickey's Magical Christmas*. Then the trailer for *DuckTales: The Movie*, stopping, starting and replaying it twenty times. He spends some time hopping, flapping, bouncing across the room. Sometimes he sits on top of the bookcase. Sometimes he perches next to me. It's his own bedtime dance. Joyous, repetitive and oddly calming.

Eventually, he switches off the TV. We brush his teeth, nearly making it to two full minutes now, thanks to a very slow five-to-one countdown, and then I guide him to bed. I tuck him in, kiss him on the head three times and say 'I love you' between each one. Then I step back, flick off the light and whisper, 'Night night, darling, sweet dreams, see you in the morning.'

As I pull the door closed, he shouts 'Luh!' from under the covers. 'Love you,' I reply. He repeats it twice more, louder each time, laughing as I call back from the hallway. He's been doing that for over a year now. Only recently have the happy tears stopped welling in my eyes each time.

By now, it's nearly midnight. I get his school uniform ready for the morning, then I watch a bit of TV, reply to some messages, scroll on my phone. I need sleep, but I also need this. Just a moment to decompress. To be me, before I become everything again tomorrow: dad, son, carer, co-parent, boss.

When I'm sure he's settled, I return to the annexe, brush my teeth, turn the sofa back into a bed and try to get some sleep. Hoping that neither Tommy nor my dad wakes me up before my alarm does. Tomorrow's a school day and a work day. But for now, this one is done. A simple day. A repetitive and somewhat predictable day. But a happy one.

There was a time when I didn't think happiness like this was possible. In those early years, the only thing I seemed to feel was fear. Every day brought new uncertainties, new challenges. I was overwhelmed by all the things Jude and Tommy couldn't do and by all the expectations I had to let go of. Family holidays, birthday parties, school events, spontaneous outings, they either stopped or looked completely different from what I'd imagined.

I always thought the most important moments would be found in the big milestones: first words, first bike rides, family holidays by the sea, days out, exam results, medals and certificates. The kind of moments you post about on social media, the ones you feel proud to tick off. And if I'm honest, some days my heart still aches for those things. Not because I want to change who my boys are but just because I wish it was easier for them to be themselves. To communicate, to understand, to process the world around them. There are still moments I find myself watching other families at a restaurant or in the park and feeling that familiar tightness in my chest. And that's OK.

Every now and then, there are still mornings when I wake

up having dreamed that I was having a conversation with my boys. That Jude and Tommy were chatting away, telling me about their day, asking questions, making jokes. Doing all the things I see my mates doing with their kids. When I wake up, there's a pang, a few seconds where I have to remember it wasn't real. And that's OK too.

Those waking moments used to break me and the ache could last for days. But now? It's just a moment. A flicker. And then I'm back. Back to the life we have and all the other ways we connect.

That's acceptance, I think. Not pretending you never wish things were easier or different. Just knowing you can hold those feelings and still feel joy. That it's all right to enjoy the amazing moments, be proud of all of the progress, the boys and young men they're turning into, love them with every inch of my heart, yet still have mixed feelings some days. Still get a little sad about the things we can't do, the life we're not living but never staying stuck there. Choosing to focus on the positives but acknowledge some of the harder emotions and moments too. That's what acceptance means to me.

Time is what's changed that perspective for me. Because somewhere along the way, I stopped counting milestones and started noticing the inchstones. The way the joy lives in the small moments. It's in those Sunday drives where Jude lights up to a '70s pop song or some old school R&B. It's in the routine Tommy has created for himself, the cake from Tesco, the *DuckTales* trailer, the late-night showers. It's in the nose taps, the cheeky laughs, the 'Tuh' Tommy shouts at me to get me to say 'Tommy!' which then causes him to crack up laughing.

It's the tiny connections that at one time felt completely

out of reach. A new word from Tommy that he repeats over and over. Jude being in the same car as his brother for a short drive. Tommy scanning our shopping at the self-checkout. Jude letting me help him shower. A day out with both boys together. A new food tried, even if it's just a bite. A full night's sleep.

These small, almost insignificant moments are huge in our world. And they still keep coming, quietly, unexpectedly and often in their own time. They remind me that progress hasn't stopped. That growth looks different here but it still happens. That there's still so much to be proud of, so much to hope for, so much more to come.

Recently, a moment like this came along that has changed my world – and, I hope, Tommy's.

I'd just settled onto the sofa after helping my dad into bed. Jude was happy in the annexe. My brain had moved on to school bags and uniform, the boys having just gone back to school after the long summer break. My phone pinged. A WhatsApp from Charlotte.

> Hallo

It was probably an accidental message, I thought or, as I watched the dots that showed she was still typing, she had hit 'send' too soon. Then:

> Dad
> Love
> You
> Tommy

CHOOSING JOY

A wave of emotions flooded over me. What was this? Tommy texting me? I quickly replied:

> Hello Tommy. Love you too.

Seconds later he messaged back:

> Night
> Dad

I wrote back:

> Night night Tom Tom. See you on Friday. Love you.

Short, sweet and straight to the point. Tears streamed down my face. Was this really happening?

A text conversation between a parent and their fourteen-year-old is an everyday experience for most families. But for us, after years spent longing for conversations and to know what the boys were thinking, this was huge. It also opened new possibilities in being able to communicate from afar and showed how much Tommy understood the concept of communicating with me when I wasn't physically with him. His AAC device has been life changing but that's only ever used in the moment, to communicate with the person physically next to him. For him to want to message me and understand that he's talking with me, even when we're not together in the same place, that was incredible.

Charlotte rang me as soon as he put the phone down.

LOVE NEEDS NO WORDS

She'd been lying in bed next to him, the same way they do every night before going to sleep, when she'd asked him if he wanted to text Daddy. Not really knowing how he'd react, she passed her phone to him, opened up a message and encouraged him to talk to me. He needed a little guidance, a gentle reminder to reply and not open up YouTube but all the words were his own.

We tried again the next night. I asked him if he'd had a good day, and he replied, 'Good.' I asked him if he was happy, to which he said, 'Book games.' I wondered if he meant that was what made him happy, as they're two things he loves.

The next week we picked up again, and I told him I'd see him after school tomorrow. He replied, 'Great.' Then he discovered GIFs. An assortment of 'I love you', 'goodnight' and pictures that he liked soon followed. He seems to love one that's a close-up of a dog, his face looking like he's smiling. A couple of weeks later he told me he'd been to a pumpkin patch and had pizza. Now it's becoming a routine. When he's with Charlotte, just before bed he'll message me and we say goodnight to each other. I tell him when I'm going to see him next, wanting to reassure him that I'm here. Every time I get a message from him I sit there excitedly waiting to see what he's going to say, never knowing how long we've got before I get a barrage of GIFs and a goodnight. These text conversations have become the highlight of my day. They're a way for us to stay connected when he's with Charlotte but more than that, they're another step towards opening up his world even more.

Sometimes I still can't believe how far we've come. Not just Jude and Tommy but me too. As a dad. As a person. Seventeen years ago, I didn't know what the word 'autism' meant. I didn't know there was a spectrum or how it impacted people's lives. I didn't know what AAC was or what a sensory profile looked like or how many different ways there are to connect with a child who doesn't speak. I didn't know the weight of advocacy, the heartbreak of exclusion or the shining joy of a single good day after months of really hard ones.

I certainly had no idea that one day I'd get to share our stories with millions of people. That our ordinary days, our inchstones, our chaos, our routines, would resonate across the world. That other parents would message me in tears, saying, *'I feel less alone.'*

Stories About Autism began as an outlet. A place to process and try to make sense of our lives. And also to show friends and family what that life looks like. The good and the bad, the happy and the sad. But it became something so much more; it became a lifeline for others – and for me too. It gave me purpose when I felt lost. It helped me step into this new version of life. And it showed me just how powerful our stories can be. It has given me friendships I never knew I needed. And it's given me opportunities too. To meet other families, to share knowledge with professionals and to talk with corporations. To launch the SAA Clothing brand and shop. To create SEND Fest and host events for families like ours. All with the goal of making the world a little more accepting, a little more understanding. To make life better for autistic kids, adults and their parents and carers too.

One of the opportunities Stories About Autism has brought me was the chance to go to Sydney, to speak at a conference for Autism Awareness Australia. Which, on the one hand, was a dream come true. I'd travelled round Australia back in 2004 and had once thought I'd revisit one day with my boys, but I'd long since given up any hope of going back. So being asked to go there to share our stories and to meet other parents seemed too good to be true. But, on the other hand, it had the potential to be a nightmare too. And that's exactly what my mind focused on: how could I possibly travel all the way to the other side of the world for a week? There was no way that Tommy would be able to cope. Any attempts over the last few years at changing his routine days with me had been a disaster, triggering meltdowns and huge anxiety. I had taken a Friday night off a few months earlier and it had taken two hours for Charlotte to convince Tommy to go inside her house. He had kept running into mine, crying, stomping, throwing things around. They had the worst evening, and it left me feeling like I'd never try to go out on a Tommy night ever again.

But, for all my doubts, Charlotte made me see it was an opportunity I couldn't pass up. And that with the right planning and the right support in place, we'd do everything we could to make it work. So, reluctantly, I accepted the offer. My brother came to stay at the house for a week with my dad, we put social stories in place for Tommy, a clear visual schedule so he could see exactly how many days it was until I was back, and we went for it.

The first night he was due to be at mine was a little tricky; it took him a while to go inside Charlotte's house and he kept checking my house to make sure I wasn't there, but he wasn't upset. And as the week went on he adapted. I sent him a video message each day, trying to make him laugh and

CHOOSING JOY

counting down the days until I'd be home. Charlotte recorded him watching each time, laughing, then saying 'love you' back to me. He went to school as usual and out with his carers at the weekend as usual, and he coped just fine. Even more remarkably, both he and Jude were together at Charlotte's house, not crossing paths too often but content.

Meanwhile, I had my first real break in six years. I spoke at the conference and loved meeting the team and the other speakers. I toured around Sydney, met up with a friend and slept. Well, kind of. Not only was having my own bed strange after three years on a sofa, but I actually found having so much space, so much time, unsettling. It was a surreal week. After so long on high alert and now having no responsibilities other than the conference, I struggled to know what to do with myself. I loved going to Sydney, I visited Manly, Bondi and spent a lot of time around the harbour and wandering round the city. I loved having a break, but it definitely brought up a lot of emotions. Having free time and no pressure will do that to you. But it was worth it – oh so worth it. And for all of us, it was the biggest confirmation of growth we could have asked for. It showed me that with the right support in place Tommy, Jude and my dad can all cope without me. It was a mark of how far both boys have come and a glimpse of a possible future where I might be able to have some more time for me. To travel, to socialise, to meet someone new. It was a sign that I can start to dream for me again.

One of the most unexpected sources of joy in recent years has been the co-parenting relationship that Charlotte and I have built. It's not something you really hear about and certainly not something I imagined when our marriage ended. At the time, things were tough and emotionally raw. But what we couldn't always manage in a relationship, we've somehow managed to build as co-parents. As friends. As a team.

We've always tried to keep the lines of communication open. Even when things between us were hard, we put the boys first. That was the starting point but over the years something else happened: the friendship grew stronger, the trust deepened and we began leaning on each other in ways we hadn't before.

And now, ten years on, we live opposite each other – which was a little strange when I first moved in but now it makes perfect sense. It's become our version of normal. Charlotte has helped with my parents countless times over the years, checking in on them when I couldn't be there, stepping in when things got too much. Comforting my mum when she was confused and lost, making meals and cups of tea for my dad, even helping him in and out of bed. She's supported me without question, always wanting the best for the people I love. I don't know what I would have done without her. And I've tried to do the same for her.

That support extends to every part of our lives now. I've got a great relationship with her daughters, Seren and Francesca. I see them nearly every day. I've taken them to school, picked them up, grabbed them sweets from the shop. Just regular, everyday acts but ones that show how far we've come, how we've built a version of a blended family that works for all of us. I love seeing them grow and progress and feel proud of the sisters they are to Tommy and Jude. I get on well with Carl too. We chat about football, about work and the kids, and I have a great deal of respect for the stepdad he's become for my boys.

And then there's SAA Clothing. When I first had the idea, it was Charlotte who helped bring it to life. She believed in it and in me. At the beginning she was there behind the scenes, helping with packing orders, setting up systems and cheering it all on. Then a few months in, she joined me full time. It has given her a new sense of purpose too, a way to be part of something bigger, a community she can connect with and contribute to. Now we work together almost every day, running a business that's all about inclusion, understanding and connection. Which, when I say it out loud, does sound a bit mad. We're exes who share two kids, co-run a business, live across the road from each other and have daily handovers with routines only we can understand. But it works. And it works because we want it to. Because we've put the past behind us and chosen to focus on what's ahead. Because we care about each other and want each other to be happy. Because, like everything else in this journey, we've found our own route through.

And truthfully, it's not just Jude and Tommy who bond us. It's the life we've lived. The things we've seen and felt that no one else truly understands. The sleepless nights. The heartbreaking meltdowns. The battles to get support. The fear of the future. The quiet 3 a.m. moments when everything felt like it was falling apart and you held it all in because there was no other choice. The joy in every inch of progress. The moments that Jude and Tommy are together and happy.

No one else in the world knows or feels those moments the way we do, because they're our boys. That connection doesn't have to disappear when a relationship ends. If anything, for us, it's deepened. It becomes something new, rooted in love for each other, even if it's no longer romantic. It's a relationship I'm proud of. There's real peace in knowing we're on the same side, that we've got each other's backs and that Jude and Tommy can grow up surrounded by love and two parents who will always be there, even if it looks different to how we once thought life would be.

None of this is what I pictured. I never imagined I'd be a carer or co-parenting or living with my dad again in my forties. I didn't imagine I'd be running two businesses from my kitchen table. I didn't imagine I'd be speaking at events and certainly not that I'd be flying to Australia to do so. We've come through some incredibly hard chapters, but somehow, we keep finding our way forward. One step at a time.

There's still so much we don't know about the future. There are so many decisions ahead; transitions, changes and challenges we've yet to face. I'd be lying if I said I didn't still get overwhelmed when I think too far ahead. But I've learned to live with uncertainty in a different way now. Not as something to fear but something to manage. To take one step at a time. I've learned to trust in our ability to adapt, to find new ways forward and to lean on others when we need to. That's what the last seventeen years have taught me, not just how to survive but how to bend without breaking. How to hold fear in one hand and hope in the other.

The future won't look like the one I imagined, but maybe it'll be better in ways I never could have seen. Because I used to think I had to fix everything. That it was my job to get us 'back on track'. I threw myself into therapies, strategies, research. I was chasing a version of normal I thought we'd somehow wandered away from.

But eventually, I stopped chasing. Jude and Tommy don't need fixing. They need space to be themselves. They need support, consistency, patience and a world that meets them where they are. They don't need to live up to any preconceived ideas or visions I had of what life would be like for them or for me. What they need is a parent who meets them where they are not where I wanted them to be.

And the more I let go of what I thought life was supposed to look like, the more space there was for something else. Something just as special. That's what this chapter is about. Not a perfect life. But a life that's real and meaningful and full of moments that are just as special. We all get told to appreciate the little things. But in our world, the little things are everything. Tommy and Jude show me that each and every day.

When I look back over the last seventeen years, especially those that have come since my divorce and the decision to separate Jude and Tommy, there have been periods where I've felt completely lost, bewildered that this is how my life has ended up. But I've also come to realise these are phases. Passages of time. Sometimes a few hours, sometimes a few days, sometimes even a few months, but there's always light amid the darkness.

That light can come from a good day with Jude or Tommy. A new skill developed, a positive report from school or even just a happy day. A day that had lots of smiles and no meltdowns. That's all it takes to lift the gloomy mood. I read once that a parent is only ever as happy as their unhappiest child, and I feel that in my bones. When they're struggling, so am I; when life is simple and fun for them, suddenly the sun comes out once more and a huge weight is lifted off my shoulders.

The light also comes from knowing my mum is well looked after in her care home. Seeing her smile when I visit, even if she has no idea who I am. Seeing photos of her happy with my aunt and cousins. The light comes from a simple, happy day for my dad. When he's slept through the night, been chatty and interactive.

The light comes from the handful of days/nights off I have each year and spend with those closest to me. The friends I wish I had more time to see but cherish every moment I get with them. It comes from the hope that in a different phase of my life there'll be more time for this. When life is less complex, I will have more free time, more nights to myself, more opportunities to socialise. To date, to meet someone new, to fall in love. To travel, to accomplish the things I want to do. I've had a taste of some of that recently, especially with SAA Clothing, my Australia trip and even in writing this book. Doing things outside of being a parent/carer, doing things for me. I spent a lot of the last ten years feeling like this was out of my reach. But maybe it's not. Maybe it's just been about waiting for the right time.

So if you're reading this and you're still in the thick of it, still grieving, still fighting, still waiting for a day that feels manageable, I want you to know: it's possible. It may not be the life you pictured. But it can still be full of joy. And hopefully, one day you'll look around at the routines, the differences, the adaptations you've made and you'll realise, this is your version of happy. Even if it doesn't look like anyone else's.

*

Last summer, I took Tommy into London to see a relaxed performance of *The Lion King*. Just the two of us. It might not sound like a big deal to some but a few years ago I wouldn't have even considered it. The thought of packed train stations, crowded theatres, unfamiliar noises and unpredictable moments, it would have been impossible. I'd have turned the invite down, already overwhelmed by the what ifs.

But we were going through a good patch. I'd seen how much Tommy had progressed. And so, for the first time in a long time, I said yes.

With the help of his school, we prepared a social story, filled with photos and symbols walking him through the entire day: train, taxi, theatre, snack, show, taxi, train, home. We made a visual schedule with Velcro pieces he could remove and mark off each stage as it happened.

I labelled the outing a 'Daddy and Tommy day out', and we talked about it for a couple of days beforehand. On the morning of the show, we drove to the station. On the train, we looked through his Mickey Mouse books and read through the social story. He clutched onto the schedule, every now and again making me read each step out loud, seeking reassurance about what was going to happen next. I could see the nerves mixed in with excitement, and I felt them too.

We got a taxi to the theatre and held hands tightly as we navigated the chaos of the West End. Tommy's social story had included a photo of the outside of the theatre, which helped him recognise where we were. Once inside, we made our way to our seats. I wasn't sure what he was expecting. I wasn't even sure what I was expecting. But I'd come prepared, sweets in hand, eyes on him constantly, just in case.

Then the lights dimmed.

The music began.

Performers paraded down the aisles dressed as animals, drumming and dancing, the theatre alive with colour and sound. And Tommy lit up. His whole body responded, eyes wide, hands flapping with joy, feet bouncing in rhythm with the music. I held him gently, sensing his urge to reach out. At one point he did try to dash towards the front, and I had to scoop him up before he made it to the stage. But aside from that, he was incredible.

He watched, stood, sat, moved but most importantly, he enjoyed it. He understood the interval. We used the toilet, got another snack and he made it through the second half. He coped with the crowds leaving the theatre, still clutching his schedule, ticking off the final stages of our plan, as we navigated the journey back to the train station and our car.

When we got home that evening, my heart was full. Not just because of what we'd done that day but because of how far we'd come. A day that once felt unthinkable had become one of the most special memories we've ever shared. I was so proud of him. I was proud of us.

And that's what redefining happiness has come to mean to me. This is not the life I once imagined, filled with milestones and neatly defined stages. But it is one built around connection, understanding and presence. The world and the pressures of everyday life haven't made this easy. It rarely does for families like ours. But within that complexity, we've carved out something beautiful, something that's completely ours.

It's the joy of knowing my boys are content in their own

ways. That they feel safe and understood and loved beyond measure.

It's the peace that comes from letting go of what should have been and fully embracing what is.

Because this life, with all its unpredictability and intensity, the beautiful highs and the heartbreaking lows, is a life worth celebrating.

Afterword

Around the time I finished writing the final draft of this book, my world was turned upside down when my dad passed away suddenly. Life had become a lot more challenging over the previous year, and finding the right balance of care to meet his needs weighed heavily on my mind. His death was completely unexpected. For me, at least.

My dad has always been there, leading by example and quietly helping to shape the man and father I've become. In recent years, he had been living with Parkinson's, and three years ago, the boys and I moved in with him. I took on the role of his carer; a role which grew as the weeks and months passed and the Parkinson's worsened. Suddenly, those caring responsibilities are over. Not only has he gone but a huge chunk of my daily routine and purpose have gone too. His passing has left a huge hole in more ways than one.

Despite the heartbreak and grief, life has had to carry on because Tommy's and Jude's needs continue. Their routines still need to be followed, daily structures kept to. There hasn't been time to wallow, to stay in bed and hide from the world. I've had to keep going. For them.

AFTERWORD

My father's death left me with the surreal feeling of not knowing what to say to my seventeen- and fourteen-year-old sons. I didn't know how much they would understand of what I told them about their grandad passing away. How do you explain death and that someone who has been such a huge part of their lives is no longer here, that he's simply gone?

Jude just carried on as usual. When my dad went into hospital it made no difference to his day, and his death seems to have had little impact on him. While I'd never want to see either of my boys upset, this breaks my heart a little. It's left me, like most days for the last seventeen years, desperate to understand what's going on in that mind of his, to have even the smallest glimpse of what he might be thinking. Most of the time he seems wholly focused on his needs being met, and it's even made me wonder if he'd miss me if I wasn't here. Would he even notice?

With Tommy, things were different. He noticed as soon as Grandad went into hospital. Whether it was the break in routine or the worry about his absence, I'll never know. In the sweetest way, Tommy had forever tried to 'control' my dad, making sure he was in his chair at certain times in the evening, wanting him in bed at a specific time and even putting his walking frame outside the bedroom door when I forgot to. Oh, how I'll miss that.

The day after my dad passed away, Charlotte gently explained it to Tommy while putting him to bed. She told him Grandad has gone to heaven now. That he's in the sky with the stars and the angels, and he'll look after us in a different way. She asked if he understood and he gave her a thumbs up. She told him that when someone dies we can't see them anymore, but we carry them with us and feel them in our hearts forever. They cuddled and she told me he seemed OK.

The next couple of nights with me he was a little emotional and erratic. I tried to talk to him but as always when Tommy is upset, he won't let you communicate with him. Then he seemed to settle and has been completely fine since. For someone so bound to routine and who struggles with change, this could have been a huge challenge so it's a relief he's handled it so well. As with Jude's lack of visible understanding, it's a little heartbreaking at the same time.

So the past few months, which should have been full of excitement as this book was being prepared for release, have also been full of sadness. I'm gutted my dad will never get the chance to read this. When I told him last year that I had secured a deal for my book and was busy writing, I know how proud he was. Life can be cruel.

I'll leave you with a few lines from the eulogy I wrote, my tribute to him from me, Tommy and Jude.

> When Tommy and Jude came along, life changed in ways none of us expected. As we learned what autism meant for them and for us, Dad was nothing but accepting. He always reassured me everything would be OK. He and Mum made their home a safe, loving place for the boys, and the boys adored them for it. Through all the ups and downs, they were always there, always offering to help, always trying to put a smile on Tommy's and Jude's faces.
>
> When I started sharing stories about the boys online, they wanted to read them, so I introduced them to social

AFTERWORD

media, which I'm not sure Dad ever really understood. Even so, a video of him went viral and gained millions of views. I reshare it a couple of times a year and every time it goes viral again. Thousands of people have found my page because of that clip, more than anything I've ever written. It's about ten years old now: Jude in a paddling pool and my dad going back and forth with buckets of warm water, making sure it wasn't too cold.

Jude reaches up, pulls him in and kisses his cheek. That was my dad – just wanting Jude to be happy. I'd tell him about the millions of views, how he was 'famous', which made him laugh, but he didn't really get it. Until I told him Paul Scholes had liked and shared it. That got his attention.

To me, he was my dad. My mate. And a really good man. The kind of man you could rely on, laugh with, learn from. The kind of man who was kind and loyal, who put others first and who never needed the spotlight. And though he didn't show it often with words, he loved his friends and family deeply.

I'll miss him every day, but I'll carry him with me in everything I do. In how I raise my boys, in how I treat people and in the small ways he showed what love really means.

Sleep well, Dad. We love you.

Acknowledgements

A few years after I hit 'publish' on my first Stories About Autism post, I started to wonder if I could one day write a book. I've loved books since I was a kid and always dreamed of being an author. I just never imagined the book would be about my life – or these topics. After years of thinking, a lot of planning and a year of actually writing – here we are. This book is in your hands.

Which means there are a lot of people to thank for helping turn this idea into a real book. I'll start with the people who moved it from dream to draft: Penny Wincer, author of *Tender* and a brilliant non-fiction book coach. We became friends online, bonding over life as carers and parents of autistic children. Penny helped me shape my first proposal, find an agent and, ultimately, secure a deal. Those hours talking about the craft of writing paid off. Thank you, Penny.

James Spackman at The bks Agency: your belief in me and this book and your clear advice at every step have been invaluable. You saw how important these topics were from the very beginning and how they could help so many others. Thank you for helping make this a reality and for enabling me to focus on the fun stuff.

ACKNOWLEDGEMENTS

I was lucky to have real interest in the proposal and the rare privilege of choosing where to take it. That choice became easy after speaking with Michelle Signore and the team at Gallery Books at Simon & Schuster UK. Michelle, your enthusiasm for this project was infectious from the first call. You made me want to write this book, reminded me why it mattered and gave me belief whenever I wobbled.

To the wider team: Kat and Maudisa, thank you for helping shape the story and for your patience with my slipped deadlines. Justine, thank you for believing in this story so deeply and for everything you've done to help it find its way out into the world. Sabah, your excitement for the book (and the tears on each read-through) made me feel this was a story worth publishing. I'm excited to see where your hard work leads. To everyone at Simon & Schuster/Gallery Books, thank you for the empathy you've shown during a year that's been challenging and unpredictable at times. You never added pressure; you gave me space when I needed it. I'm forever grateful.

Next, to everyone who's been part of Stories About Autism, thank you. For every like, comment and message. For celebrating each step of progress, every inchstone and for standing with us on the harder days too. You've told me our stories helped you but the truth is you've helped me just as much. Life has been incredibly lonely at times, and you've always been there for me and the boys. This page has given me real friendships and helped me feel less alone. The interest you show in our daily lives, the love you show us – it's been life-changing. This book is for you and for all the families like ours across the world. Without you, this book wouldn't exist. Thank you for being here and for choosing to read it.

Now for some of the more emotional thank-yous.

My love of reading and writing came from my mum. From an early age she encouraged me to read, took me to the library and always found me another book. I'm devastated I've gone through this whole process without her, never able to talk to her about it. I know how proud she'd have been to see my book on her shelf. Thank you, Mum, for everything.

And to my dad, who, as I share in the afterword, never got to see the finished book either. Over the last year he'd regularly ask how it was going. I'm heartbroken you're not here to read it and enjoy this moment with me. The dad I am to Tommy and Jude and the person I am is because of how you and Mum raised me. I'll be forever grateful.

Writing about caring for both my parents was tricky and, at times, upsetting. But like everything else in this book it's real life, a phase many readers are going through or one day will. It matters. I hope I did you proud.

To my cousins Carly and Freddie: thank you for the support from the sidelines, the encouragement you've shown for Stories About Autism and for this book, the belief you had in me when I couldn't find it myself and the care you showed my mum over these last few years.

To John: for having enough excitement for the both of us about this book and every other small accomplishment over the years; for turning up to every event and for always checking in.

To Caz, Jody, Victoria and the other carers who've played such a big part in Tommy's and Jude's lives: we wouldn't be where we are without your love and support. Your hard work with the boys has made their lives better and in turn mine and Charlotte's too. Thank you.

ACKNOWLEDGEMENTS

And to Charlotte. Where do I start? To outsiders our relationship and the lives we lead can seem a bit unusual but anyone who knows us gets it. Thank you for everything: for encouraging me to hit 'publish' that very first time; for being a sounding board whenever I needed to work out how best to talk about our boys; and for believing in me, especially when I didn't. Divorce and co-parenting can be tricky, impossible for some, but you've always made sure that hasn't been the case for us. In a strange way it's brought us closer as friends. You've always wanted the best for me, you've gone above and beyond for my mum and dad and I'm so proud of all you're doing online and with SAA Clothing. Stories About Autism and this book wouldn't have been possible without you. Thank you.

And finally, to Tommy and Jude. The last seventeen years have been a rollercoaster but always full of love. I wish you knew how much joy and hope you bring to people every single day but maybe that's part of the beauty of your stories. You're just living in the moment, doing what makes you happy. You've been my biggest teachers and completely changed my life and what I value. I'm the one who gets to share your story with the world – and what a story it is. My life will always be dedicated to being your dad, making sure your needs are met and helping you get everything you deserve from life. This book is for you. Love Needs No Words.

Notes

Chapter 3

- Gina Ford, The Contented Little Baby Book (London: Vermilion, 1999)
- Jerry Maguire, dir. Cameron Crowe, Gracie Films/Triad Pictures, 1996.

Chapter 14

- Naoki Higashida, The Reason I Jump, trans. KA